FIGHT

★★★ *for* ★★★

LIBERTY

FIGHT
★★★ *for* ★★★
LIBERTY

DEFENDING DEMOCRACY
IN THE AGE OF TRUMP

edited by MARK LASSWELL

a project of The Renew Democracy Initiative

PUBLICAFFAIRS
New York

PublicAffairs
Hachette Book Group
1290 Avenue of the Americas, New York, NY 10104
www.publicaffairsbooks.com
@Public_Affairs

Printed in the United States of America

First Edition: October 2018

Published by PublicAffairs, an imprint of Perseus Books, LLC, a subsidiary of Hachette Book Group, Inc. The PublicAffairs name and logo is a trademark of the Hachette Book Group.

The Hachette Speakers Bureau provides a wide range of authors for speaking events. To find out more, go to www.hachettespeakersbureau.com or call (866) 376-6591.

The publisher is not responsible for websites (or their content) that are not owned by the publisher.

The Library of Congress has cataloged the hardcover edition as follows:
Names: Lasswell, Mark, editor.
Title: Fight for liberty : defending democracy in the age of Trump / edited by
    Mark Lasswell
Description: First edition. | New York : PublicAffairs, 2018. | Includes bibli-
    ographical references.
Identifiers: LCCN 2018020917 (print) | LCCN 2018029408 (ebook) | ISBN
    9781541724150 (ebook) | ISBN 9781541724167 (pbk.)
Subjects: LCSH: Democracy. | Freedom of speech | Freedom of the press. |
    World politics—21st century. | Democracy—United States. | Freedom of
    the press—United States. | Freedom of speech—United States. | Political
    culture—United States. | United States—Politics and government—2017– |
    Trump, Donald, 1946– Influence.
Classification: LCC JC423 (ebook) | LCC JC423 .F42 2018 (print) | DDC
    321.8—dc23
LC record available at https://lccn.loc.gov/2018020917

ISBNs: 978-1-5417-2416-7 (trade paperback original),
978-1-5417-2415-0 (ebook)

LSC-C

10 9 8 7 6 5 4 3 2 1

Contents

CONTENTS

CONTENTS

Preface

The Renew Democracy Initiative began in the months following the 2016 American presidential election. Three of us met over coffee to talk about what might be done to counteract the troubling trends we had seen playing out over recent years: the degradation of civic dialogue, the erosion of faith in basic institutions, the denigration of expertise as "elitism"—and a resurgence of political authoritarianism and extremism.

This resurgence, of course, did not begin or end with the US presidential election and the strong populist currents it revealed on both sides of the ideological spectrum. Nor was it confined to the United States. Across Europe, separatist movements and populist parties were gaining traction. Strongmen were ascendant from Turkey to Russia to the Philippines. Fanatics and terrorists continued to pose a global threat.

Our small group expanded rapidly. Our concerns were widely shared by members of both the left and the right searching for common ground in a new center. The growing threat from all sides to what used to be called "liberal democracy" had sounded an alarm bell.

Traditional bipartisan consensus is under assault on issues including free trade; a system of alliances and the postwar, rules-based order; and the need for political compromise. Even more troubling, confidence in democratic institutions and the individual rights they exist to safeguard is failing. The rise of a new illiberalism has launched a wave of nativism, isolationism, militant identity politics, and hostility toward dissenting views. It is crowding out and undermining the spirit of freedom, meritocracy, and tolerance that characterizes the most cherished ideals of liberal democracy.

We have assembled a coalition of diverse voices—writers, diplomats, statesmen, artists, entertainers, business leaders, academics, lawyers, a Nobel laureate, even a certain chess champion—from around the world to defend these "first principles." At the Renew Democracy Initiative, old points of division—marginal tax rates, health-care reform, military spending—have faded quickly into the background as we focus instead on how much we have in common: a belief in the fundamental ideas that for generations have made so much of the world free, prosperous, and safe. But shared beliefs are not in themselves sufficient. They must be defended, and this demands action.

What step to take first? Should we start a new political party—internationally engaged, fiscally responsible, socially tolerant? A new think tank? One of our founders, Bret Stephens, argued that ideas were at the forefront of any serious change. And, indeed, those who care deeply about these first principles of liberty and democracy have not been vigilant enough in defending them, in articulating why the siren song of the demagogues, extremists, and cable news talking heads is dangerously wrong. Believing in the principles of liberal democracy is not enough. It is essential to communicate why these principles have improved lives wherever they have flourished and why they are still the best hope for spreading prosperity and security in the future. So short is the collective memory of fascism, communism, and other forms of totalitarianism that many young people today no longer consider living in a democracy to be important. The situation is urgent.

And so RDI came into existence—an effort to reinvigorate democracy from the ground up, based on common ideals and ideas. Our goal is to remind, to educate, and to advocate for liberty. This book, inspired by the *Federalist Papers*, is our inaugural publication. The essays collected here lay out first principles, describe the most serious threats to liberal-democratic values, and outline solutions to meet those threats. We have no partisan agenda; we embrace any citizen, of any political persuasion, of any nation, who values these principles.

"Freedom is never more than one generation away from extinction," Ronald Reagan warned. How to preserve it? Franklin Roosevelt illuminated our path when he said: "The real safeguard of liberty is education." Education, that is, about the principles that inform the politics and values and processes of democracy. RDI seeks to inspire whomever we can, wherever we can, to help create a cultural and political climate that stirs pride, not alarm. So join us. Visit our website and add your name to our manifesto. Sign up for our mailing list and spread the word. Above all, engage in citizenship to the fullest.

Fight for liberty!

—The Renew Democracy Initiative
Garry Kasparov, Chairman
Richard Hurowitz, President
Anne Applebaum, Director
Max Boot, Director
Karl-Theodor zu Guttenberg, Director
Igor Kirman, Director
Mark Lasswell, Director
Richard North Patterson, Director

Introduction

★ ★ ★

JON MEACHAM

Everything seemed to be falling apart. After his election to the presidency in November 1932, Franklin D. Roosevelt received a talkative friend. If FDR could rescue America from the Great Depression, the caller said, then Roosevelt would be remembered as the greatest of presidents; if he failed, then he would go down as the worst. There were live alternatives to democratic capitalism afoot in the world: European fascism in Germany and Italy, Soviet Communism in Russia. Roosevelt responded matter-of-factly: "If I fail, I shall be the last one."

And so, to some extent and some degree, we've been here before: a sense of crisis, of crumbling order, of facing destructive forces

---

Jon Meacham is a distinguished visiting professor at Vanderbilt University. His books include *American Lion: Andrew Jackson in the White House*, awarded the Pulitzer Prize for biography in 2009.

JON MEACHAM

that may prove beyond our control. America and its allies survived
the 1930s and World War II not least because FDR did not fail.
For all his shortcomings—and they were legion—Roosevelt was,
however, a rare spirit. "Men," the *New York Times* wrote after his
death in Warm Springs, Georgia, in April 1945, "will thank God
on their knees a hundred years from now that Franklin Roosevelt
was in the White House when a powerful and ruthless barbarism
threatened to overrun the civilization of the Western World." Such
an encomium seems unlikely when the newspaper comes to assess
the life and legacy of the forty-fifth president.

The issue at hand, though, is larger than any single figure.
Once thought to be firmly entrenched in the Western world,
democracy—or at least the democratic norms we have taken
for granted since the crisis of capitalism in the 1930s—is under
global assault. The essays collected here survey the scene with
dispassion and clarity. From Putin's Russia to Trump's America
(the two, alas, have more in common than is even remotely comfortable), freedom of speech and of the press, the rule of law,
fair play in the marketplace and in the movements of ideas and
of people across borders, and confidence in the integrity of the
governing classes are all in danger. The forces of authoritarianism, nativism, and kleptocracy are ascendant. The concerns that
have prompted this project are not those of a single news cycle;
neither are they driven by partisan animus or by an ad hominem
obsession with the current occupant of the Oval Office. The
contributors to this book are motivated by fact, not ideology; by
reason, not passion; and, crucially, by hope, not fear.

The essayists are working within an old and important American tradition, one articulated by Frederick Jackson Turner, the

2

great historian of the frontier. "Other nations have been rich and prosperous and powerful," Turner wrote nearly a century ago. "But the United States has believed that it had an original contribution to make to the history of society by the production of a self-determining, self-restrained, intelligent democracy." In 1944, the Swedish economist Gunnar Myrdal, writing his landmark *The American Dilemma*, quoted the African-American Nobel Peace Prize laureate Ralph Bunche in an effort to define an American creed. "Every man in the street, white, black, red, or yellow," Bunche observed, "knows that this is 'the land of the free,' the 'land of opportunity,' the 'cradle of liberty,' the 'home of democracy,' that the American flag symbolizes the 'equality of all men' and guarantees us all 'the protection of life, liberty and property,' freedom of speech, freedom of religion and racial tolerance." For Myrdal, such a definition of human liberty and of aspiration gave the American creed global significance. "And even the skeptic," he wrote, "cannot help feeling that, perhaps, this youthful exuberant America has the destiny to do for the whole Old World what the frontier did to the old colonies."

So it has largely proven in the decades since World War II. Now a variety of factors has put the Western experiment with liberty in jeopardy. Self-government in the American mold, with its roots in the parliamentary and common-law traditions of Britain, was always understood to be the most fraught and perilous of undertakings. "Probably, prudence, wisdom, and patriotism were never more essentially necessary than at the present moment," George Washington wrote in the early autumn of 1788. In a letter to the Marquis de Lafayette a few months later, on the cusp of assuming ultimate power in the young republic,

Washington emphasized, "Nothing but harmony, honesty, industry and frugality are necessary to make us a great and happy people."

The key insight of the founding fathers—one that has informed every successive generation—was that such virtues are not always in abundant supply. Hence the checks and balances of the constitutional system and the emphasis on the cultivation of republican virtues. "National passions and habits are unwieldy, unmanageable, and formidable things," John Adams wrote, and the point of divided sovereignty, the rule of law, and a free press was to give reason a fighting chance in the perennial struggle against the appetites and ambitions of the factions of the moment.

The unavoidable truth of the matter is that passion is gaining the upper hand on reason in too many ways, in too many countries—including America. There are sundry causes for the crisis of the hour, and the essayists here explore not only the underlying forces driving the current discontent but also offer possible solutions. It is not the work of a day, or of a week, or of a single election. Recovery and restoration, rather, require constant vigilance and perennial devotion.

History is an ally in this struggle, for an empirical, commonsense case can be made—and must be made—that liberal democracy has always grown stronger the wider it has opened its arms. One sign of the strength of the system, in fact, is the ferocity of the reaction against the infrastructure of liberty in the first decades of the twenty-first century. The forces of fear are mighty, but the armies of hope and of equality of opportunity have much to draw on in this fight.

In the twilight of his life, Franklin Roosevelt, one of the most accomplished purveyors of hope in American history, recalled the words of his old Groton School headmaster, Endicott Peabody: "Things in life will not always run smoothly. Sometimes we will be rising toward the heights—then all will seem to reverse itself and start downward. The great fact to remember is that the trend of civilization itself is forever upward, that a line drawn through the middle of the peaks and the valleys of the centuries always has an upward trend." It can be difficult to recall that fact in the maelstrom of the moment, but it is a fact—and, as John Adams reminded us long ago, facts are stubborn things.

PART ONE

First Principles

Liberal democracy has flourished because it is undergirded by certain basic values. These values merit fresh discussion to help reinvigorate them in the battle against illiberal forces now spreading across much of the world. In today's supposed post-truth moment, the first step is to assert the seemingly obvious: truth exists, truth matters, truth must be defended. The Enlightenment—progenitor of liberalism and the veneration of individual freedom—was fueled by reason and by the search for its soul mate, truth. To demean and discredit the idea of truth is to attack the foundations of democracy itself.

The reassertion of other liberal-democratic first principles will also help counter the illiberal tide: Individual liberty is not a "Western" concept, nor is it reserved for only those particular peoples deemed capable of appreciating and defending it. Economic freedom nourishes the expression of all other freedoms. The valorization of civics and civility is essential to discouraging the spread of hatred and partisan extremism that hobbles democracy and invites exploitation by demagogues. Globalization knits nations together in peace and prosperity, buttressing liberal democracies and turning a spotlight on freedom's blessings; economic nationalism accomplishes none of this. Finally comes a distinguishing characteristic of democracy that is a standing rebuke to illiberalism everywhere: the toleration of dissent.

The Need for Truth

★ ★ ★

ROGER SCRUTON

"There are no truths," wrote Nietzsche, "only interpretations." True or false? If true then false, hence necessarily false—false under every interpretation. That ought to have been an end to the matter. In fact, it was only the beginning. Not long after Nietzsche made this declaration in the late nineteenth century, relativism began to gather momentum. Faced with a world in which people acknowledged rival authorities but no shared method of discussing them, many were tempted to abandon entirely the old distinction between the true and the false. What you say is true from your point of view, was the mantra, what I say is true from

---

Sir Roger Scruton is a professor in the Humanities Research Institute at Buckingham University in Britain and a fellow at the Ethics and Public Policy Center in Washington, DC. His books include *On Human Nature*, *Notes from Underground*, and *Confessions of a Heretic*.

mine. Hence there is no disagreement, no conflict, nothing to be resolved, and no way of resolving it in any case. Truth, fact, reality—all such notions were relativized, and the search for the objective standpoint, from which the evidence could be assessed and the facts determined, was abandoned as delusory.

"Cultural relativism," as it was called at first, looks like a positive step toward toleration. On examination, however, what seems like the acceptance of difference shows itself to be the opposite. If there are no facts, if people cannot judge or be judged save from their own point of view, then all that we say, think, or do is beyond external criticism. Nobody has grounds to protest or to argue, because to do so would be to impose a point of view that has no authority for the person being criticized. All people exist in the bubble of their own opinions and are granted the absolute permission to be who they are regardless. In which case, all people are a potential threat to their neighbors.

Human beings will continue to want those things—possessions, comfort, survival—that power alone can secure for them, and in pursuing those things they will continue to be in competition with the rest of us. If there is no truth, then we cannot accommodate and conciliate our conflicts by agreement, because the idea of agreement suggests a cooperative search for the facts. A world without truth is a world without trust, and in particular without the trust between strangers on which all societies ultimately depend. Take away trust, and you take away all that makes it possible to tolerate difference and to build together with your neighbors a shared form of government.

That a priori argument is not without empirical support. In the emerging "post-truth" culture of young people today, we find an extraordinary burgeoning of intolerance. If there is no truth but only opinion, opinions become the shaping force of social identities. People begin to define themselves in terms of them, and to create networks of conformity where they feel safe among people like themselves. Social media encourage their users to approach opinion in that way. Opinions are part of you and not to be judged. Opinions, like selfies, are things that you share.

The search for safety goes hand in hand with suspicion of the intruder. Hence social media abound in expressions of malice and belligerence toward those who challenge the opinions of the day. When young people find themselves in an academic milieu where thinking is required of them, their first instinct is to escape from all rival forms of thought. In countless universities in the Western world, we have seen students preventing the expression of unwanted opinions, at the very same time as affirming the dogma that there is no objective standard from which any opinion can be judged. Truth has gone, but power and identity remain. And the contest is fought without any possibility of compromise or conciliation, because those both depend upon the belief that there is a fact of the matter and that it is the purpose of discussion to discover it.

Before the advent of social media, the biggest boost for the flight from truth came from the universities themselves. Since the 1960s, humanities departments have surrendered to a wave of relativist scholarship, some of it originating in Paris at the time when the postwar baby boomers knocked the old scholars from their perch. Structuralism, poststructuralism, and deconstruction had a viral effect on the French curriculum, consigning all ideas of objectivity to the trash can. And, in a similar development in

America, the once respectable "pragmatism" of William James, Charles Sanders Peirce, and John Dewey was recycled as an attack on the very concept of truth. Pragmatism came to denote the view that truth is "what works," where "what works" means "what works for me."

The scholars who fostered this post-truth culture tended to come from the left. But they may have unwittingly helped create the milieu in which Donald Trump has flourished. His thoughts, attuned by their very nature to the limits of a Twitter account, make no distinction between the true and the false, and assume that no one else makes such a distinction either. Should the FBI show that Trump colluded with the Russians in manipulating the presidential election, that would not be a fact but simply "fake news," of no greater authority than his own homegrown alternative, which will have the added advantage of being contained in a tweet, so that we can read it quickly and move on.

The president owes his election in part to the astute use of social media, themselves the most powerful instruments in the demotion of truth from its once exalted position in the human psyche. We have yet to get used to the damage done to rational argument by the Internet's conversion into one great seething cauldron of opinions, most of them anonymous, in which every kind of malice and fantasy swamps the still, small voice of humanity. Maybe someone will create software that will worm through the system, systematically deleting all that is false and destructive. But until then we live in a post-truth culture.

An influential proponent of this culture, Michel Foucault, argued that behind every practice, every institution, every system of belief lies power, and that the goal of the historian is to unmask that power and to liberate its victim. Foucault originally described his method as an "archaeology of knowledge" and his subject matter as truth, suggesting that truth and knowledge were the goals of his inquiry. But, in his seminal 1966 work *Les mots et les choses* (published in English in 1970 as *The Order of Things*), he made clear that "truth," for him, would always appear in scare quotes, because "truth" is the product of "discourse," and discourse the voice of power. Foucault's "truth" does not exist independently of the opinions that give voice to it but is created and re-created by the prevailing discourse. Hence, there are no received truths that are not also convenient truths, and truth itself has no existence independent of the political structures that it serves.

In a series of striking books, Foucault showed—to the satisfaction of his youthful readers—that the entire understanding of the world on which French postwar society had been built was simply a mask for the power of the bourgeoisie. "Truth" has no authority outside the social structures that are propped up by it and that in turn prop it up. The whole castle of illusions will come tumbling to the ground just as soon as a rival discourse replaces the old "truth" with a new "truth" of its own.

This is not the place to explore all the ways in which the concept of truth has been marginalized by thinkers like Foucault. But one thing is sure: students who have suffered three or four years of Foucault, Gilles Deleuze, Jacques Derrida, Richard Rorty, and Slavoj Žižek are not likely to believe that there are real truths about the human world and certainly not that it is the business of a university to discover them. On the contrary, they will come away from their studies in the same condition as they began them, acknowledging no distinction between truth and opinion, and confident that their own opinions are the right ones because they are shared by everyone in the same "safe space" as themselves.

The fact is, however, that truth is an indispensable concept, as necessary to the advocates of a post-truth society as to its opponents. Moreover, it is a concept that is more securely founded than any other. Language itself testifies to this. There is no way of expressing an opinion without the implicit assertion of its truth; the first moves in dialogue—"yes," "no," "I agree," "you are wrong"—are ways of establishing a shared commitment to truth. Those who tell lies depend on the distinction between the true and the false, and on the human capacity to engage with it. Our outrage at being lied to by politicians, misled by preachers, and corrupted by seducers is the outrage felt by truth-directed creatures when others have set a trap into which the truth seeker is likely to fall.

Scientific theories aim at truth, and it would be impossible for science to proceed except by conjecture and refutation. To refute a theory is to show it to be false, and even if there are philosophers of science like Paul Feyerabend who believe that any scientific theory can be retained in the face of the evidence, no practicing scientist takes them seriously. The scientific community is founded on debate and challenge, and you cannot debate if you think there is no truth to be aimed at.

Nor is science some isolated sphere to which old-fashioned and eccentric ideas of objectivity retreat from the surrounding intellectual disorder. In every sphere where there is genuine thought and real opinion, the laws of logic apply. All who think are obliged to stand by the implications of what they think. But one proposition implies another if the first cannot be true without the second being true. Logic tells us that every proposition p is equivalent to the proposition that p is true. We cannot reason if we deny the law of noncontradiction, which tells us that p and not p cannot both be true together. At every juncture we encounter the absolute and all-pervasive nature of the concept of truth, which guides our thinking even when it is never mentioned. It is a concept so deeply implanted in the human psyche that only sophism can have any force against it, and those who take refuge in these arguments will not stand up for long.

All this needs to be said now for two reasons. One, as mentioned, is that the relativizing of truth, which seems to its advocates to be a form of toleration, is in fact a recipe for conflict: it closes the door to the very possibility of dialogue. Failure to discuss our differences is a sure way to enhance them, and the first result of the post-truth culture has been the "no platform" and "safe spaces" habit of the modern campus. Post-truth culture is not the friend of toleration but its enemy.

The other reason is that, without the concept of an objective reality, human beings adopt a posture of retreat. In all areas where decisions are required, people lose confidence that there is either a real objective goal or a sure method of pursuing it. Everything becomes veiled in hesitation—a syndrome that can be observed in the very language of so many young people today, for whom all expressions of opinion and decision come padded with "like," "sort of," "basically," and "whatever." The outgoing, definite, and courageous person is a rare product of the post-truth culture, yet one on whose existence the future of society depends. Without such people the democratic process, in which real and urgent issues are confronted in a spirit of open-minded discussion and a preparedness to accept the facts and act on them, will be jeopardized. If so many young people today are losing the sense that the democratic process matters, it is surely in part because they are losing the capacity to take part in it, not knowing what the point of discussion might be. The first goal of a university education should be to impress on them that truth exists, that it is distinct from mere opinion, and that we discover it by arguing with those who dispute what we say.

Values Without Borders

★ ★ ★

ELIZABETH COBBS

A reproach of our age is that "the West" foists its beliefs on other regions of the world. This is like claiming that biology teachers foist an interest in sex on teenagers.

History shows that values considered Western are not. It is patronizing to assume otherwise. People around the world have the same stake in conflict resolution, democracy, and free markets. Starting around 1648, quickening in 1776, and culminating with the 1991 breakup of the Soviet Union, multitudinous nation-states replaced a handful of empires. Today they number nearly two hundred. The global system to which they belong enjoys transnational norms that have dramatically increased life expectancy. That's something everyone values.

Elizabeth Cobbs is Melbern G. Glasscock Professor of American History at Texas A&M University and a senior fellow at Stanford University's Hoover Institution.

These norms arose from survival instincts. Survival means not dying prematurely from violence or starvation. Every human community has historically viewed peace and prosperity—the avoidance of war and poverty—as supreme goods.

For millennia, most assumed that the best, and sometimes only, way to achieve these goals was to steal. Emperors and commoners alike justified foreign conquest and domestic slavery by dehumanizing others as less deserving. Since the mid-seventeenth century, this view has gradually lost ground to the belief that all humans are created equal. That belief eventually led to decolonization and the abolition of slavery. It explains the one-country-one-vote United Nations.

This advancement happened because humans discovered that societies based on equality function better than strictly hierarchical ones. They are wealthier and more peaceful. The United States provided a compelling example early on. Immigrants flocked to its shores and brought their families. Other nations gradually copied aspects of America's system, which itself was an amalgam of ideas that originated elsewhere.

Global convergence is not surprising. Humans have always swapped and even swiped useful technologies, from silkworm cultivation to artificial intelligence. Proven ideas reseed quickly. Like the invention of the wheel in Mesopotamia or hybridization of corn in Mesoamerica, geographical origin does not matter greatly in the long run. No one has to make people buy iPhones or eat tacos. They line up.

"Best" political practices are another technology that humans appropriate when useful. God did not ordain them just for chosen peoples. In recent centuries, three techniques of governance have been widely adopted. They are *arbitration* of disputes, *access* to opportunity in government and business, and *transparency*. Such terms do not carry the emotional appeal or historical baggage of "life, liberty, and the pursuit of happiness." For that reason, they may help us understand why these trends became universal across cultures—and why we should treasure them.

Arbitration means negotiating rules rather than grabbing the nearest club. There are countless examples within societies that practice the rule of law, but arbitration is particularly vital with regard to the most catastrophic form of violence: war.

It is commonplace to credit (or blame) Woodrow Wilson for idealistic notions of collective security. This connotes American responsibility for the system's success, failures, and maintenance. It suggests that Washington may have imposed rules of world order mainly to serve itself. But history shows that others were just as deeply committed and still are.

The story goes back to the Peace of Westphalia, which ended papal authority over Europe in 1648. This first European congress sought to reconcile sworn enemies. Combatants of the wars of the Reformation considered one another so sinful that they refused to meet in the same city. Delegates from Protestant nations convened in one town while Catholic representatives deliberated thirty miles away. Despite their mutual hatred, they made peace by confirming the right of sovereign states to choose their own faith.

The agreement set two precedents. First, it established a doctrine of tolerance for the religious and cultural diversity of nations. Second, it showed the potential of multilateral negotiation—in effect, arbitration.

Philosophers worked through the implications in the following century. With religious authority at an end, jurists articulated a secular "law of nations." In 1758, the Swiss diplomat Emer de Vattel wrote *The Law of Nations*, much admired by George Washington. The Peace of Westphalia, Vattel asserted, established three laws of sovereignty: states are legally equal, they have a right to self-determination, and no state can intervene in another.

There was a catch, however. Without a pope, each state was its own enforcer of these laws. If some bruising enemy made a nation its vassal, there was little the victim could do unless equipped with sufficient lethal force. Poland's disappearance in 1795, when neighbors carved and swallowed it, set a sad example.

The founders of the United States were aware of this defect. When they wrote the Constitution, they not only guaranteed the Westphalian sovereignty of the thirteen states, smallest to largest, but they also set up a commonly elected arbiter to enforce rules to which they had all agreed. In *Federalist 4*, John Jay called the federal government an "umpire" to "decide between them and compel acquiescence."

Alexander Hamilton cautioned against the alternative. Human experience going back to Athens, Sparta, and Rome was a record of "carnage and conquest," he wrote in *Federalist 6*. Europeans would attest that "neighboring nations are naturally enemies of each other." In his concluding essay, Hamilton admitted a "trembling anxiety" should the states fail to adopt the Constitution.

The system turned out to work astonishingly well. Competitive neighbors did not come to blows over resources. No state invaded or annexed another. Itty-bitty Rhode Island enjoyed the same privileges as giant New York. Aside from a civil war over slavery, in which the federal government used force to corral members considered in violation of the compact, domestic disputes were resolved without violence. Together, the states warded off external threats as well.

This arrangement was anomalous. Around the globe, conflict routinely surfaced. Innumerable peoples endured conquest and colonization in the nineteenth century. Empires clashed. "The government of the United States has no model in ancient or modern times," wrote François Barbé-Marbois, the French diplomat who arranged the sale of Louisiana, from which another fifteen states were soon admitted on a basis of equality with founding members.

Visionaries elsewhere called for similar mechanisms. In the decades after Napoleon Bonaparte bled Europe white, hundreds of peace societies sprang up globally. From Austria to New Zealand, they advocated for a "Federation of the World." Poet Alfred Lord Tennyson called for a "Parliament of Man." Novelist Victor Hugo predicted a "United States of Europe" to replace "bullets and bombshells."

Nicholas II of Russia made the first moves toward world organization, well ahead of Woodrow Wilson. In 1899, the czar invited twenty-six nations, including China, Japan, Persia, and Thailand, to the first Hague peace conference. They founded the Permanent Court of Arbitration, which still adjudicates international disputes. Two years later, Latin American nations joined.

The Permanent Court of Arbitration's powers were too narrow to prevent World War I, and the hobbled League of Nations failed to prevent World War II. But they set the trajectory for the United Nations, the European Union, the Organization of African Unity, the World Trade Organization, and other international bodies designed to arbitrate disputes and coordinate interests.

Arbitration is the first pillar of the modern world. Less powerful nations benefit the most. How do we know? Unlike in all preceding eras, these nations have proliferated.

Access to opportunity is the second pillar of modernity. Although every faith enjoins members to treat one another as brothers and sisters, wars of religion ironically helped make equality between individuals, as between nations, a secular value, too. This produced liberty, or access to opportunity.

Liberty is the practice of equality. Equals can't tell one another what to do. The powerful can't withhold rewards for which everyone is entitled to compete. In open societies, the law protects an individual's right to strive for political input and personal gain. A caste system, by comparison, designates hierarchies and allots opportunities. Once an untouchable, always a garbage collector.

The trend toward liberty gathered momentum in England following a century of religious fratricide. The 1689 Bill of Rights diminished the authority of the monarch and increased the people's access to political power. John Locke famously articulated the rationale. Equally possessed of reason, all men had a natural, unalienable right to "life, liberty, and property." Monarchs were contractually obligated to defend their subjects' liberties in exchange for obedience. If kings failed, Locke wrote, citizens of property "might as often and as innocently change their Governors, as they do their Physicians."

The English Bill of Rights enshrined representative government. Americans took it further. They ditched the king and spread the franchise. Other colonial peoples paid heed. Before Thomas Jefferson died in 1826, a dozen countries in the Western Hemisphere had declared independence. They took liberty further yet, becoming first to abolish chattel slavery.

Liberty also had an economic component. It challenged closed systems that harmed prosperity. Adam Smith argued in 1776 that aristocratic monopolies perpetuated backwardness. Open markets stimulated competition. Britain's experience confirmed this. Inventive commoners engineered the Industrial Revolution and made the British people the wealthiest in the world.

The United States took economic openness another step by creating the first common market. Under the Constitution, the sovereign states took down trade barriers erected against one another after the Revolution. No duties, no tariffs. Citizens of any state had access to the markets of all. They could easily start businesses as well. In 1811, New York passed the world's first general incorporation law, allowing almost any group to form its own limited-liability enterprise.

It took another century for the values of political and economic access to gain consensus globally. For Asians and Africans, adoption was hastened by a determination to run their own countries. Far from liberty being thrust upon them, they demanded it. Sometimes, they fought for it. Many found independence a challenge, and some instituted dictatorships as closed as the imperial systems they replaced, but the world order established by the United Nations allowed them to pursue their destinies without fear of recolonization.

Economic openness generally trailed political change. Jealous of their hard-won autonomy from grasping outsiders, China and India, the two most populous countries, closed their markets in the mid-twentieth century. But experience revealed that dictating what individuals could do to earn a living stifled growth. When China in 1978 and India in 1991 reversed these policies, hundreds of millions climbed out of poverty. Income inequality with the West declined.

Allowing common folk to explore their hopes led to global advances in every field, most crucially food, medicine, and hygiene. Human life expectancy climbed from an average of thirty-six years in 1900 to sixty-six years in 2000. In many countries, it zoomed past eighty. Access—the practical expression of liberty—benefited everyone, but especially the poorest.

Transparency undergirded arbitration and access, which were not possible without information and clear rules.

Historians divide world history at 1492. When Columbus sailed the ocean blue, monarchs held information so tightly that even maps were state secrets. The world became modern as governments unclenched their fists. In 1777, the Continental Congress decreed that its proceedings would be published for citizens' inspection. In 1803, the British Parliament looked the other way when a private company began doing the same.

Mikhail Gorbachev based his 1985 reforms of the Soviet Union on perestroika (opening the closed economy) and glasnost (transparency). Like Chinese leaders seven years earlier, he acted in the national self-interest. In the 1980s, the entire city of Moscow could handle only sixteen long-distance telephone calls at once. Glasnost, perestroika, and détente persuaded other countries that they could safely share advanced technologies with the Soviets. Transparency proved more conducive to Russian well-being than secrecy.

Around the world, business leaders also hastened the expansion of transparency. Global capital markets lend money only to foreign borrowers willing to open their spreadsheets. As South Korean sociologist Yong Suk Jang has observed, the global spread of accounting standards shows "the worldwide development of the transparency model."

Private citizens carry the banner, too. Transparency International formed in Germany in 1993 to expose government corruption. It now has chapters in more than one hundred countries. In 2010, entrepreneurs in India started Ipaidabribe.com to expose graft. Reformers in Kenya and Bhutan copied it.

From the most democratic to the most autocratic, world leaders—many of them, anyway—tend to hang their heads when spotted fudging facts. On his first day as president, Barack Obama promised transparency. Then came revelations of spying on world leaders—and he apologized. On the opposite side of the globe, the Saudi minister of health suppressed information on the outbreak of Middle East respiratory syndrome, or MERS. King Abdullah fired him. His successor pledged adherence to "the principles of transparency."

How do we know that transparency has become a world value? People of every ethnicity are mortified when caught violating it—unless they have no shame. That itself is a warning sign.

Arbitration, access, and transparency are the three pillars of modernity. They help us evaluate our leaders, as Locke pointed out, and are our best tools for keeping ourselves safe. Like the Sumerian practice of farming—and for the same reason—they spread around the globe. The West doesn't own them. We all do. They improve survival.

Civics and Civility

★ ★ ★

MICHAEL SIGNER

In August 2017, hundreds of white supremacists, neo-Nazis, nationalists, and other alt-right adherents descended on Charlottesville, Virginia. They were intent on staging a rally they called "Unite the Right." The rally's supposed rationale was to protest the city's planned removal of a statue of Robert E. Lee, the Confederate general who waged war to defend slavery. The night before the rally, they marched carrying torchlights, in a frightening echo of similar displays by Hitler Youth in the 1930s.

One practical effect of this grotesque undertaking in Charlottesville was a reminder to the world that civics and civility are

---

Michael Signer, former mayor of Charlottesville, Virginia (2016–2018), is the author of *Demagogue: The Fight to Save Democracy from Its Worst Enemies* and *Becoming Madison: The Extraordinary Origins of the Least Likely Founding Father*.

27

vital elements of democracy, and that they must be defended from illiberal forces gaining traction in the United States and elsewhere around the globe.

I was the mayor of Charlottesville at the time of the onslaught. These invaders were not only bigots. They were also like arsonists, setting fire to the essential pillars of deliberative democracy. Over a period of twenty-four hours, they succeeded in instigating the violent chaos that they clearly hungered for. They came girded for battle and taunted counterprotesters, many of them African American, with disgusting insults, including, according to the *Washington Post*, "Dylann Roof was a hero!"

Dylann Roof is the white supremacist who in 2015 shot to death nine black worshippers at a church in Charleston, South Carolina.

In Charlottesville, a man named James Alex Fields Jr. drove his car into a crowd of those protesting against the white supremacists, according to police, and killed thirty-two-year-old Heather Heyer, and injured dozens more. At the time of this writing, Fields was awaiting trial for first-degree murder.

Some of the white supremacists in Charlottesville wore red "Make America Great Again" caps, and the president who campaigned on that slogan quickly waded into the aftermath of this tragic, enraging story, declaring in a news conference that there was "blame on both sides," and that "you also had some very fine people on both sides." But he did not—indeed, he could not—specify who the "very fine people" were among the white supremacists and neo-Nazis.

Now, consider that the white supremacists' torchlight march occurred on the grounds of the University of Virginia, founded by Thomas Jefferson. As Jefferson and the nation's other founders knew, the health of a democracy depends on its citizens' appreciation for the rights and duties of their citizenship—or civics. Another founder, James Madison, once wrote of constitutional liberty, "The people who are the authors of this blessing must also be its guardians." That guardianship is looking threadbare in these hyper-partisan times. Today's constant drumbeat of attacks on democratic institutions, including Donald Trump's attacks on the judiciary and the press, is deforming even basic notions of citizenship.

Instead of honoring the democratic process, Trump fights investigations into Russia's interference in the 2016 election. Instead of encouraging an informed citizenry, the president routinely denounces accurate reporting as "fake news." Instead of embodying the spirit of a nation with the motto "e pluribus unum," he demonizes immigrants.

But Trump is not entirely to blame. In many ways, he is a symptom as much as a cause, exploiting a creeping modern neglect of democracy's building blocks. Civic knowledge—about how the branches of government work, about legal rights and the courts, about election processes and voting rights, about free speech and freedom of religion—is essential to a citizenry that knows its own rights and respects the rights of others. That knowledge goes hand in hand with *civility*: the expectation that people treat other with the respect due to fellow members of a great democratic enterprise. When civic understanding *decreases*, so does *incivility*, as people begin to regard others not as fellow citizens but as competitors or enemies. The notion of bipartisanship or compromise falls by the wayside, and the public square becomes a boxing ring.

The stakes of this democratic erosion are both reflected and reinforced in current trends. In 2017, Roberto Stefan Foa and Yascha Mounk, writing in the *Journal of Democracy*, found disturbing trends in public opinion polls of the "deconsolidation" of American democracy, particularly among the younger generations. When asked to rate on a scale of 1 to 10 how "essential" it is for them "to live in a democracy," 72 percent of those born before World War II chose 10. But among the millennial generation the number was dramatically lower: around 30 percent. The authors also found that over the past three decades, the share of US citizens who think that it would be a "good" or "very good" thing for the "army to rule" has steadily risen. In 1995, just one in sixteen respondents agreed with that position; now, one in six agree. Today, while 43 percent of older Americans don't believe it can be legitimate in a democracy for the military to take over when the government is incompetent or failing to do its job, the figure among millennials is 19 percent.

Meanwhile, in their 2018 book *How Democracies Die*, the political scientists Steven Levitsky and Daniel Ziblatt find that four criteria distinguish the leaders of faltering democracies: The leader (1) shows only a weak commitment to democratic rules, (2) denies the legitimacy of opponents, (3) tolerates violence, and (4) shows some willingness to curb civil liberties or the media. They write, "With the exception of Richard Nixon, no major-party presidential candidate met even one of these four criteria over the last century." Today, the authors find, "Donald Trump met them all."

Civic institutions, from every level of government to schools of all types, can start to reverse these disturbing trends by taking firm steps to burnish the democratic practices that are the heart of the shared civic project. This is not just a call for a renewed commitment to civic education—though that is certainly needed, as civics has fallen out of fashion in high school curricula. With social media and online platforms leading so many to rush to the polar extremes of debate, a broad national campaign is necessary to make deliberation work again. Millions of people must be stirred to appreciate anew the essential democratic trait of listening to opposing opinions instead of trying to shout them down in person or on Twitter; to approach with respect those with whom they disagree; to elect leaders who believe in the virtue of compromise and will show generations to come how it's done; and, above all, to restore "civil" to its rightful place beside democracy.

American companies could do more to fight the promulgation of incivility that festers until it turns into hate, and companies should do more to promote civility itself. In the days before the "Unite the Right" rally, Airbnb boldly chose to cancel the reservations of protesters coming to town for the white supremacist gathering. In so doing, the company threw down an important gauntlet. Too many online companies have taken a passive attitude toward the rising tide of hate and menace. It is plain now that the laissez-faire approach has created not only a Wild West on the Internet but also a tilt toward might makes right, will to power, and the stirrings of humanity's worst demons.

I'm often asked whether I'm an optimist or a pessimist after what happened in Charlottesville. I'm an optimist because I firmly believe that America can overcome this ugly chapter in its history, just as it has overcome other stains, like McCarthyism and Jim Crow, by emphasizing the very values and principles that have guided the nation since its inception.

But nothing will happen because of ideas, or arcs of history, or pendulums, or any other evocative but empty metaphor that doesn't require *action* by people dedicated to the tenets of liberal democracy itself. That means specific acts, millions of them—some quotidian, some extraordinary, but all of them essential—to make manifest the values of democracy. We must not yield to the premise that individual human beings in their ability to choose, to grapple, to reckon, to aspire to wisdom, are less powerful than abstract history operating through them. Widespread cynicism, mistrust, and incompetence created a vacuum that the nihilistic alt-right rushed to fill. The antidote for that poisonous development is a reinvigorated focus on democracy—an institution that depends on a self-fulfilling belief by citizens and leaders that they can effect changes both large and small.

It comes down to a matter of day-to-day life, of what Americans choose to do. This work is available, and necessary, in virtually every arena, from the grand to the intimate, from public to private lives. It means calling out the unacceptable and educating those who need to know more. It means hard conversations and confrontations among the family at the dinner table, elected officials at a city council meeting, teachers and students in a high school classroom, executives and employees in a corporate boardroom, editors and reporters in editorial meetings, and judges and law clerks in chambers. And it means restoring civic education to classrooms, not teaching just about history but also about the dynamic principles of conscience that inform a vigorous and alert constitutional democracy.

Does this sound too idealistic, too optimistic for these angry times? It shouldn't. This is all within reach. Indeed, events like the massive voter turnout in Virginia against Trumpism in November 2017, in the wake of the "Unite the Right" rally in Charlottesville, are cause for real hope. Voters were breathing life into Thomas Jefferson's observation about the combination of personal agency and the upward, optimistic model of history: "Where is our republicanism to be found? Not in the Constitution, but merely in the spirit of the people." For the framers, this constitutionalism was the muscle that would give life to the skeleton of the document's famous checks and balances. Another founder, James Madison, once wrote of constitutional liberty, "The people who are the authors of this blessing must also be its guardians."

The ultimate civics lesson is that America's true system of checks and balances lies not in its institutions but in the people themselves. And there's no time like the present to take action.

In Praise of Globalization

★ ★ ★

JAGDISH BHAGWATI

G lobalization, I once joked, was doomed to condemnation in public discourse because the letters in the word added up to thirteen.

Today, the joke looks like prophecy. Far from having become accepted as desirable once impassioned tempers yielded to reasoned response, globalization is increasingly the object of much malign, if ill-informed, commentary. Contrary to the expectations of many, such as *New York Times* columnist Thomas Friedman, that globalization is here to stay, its opponents see it as vulnerable and seek to dismantle it. Yet the fact remains: many countries over the past half century have improved by

Jagdish Bhagwati, University Professor (economics, law, and international affairs) at Columbia University, is the author of *In Defense of Globalization* (2004), with a new afterword (2007).

many measures, including life expectancy. One may plausibly argue that these improvements have tended to occur in countries where the liberal-democratic values of liberty and openness to the world prompted them to welcome trade and foreign investment. But the critics of such globalization have remained hostile to its merits.

Before weighing the debate over globalization, we should note that discord often arises just because commentators have different ideas in mind when they think of globalization.

The simplest definition is the best: globalization is the integration of the national economy into the international economy. This integration can happen in different realms: trade, direct foreign investment, portfolio capital flows (cross-border stock and bond investment, for example), intellectual property, and movements of humanity (both economic migrants and refugees fleeing war, pestilence, and discrimination).

These facets of globalization must be identified and acknowledged so that the debate can be conducted on rational terms. Critics who are worried about free trade—like some of President Trump's misguided advisers—are to be distinguished from those who worry about free capital flows. One can thus be for free trade (as I am) but not buy into free capital flows (as I don't). The distinction may seem obvious, but anti-globalization intellectuals have been surprised to discover that nuances can exist on the pro-globalization side.

So, what was it about globalization originally that made critics raise a battle cry?

In the 1970s, the Chilean sociologist Osvaldo Sunkel led the charge against what he called "transnational capitalism and national disintegration." His focus was the deleterious effects on "the national economy." No mention of distributional questions that would come later. Nor of social impacts on democracy, on the environment, on child labor. And the concern of these early critics was strictly about the effect of "national disintegration" in developing countries (i.e., underdeveloped countries, before the reign of euphemisms began). As I said at the time, in contrast to existing mutual-gain models, under which there would be a "benign impact" outcome for the developing countries, they faced the possibility of a "malign impact" outcome. It seemed reasonable to the anti-globalizers that competition between the rich and the poor countries would only impoverish the latter: the strong would overcome the weak. Yet that hasn't proved to be the case.

The critics of globalization have moved on in two important ways: first, the concern now focuses more on social issues; and, second, in an ironic role reversal, the fear of a malign impact has now shifted to the rich countries. While the poor countries, and their people, now see globalization as enhancing their opportunities, rich countries face protests from populists and other militant critics who fear that competing with the poor counties will diminish their own opportunities.

The concern with social issues came of age at the World Trade Organization meeting in Seattle in 1999. I was present there and was teargassed as protesters turned violent. It became apparent to me that the protesters were concerned not about "national welfare"—that was a losing argument, because we economists could present them with voluminous evidence that showed unambiguously how international trade and investment had been beneficial in the postwar period of liberalization and opening of national markets. Instead, the protesters assailed globalization because it was failing on social issues.

On returning to Columbia University, I began work on what would become *In Defense of Globalization* (2004), where I took up several social concerns, such as child labor, the environment, gender rights, democracy, culture, wages, and labor standards, and examined the myriad skeptical and hostile arguments. I concluded that globalization, in the shape of trade and direct foreign investment, was a force to be celebrated, not lamented.

The opponents of globalization, now in rich countries, are seized with fear that they will not be able to compete with poor countries. Some labor unions argue that free trade with poor countries will produce paupers in rich ones, so they propose restricting free trade to "like wage" countries: free trade with Canada is fine but with Mexico is disastrous.

Reinforcing what might be called the Age of Fear, there is also the Age of Rage. Manifestly, rage is running through some anti-globalization groups. This comes from the presumption that globalization benefits elites ("the 1 percent") but harms the poor at the bottom of income distribution (the bottom 30 percent). The inevitability of income distribution worsening in an open economy is implausible in the absence of convincing economic modeling. Nor are the wealthy a static group; people fall out and new ones enter.

The rage today is also fed by the wealthy themselves, often a part of a global elite, indulging in conspicuous consumption as never before, their ostentatious habits on display for the Internet's ogling eye and available for examination anywhere in the world. Does the World Economic Forum really need to be held at a luxurious, remote ski resort in Davos, Switzerland? I am regularly struck by the strangeness of the current moment when I see the *How to Spend It* weekly magazine supplement for my favorite newspaper, the *Financial Times*, which often lectures against inequality. As do plenty of the paper's wealthy readers. The greater good would be well served if our elites dialed back their often offensive and incendiary hypocrisy. Go and buy a castle in the Rhine Valley each week, for all I care, but don't post about it on Instagram.

A relatively new target of globalization's critics is immigration. Many in the United States, the European Union, and elsewhere believe that it is the elites who favor immigration, even if it harms the working poor. There is some truth in this, I fear. Years ago, in the 1990s, when I argued for freer immigration, I had a friendly argument with economist Paul Krugman, formerly one of my star pupils. He believed that the proponents of more immigration were interested in cheap labor for their assembly lines. Bill Clinton was for a border wall. Hillary Clinton wanted cruelly to deny driver's licenses to illegal immigrants. Times have changed. Formerly a boutique issue, immigration has grown in importance, with new battle lines being drawn and redrawn as it took center stage in the globalization debate. Sensible, fair-minded immigration reform is needed—not least because then nationalists and populists couldn't use it as a cudgel against a phenomenon that has inarguably been a net good for the world. They would of course move on to other illiberal tactics, so the debate is far from over.

The Centrality of Dissent

★ ★ ★

NATAN SHARANSKY WITH
RACHEL FRIEDMAN

L iving under totalitarian rule confers few advantages, particularly for someone who is also unlucky enough to find himself at odds with its reigning ideology. Yet one advantage that my
experience in the Soviet Union did provide is that it revealed to
me, with great clarity, what distinguishes free societies from unfree ones—namely, tolerance of disagreement or dissent. Without cultural and institutionalized respect for this principle, those
whose views deviate from the ruling orthodoxies of their day will
find themselves intimidated into silence or, when they do speak,

---

Natan Sharansky, a human-rights activist and former political prisoner in the
Soviet Union, is an Israeli public figure and until recently served as head of the
Jewish Agency for Israel. Rachel Friedman, who provided research assistance
for Sharansky's *The Case for Democracy*, holds a PhD in political science from
Harvard and is a postdoctoral fellow in Israel.

penalized with the loss of their livelihoods, physical freedom, and even their lives. The way in which a regime reacts to dissent is perhaps the most powerful indicator of its basic character and future prospects. It is therefore incumbent on liberal democracies to pay close attention to dissidents around the world, to support freedom fighters in the struggle for basic rights, and to vigilantly guard their own citizens' ability to disagree without fear of retribution.

In 2004, Ron Dermer and I published *The Case for Democracy*, describing what I had learned as a dissident in the Soviet Union about the fundamental distinction between free and fear societies. Free societies allow citizens to express their views without risk of arrest, imprisonment, or physical harm. Fear societies do not. A simple way to determine which category a society falls into is to apply what we called the town square test: Can a person walk into a busy public square and express her views without fear of physical harm? If so, she lives in a free society; if not, it is a fear society.

When a government is unwilling to accept the natural diversity of human opinions, its only course is to indoctrinate citizens into a rigid belief system that it alone controls. As people grow dissatisfied and begin to question those beliefs, the regime will resort to intimidation and terror to preserve its ideological monopoly. The more questioning there is, the more energy and resources the government will have to spend to control its own people. In addition, it will invent various external threats to galvanize and unify its citizens. This perpetual need for external enemies renders dictatorships inherently aggressive. It also means that the struggle of democratic dissidents, who wish to replace their tyrannical governments with liberal ones, is aligned with the fundamental interest of free societies to live in peace.

Every fear society comprises three types of people. True believers are those who genuinely believe in the regime's official ideology. Doublethinkers, by contrast, have begun to question the reigning dogmas but are too afraid of the consequences of dissent to speak out. Finally, dissidents are those who have crossed the fateful threshold from silent questioning to open critique. Compelled by a deep-seated longing to be free, dissidents brave the consequences of disagreement—harassment, imprisonment, torture, even death—for the right to speak their minds and for others to do the same.

The proportions of these three groups are constantly changing. Although it is impossible to know how many doublethinkers there are, their number tends to increase all the time, as daily restrictions and indignities make people question the justice of their government and the validity of its official creed. Dissidents, for their part, will be few at first, but their courage often inspires others to become outspoken critics themselves. Revolutions take place when enough people simultaneously cross the line from doublethink to open dissent that the regime can no longer contain the upsurge of opposition and must make liberalizing concessions or collapse.

I am convinced, based on my own experiences and those of other dissidents around the world, including in China, North Korea, Egypt, Syria, and Iran, that doublethink is a universal phenomenon. I am also convinced that it is inherently and deeply uncomfortable, involving constant self-censorship and anxiety lest the wrong words come out. The natural drive to shed this burden means that the dynamic of questioning, dissent, and revolution is not culturally or geographically specific. Deep down, all people desire to live freely in the sense I am describing.

Given this understanding of life under dictatorship, it has been one of my lifelong aims to persuade the leaders of free societies to see democratic dissidents as their most important strategic allies. Dissidents are both prophets of revolution and key partners in promoting the spread of freedom.

Dissidents are prophets because they alone perceive the extent of internal opposition to a regime. Because it is impossible from the outside to distinguish a doublethinker from a true believer, foreign observers will have difficulty knowing how much of a population has broken faith with its rulers. It may even appear from public demonstrations that masses of citizens support the regime, leading outsiders to misunderstand domestic dynamics. Dissidents, by contrast, see the unraveling of true belief from within, and they see the regime's frantic efforts to preserve itself in the face of growing resistance.

For example, farsighted Soviet dissidents such as Andrei Amalrik had predicted the fall of the Soviet Union many years before its collapse. Amalrik's account struck a nerve with Soviet leadership, which understood the power of dissident ideas and its own vulnerability to citizens' longing to be free. His explanation of how and why the regime would fall also corresponded to what in fact transpired, as the Communist government weakened and eventually lost control of its subjects. Yet most Western observers, having failed to take heed, were caught off guard when his predictions came to pass.

Similarly, Egyptian and Syrian dissidents had warned that their governments were susceptible to collapse years before revolution and civil war engulfed those countries. Yet just two weeks before the fall of Hosni Mubarak's regime in 2011, American secretary of state Hillary Clinton gave her assessment "that the Egyptian government is stable." In March of that same year, John Kerry—who in 2009 had called Syria "an essential player in bringing peace and stability to the region"—acknowledged Bashar al-Assad's supposed good faith and predicted that his regime would change for the better. While such misguided outsiders were busy touting dictators as guardians of regional order, perceptive observers on the inside understood that many of their fellow citizens were already doublethinkers, and that most of their rulers' energies were therefore directed to suppressing opposition and cultivating external enemies. In short, it was again dissidents—not foreign leaders or experts—who perceived their regimes' weakness and foresaw what was to come.

Dissidents are also critical partners for the free world because, by supporting them, our leaders affirm their moral commitment to liberty and advance their most basic interest in international peace.

It is important to stress that not all dissidents are strategic allies, but only those who seek to promote liberal and democratic principles. It is also essential to remember that revolution and elections do not guarantee stable democracy, because the latter requires fair elections in a free society, which can take generations to realize. Once the spirit of popular revolt is unleashed, outsiders cannot control what will happen. But, by identifying,

NATAN SHARANSKY WITH RACHEL FRIEDMAN

listening to, and cultivating democratic dissidents over the long term, the leaders of liberal democracies can support the creation of civil society and increase the odds that revolution will lead to freedom. Prodemocratic dissent is thus a free society's most potent unconventional weapon, because it both destabilizes dictatorships from within and, when consistently bolstered over a course of many years, supports local institutions and values that are sympathetic to liberty.

During the Cold War, there were a handful of world leaders who understood this and who made it a point to meet with dissidents, call out human rights abuses, and link their governments' cooperation with Moscow to the latter's respect for human rights. This moral and practical support was crucial for those of us fighting the Soviet regime. It gave us the confidence to continue our struggle, knowing that we had not been forsaken by our powerful friends. The combination of external and internal pressure led to liberalizing reforms that weakened the Communist government's control and ultimately brought down the Iron Curtain.

This understanding of the centrality of dissent to a free society implies two crucial lessons for today.

The first is that world leaders must pay more attention to the words and the fate of democratic dissidents. President George W. Bush took a unique and laudable interest in freedom fighters, meeting with dozens during his time in office and developing personal relationships with many. Yet his successor was far less keen to do the same, and as a result the Obama presidency was full of missed opportunities to promote liberty and undermine dictatorships, particularly in the Middle East.

The Green Movement in Iran in 2009 and, the following year, the series of uprisings that became known collectively as the Arab Spring had disappointing outcomes. Nevertheless, the democratic sentiment that fueled them confirmed both my belief that the desire for freedom is universal and my understanding of why democratic revolutions occur. These events stemmed above all from ordinary people's refusal to accept government control over their thought, speech, and livelihoods. In each country, a few acts of daring resistance paved the way for mass uprisings, as thousands of ordinary citizens crossed the line from doublethink to dissent. In many instances, as a trickle of opposition became a flood, regimes discovered that they could no longer control their people through fear. As a result, these governments proved brittle and several collapsed. Like all fear societies, they could survive only as long as they were able to intimidate their citizens into submission.

Unlike Soviet dissidents, however, who counted on the consistent support of the West, freedom fighters in Arab and Muslim countries found themselves abandoned by the leaders of the free world. The latter, having lost their faith in liberal democracy, were wary of promoting their principles abroad or "imposing" their way of life on others. They also mistakenly regarded authoritarian regimes as the keys to stability and feared that by pressing for internal changes they would alienate their supposed allies.

This view seems to have motivated President Obama's response to the Iranian prodemocracy movement, in particular the mass protests that erupted in 2009 over Iran's rigged presidential election. In a speech earlier that year directed to Iran's leaders, the American president had renounced a policy of "threats" in favor of "engagement…grounded in mutual respect" with the Islamic republic. Then, just before the Iranian election, he sent a letter to Iranian supreme leader Ali Khamenei, reportedly conveying his desire to improve relations and his assurance that he would not interfere in Iran's internal affairs. Obama's stance apparently emboldened Tehran to launch a massive crackdown on regime critics and human-rights activists in the election's wake. As Iranians began to pour into the streets to demand freedom, and, as masses of ordinary citizens debated whether to cross that fateful line between doublethink and dissent, the American government effectively told them all to stay home.

According to dissidents with whom I have spoken, what Iranian democrats needed most during those protests was for the American administration to state unequivocally that it supported their goals and stood firmly as their ally. Yet such rhetorical encouragement, to say nothing of material aid, never came. America's commitment to the political status quo had the effect of pouring cold water into an almost boiling pot: it discouraged revolutionary fervor at the precise moment when it could have led to meaningful change. Today, Iran remains a dictatorship bent on intimidating its citizens, acquiring nuclear weapons, supporting international terrorism, and destroying the state of Israel.

To his credit, President Donald Trump does appear to intuitively understand the importance of offering rhetorical support to dissidents, as he did during the January 2018 protests that took place across Iran. Yet it is not clear whether this instinct will be translated into a consistent policy. Moreover, he was nearly alone in backing the protestors, as few if any democratic leaders today have the moral clarity and strategic vision to support the forces of freedom over the long term.

To those legitimately wary of war and other open-ended involvements in foreign lands, I must stress that a policy of consistent support for democratic dissidents requires neither military conflict nor a rejection of diplomacy. During the string of democratic transitions that took place around the world between 1974 and 1990, external powers used a variety of tools to pressure authoritarian regimes to open up and respect their citizens' rights. The Helsinki Final Act, for example, proclaimed the international priority of human rights and, through the mutually reinforcing efforts of dissidents and foreign leaders, led to effective rights-monitoring systems within various countries. During the same period, the European Community promoted democracy by using membership as an incentive for liberalization, while the United States used economic pressure, support for prodemocratic forces, and multilateral diplomacy to encourage internal changes, all to significant effect. As a result of this international political climate, dissidents had good reason to hope that their efforts and personal sacrifices would not be in vain. Those of us who created the Helsinki Group in Moscow, for instance, knew that we would be arrested for highlighting Soviet abuses, yet we also believed that foreign leaders were listening to us and that our oppressors would in some way be held to account.

We cannot know what consequences a similar approach would have had for the Iranian prodemocracy movement or the Arab Spring. But we do know that dissidents today no longer enjoy the level of international support that my colleagues and I did. We know that it is possible for liberal leaders to stand unwaveringly with their true allies: to speak about the plight of dissidents, to offer them assistance in cultivating the institutions of civil society, and to condition relations with their rulers on respect for basic rights. And we know that when they do not do these things, they have even less chance of nurturing freedom where it is most lacking.

In fact, indifference to the fate of freedom fighters is especially dangerous now, when some of the world's most powerful countries, in particular China and Russia, are growing ever more hostile to dissent. Dictators can certainly be *tactical* partners to democracies: Abdel Fattah al-Sisi, for example, has been helpful in fighting Muslim fundamentalism in Egypt. But we must remember that these are not *strategic* alliances, because they do not serve the long-term goals of promoting liberty and peace. The more a dictator is hated by his own people, the less of our allegiance he merits.

The second lesson that we should draw from my analysis is that, to remain free, liberal democracies need to vigilantly protect their own citizens' right to openly speak their minds. This is not to say that free societies cannot place reasonable restrictions on the type and manner of speech they allow. Rather, the town square test simply dictates that ordinary people be able to express their own opinions in public without fear of violence or official retribution.

Recently, a number of American and Canadian college campuses have managed to fail this simple test. The list of distinguished speakers who have been uninvited, forced to withdraw, or bullied during their talks at various colleges includes Ayaan Hirsi Ali, Henry Kissinger, Narendra Modi, Anna Quindlen, Condoleezza Rice, Lawrence Summers, James Watson, and many others. What is more, a recent survey by the Brookings Institution revealed that a majority of college students think it is acceptable to shout down a speaker with whom they disagree, and nearly 20 percent go as far as to condone violence in that situation.

Of course, those who articulate unpopular opinions on campus do not face the same dangers as dissidents in fear societies, and they usually have the protection of law enforcement, a crucial distinction. But they do face real threats to their livelihoods and well-being for the simple act of speaking their minds or listening to an alternative point of view.

At one of my own talks at a Canadian university, for instance, a group of aggressive anti-Israel protestors took to shouting me down and bullying the students who had come to listen. Based on the passive reaction of the faculty members and administrators there, it seemed as though this was a common occurrence, part of everyday campus life. Indeed, when one of the students in the audience began to cry, I asked one of the organizers why she was so distressed, and he responded that, while I would soon get to leave that toxic environment, she and the others would have to stay, facing intimidation and hostility on a daily basis.

Israel is of course only one issue about which a climate of fear prevails on college campuses. There are many others, and it appears that the forces working to silence disagreement are only growing stronger. The fact that many citizens, especially young adults, in free societies have such a poor understanding of the importance of dissent does not bode well for the future of their countries. Liberal democracies must remember that failure to protect this most fundamental of freedoms can easily put them on the path to fear. The resulting loss would be not only theirs, but the rest of the world's as well.

At the Heart of Freedom: Economic Liberty

★ ★ ★

DEIRDRE NANSEN MCCLOSKEY

Since the rise during the late 1800s of socialism, New Liberalism, and Progressivism, it has been conventional to scorn *economic* liberty as vulgar and optional—something only fat cats care about. But the original liberalism during the 1700s of Voltaire, Adam Smith, Tom Paine, and Mary Wollstonecraft recommended an economic liberty for rich and poor that was understood as not messing with other people's stuff. When Adam Smith spoke of "the liberal plan of equality, liberty, and justice," the liberty he referred to was economic. It was a good

Deirdre Nansen McCloskey is an economist and historian. Her latest book, the last in her trilogy The Bourgeois Era, is *Bourgeois Equality: How Ideas, Not Capital or Institutions, Enriched the World.*

idea, new in 1776. And in the next two centuries the liberal idea proved to be astonishingly effective at improving the lives of the formerly desperate and poor.

Well into the 1800s, most thinking people, such as Henry David Thoreau, were economic liberals. Thoreau around 1840 invented procedures for his father's small factory making pencils, enabling it to become, for a decade or so, America's leading pencil maker. Thoreau was a businessman as much as an environmentalist and civil disobeyer. When high-quality imports finally overtook the Thoreau pencils, the family business adapted by turning to making graphite for the printing of engravings.

That's the economic liberal deal. You get to offer in the first act a betterment to customers, but you don't later get to arrange for protection from competitors. After making your bundle in the first act, you face competition in the second. Too bad. In *On Liberty* (1859) the economist and philosopher John Stuart Mill declared that "society admits no right, either legal or moral, in the disappointed competitors to immunity from this kind of suffering; and feels called on to interfere only when means of success have been employed which it is contrary to the general interest to permit—namely, fraud or treachery, and force." No protectionism. No economic nationalism. The customers, prominent among them the poor, are enabled in the first through third acts to buy better and cheaper pencils.

Economic liberty is the liberty about which most ordinary people care. The protagonist of *Forever Flowing* by Vasily Grossman (1905–1964), the only example of a successful Stalinist writer who converted wholly to anti-communism, declares that "I used to think liberty was liberty of speech, liberty of the press, liberty of conscience. Here is what it amounts to: you have to have the right to sow what you wish to, to make shoes or coats, to bake into bread the flour ground from the grain you have sown, and to sell it or not sell it as you wish;...to work as you wish and not as they order you." In eighteenth-century Britain, the blessed Adam Smith was outraged by interference in the right of workers to move freely to find profitable work: "The property which every man has in his own labor, as it is the original foundation of all other property, so it is the most sacred and inviolable. To hinder him from employing this...in what manner he thinks proper without injury to his neighbor, is a plain violation of this most sacred property." Not as they order you.

And economic liberty has massively enriched the world in goods and services. How much? In 1800 the income per person of a country like Sweden or Japan, expressed in 2018 prices, was about three dollars a day. Now it is more than a hundred dollars a day, a 3,200 percent increase. Not 100 percent or even 200 percent, but 3,200 percent. No starvation. Taller people. Doubled life expectancy. Bigger houses. Faster transport. Higher education.

The usual explanations of the Great Enrichment from economists and historians don't compute. Accumulation of capital or the extractions of empire were not the causes. Ingenuity was, and the ingenuity was spurred in turn by a new liberty after 1800. The liberal plan of equality, liberty, and justice made masses of people bold—first the free and wealthy men, then poor men, then former slaves, then women, then gays, then the handicapped, then, then, then. Make everyone free, it turned out (the experiment had never been tried before on such a scale), and you get masses and masses of people inspired and enabled to have a go. "I contain multitudes," sang the poet of the new liberty. And so Walt Whitman did. He and his friends and countrymen and their descendants had a go at steam engines and research universities and railways and public schools and electric lights and corporations and self-service grocery stores and containerization and open-source engineering. We became rich by giving ordinary people their economic liberty.

And the "we" keeps growing. China after 1978 and India after 1991, for example, began to abandon the illiberal theory of socialism, devised by Europeans in the middle of the 1800s and exported by the 1970s to a third of the globe. Turning toward economic liberalism meant that the annual growth of goods and services per person available to the poorest in China and India rose from its socialist level of 1 percent (or sometimes negative growth) to 7–12 percent. At such rates it will take only two or three generations for both countries to attain European standards of living. Such a prospect for this four in ten humans on the planet is no pipe dream. Similar enrichments were achieved over a similar span in Hong Kong, South Korea, Singapore, and Taiwan, with other startling success stories for new economic liberalism and reasonably honest government in Ireland and Botswana.

An economically illiberal government can of course borrow from countries honoring liberty. The Soviet Union did that from 1917 to 1989, for example, and for a long time even many economists in the West believed its fairy tale that central planning worked. When Communism fell in 1989, the world discovered decisively that planning did *not* work, not for the economy or the environment or for other liberties. Singapore is sometimes cited as an example of intelligent tyranny. And so is China, dominated still by an elite of Communist Party members. Both, however, practice substantial economic liberty, despite their lamentable habit of jailing political opponents.

And enrichment in the end leads to demands for *all* liberties, political as much as the economic liberties causing the initial enrichment, as it did in Taiwan and South Korea. Enriched people will not long put up with the trappings of serfdom. And, anyway, the *average* record of tyrannies is economically disastrous, such as in Zimbabwe, next door to prosperous Botswana, or for that matter in the long and dismal history of illiberalism worldwide from the invention of agriculture down to 1800.

The Christian Gospel says properly, "For what shall it profit a man, if he shall gain the whole world, and lose his own soul?" The claim against economic liberty has always been that even if we gain the world in goods, we lose our souls. Yet mutually advantageous exchange is not the worst ethical school. It is better than the violent pride of aristocrats or the violent insolence of bureaucrats. And in economic liberalism the human desire to excel is given millions of honorable paths, from model-railway building to show business, as against in illiberal societies the narrow path to eminence at the court or politburo or army. We do not lose our souls in commerce but cultivate them. The military, admired nowadays even in liberal societies, is commended daily for its "service." But every economic act among consenting adults is service. The ethical habits of commerce are expressed daily in a shopkeeper's greeting of customers: "How can I help you?"

The upshot? The concert halls and museums of well-to-do countries are marvels, the universities thrive, and the seeking of the transcendent, if not always in established churches, is expanding. One cannot attend much to the transcendence of art or science or sports or family or God when bent over in a field from dawn to dusk.

The sure way to make people bad *and* poor is the illiberality of communism and fascism, and even the slow if sweetly motivated socialism of overregulation. Women in the theocratic despotism of Saudi Arabia are quartered at home, thwarted from achievement. The economic nationalism of the new alt-right in America is impoverishing, and anyway would close off ideas from the wider world. If the general betterment is slowing in the United States—a widely held if doubtful claim—then all the more reason to invite the betterment coming from newly enriching countries such as China or India, and not close off the country to "protect jobs." Protectionist logic would have every product—breakfast cereal, accordions, computers—made in the USA. It is childish as economics, though stirring as nationalism.

At the heart of communism and fascism, and of the impulse toward overregulation, is the yearning to massively mess with other people's stuff. The usual political spectrum—which does not include true liberalism—is a spectrum merely of alterative coercions by government. In the United States more than one thousand occupations require licenses from the government. Opening a new hospital requires the existing hospitals to grant their potential new competitor a certificate of need. In Tennessee, if you wish to open a furniture-moving company, such as two men with a truck, you are required by law to ask permission of the existing moving companies. The protection of jobs has created worldwide an enormous and politically explosive army of unemployed youths. One-quarter of French people under twenty-five and out of school are unemployed. It's worse in South Africa.

Yet true and humane liberals are not anarchists (Greek *anarchos*, "no ruler"). One can admit that it can be good to abridge economic liberty a little to the extent of taxing the well-to-do to give a hand up to the poor, such as through publicly financed education. No serious argument there—Smith and Mill and even Thoreau agreed. (True, big government routinely also gives a hand up to the rich and powerful, such as protections for farmers in the United States and the Common Market. Governments follow too often the nasty version of the Golden Rule, namely, those who have the gold, rule.) And one can admit that if those wretched Canadians invade the United States, economic liberty might usefully be abridged for the duration, if it is prudent for defense. No argument there, either. (Yet governments routinely break the peace in pursuit of glorious conquest. Fear those Canadians or fear Washington.)

The solution, traditional liberals believe, is to restrict the power of government, even when the government is popular. Fascism often and communism sometimes, sadly, are popular. Moderate versions of both, in nationalism and socialism, are very popular, until they go wrong. People favor, for the nonce, the alleged glory of governmental aggressions against foreigners (see Europe in August 1914) and the alleged free lunches of governmental control of the economy (see Venezuela in August 2017).

Better to keep the government on a short leash. Of the 176 countries in the world ranked by Transparency International for its Corruption Perceptions Index (ranging from Denmark and New Zealand at the top to Zimbabwe and North Korea at the bottom), consider, generously, the top thirty governments as reasonably honest. They are perhaps worthy of, say, fresh infusions of taxpayer dollars. Portugal is the margin. Italy ranked 60th out of the 176, just below Cuba and Romania, and just above Saudi Arabia. What percent of world population was governed by the better governments, such as France or the United States? Ten percent. That is to say, 90 percent of the global population lies under governments agreed to be corrupt on the level of below-Portugal.

The calculation shows why the optimism among amiable people on the left, and among not so amiable people on the right, about extending the illiberal powers of government is naïve. Thoreau wrote, in true liberal style, "I heartily accept the motto,— 'That government is best which governs least,' and I should like to see it acted up to more rapidly and systematically."

Yes, with a few modest exceptions.

PART TWO

Threats

Threats to democracy today come in many forms, from many sources. Some of the danger is geopolitical, with Russia and China increasingly bold in their anti-democratic designs, and with authoritarianism and ultranationalism elsewhere rattling the international order. The proliferation of failed states, of Islamist extremism, of malicious technology, of the nuclear menace—all contribute to a climate that is hostile to democracy. But danger also lies within democracies as citizens lose sight of the values that safeguard their freedoms. Some are losing confidence in democracy itself, while others feel an unwarranted complacency. Hyper-partisanship that crowds out the possibility of debate and compromise further saps the democratic spirit. When the free press is regularly attacked in the land of the First Amendment, the reverberations are felt everywhere in the free world, and in the unfree one too. Meanwhile, illiberals of every anti-democratic persuasion gloat and plan their next assault on liberty. The dangers to democracy are real, and they are rising.

The Anti-Democratic Contagion

★ ★ ★

GARRY KASPAROV

The global spread of democracy once seemed unstoppable. Republican forms of government replaced empires, monarchies, and other autocratic regimes in the twentieth century, a surge based on the precepts of liberal democracy: that leaders should be elected and held accountable by the people, according to the principles of individual freedom, human rights, civil liberties, and the rule of law. By the turn of the millennium, the belief in the superiority of such systems looked well on the way

Garry Kasparov is chairman of the Human Rights Foundation and the author of *Winter Is Coming: Why Vladimir Putin and the Enemies of the Free World Must Be Stopped*. A former world chess champion, he retired in 2005 to join the Russian prodemocracy movement.

to becoming universal, bolstered by the economic and cultural dominance of open societies, especially the United States.

There were still many authoritarian states, but it was taken for granted that a majority of their citizens did not share their leaders' devotion to autocracy. In 2010, a wave of revolutionary uprisings rolled across the Middle East—one of the most repressive areas of the globe—dubbed the Arab Spring. It was easy to believe that the revolts were another step toward the inevitable triumph of worldwide democracy.

Things look quite different today. Far from fading away, the world's dictatorships are gaining confidence and influence while authoritarian tendencies are finding new footholds in the free world. The Arab Spring has turned to winter, with only Tunisia producing a democratic transformation while much of the region became engulfed in civil wars and even greater repression. Russia and China are flexing their economic and military might abroad while keeping a firm grip at home. Virulent nationalism has come to the surface in young European democracies like Hungary and Poland and in old ones like the United Kingdom. Bellwether Germany saw an extremist far right party gain parliamentary seats for the first time since the 1940s. America, the "shining city on a hill," elected a president who calls millions of his opponent's votes illegal, attacks the free press, and speaks admiringly of despots past and present.

Democracy is in crisis. When voters bother to show up to the polls at all, they increasingly do so to support extremist candidates and illiberal policies. Surveys show a frightening degree of sympathy for the idea that democracy as a system is nothing special, and respect for core concepts like political dissent and free speech have less support than ever before.

This trend is certainly frightening to anyone like me, born in the totalitarian Soviet Union in the middle of the Cold War. That the free world could turn its back on the democratic values we so envied and coveted is a terrible disappointment. This drift also has echoes of the downfall of Russia's all-too-brief democracy, at which I also had a front-row seat. The return to repression in Russia was swift—just eight years from tearing down Soviet monuments to building up Vladimir Putin's mafia regime. It painfully illustrated that Ronald Reagan's formulation, "freedom is never more than one generation away from extinction," is not only true but a generous estimate.

What could lead so many of the world's freest and wealthiest citizens to lose faith in the system that produced their freedom and riches? How can the nations that won the Cold War by exemplifying and promoting the values of democracy now cast doubt on those values? Let us go back to that high point that freed so many millions, myself included, and consider that democracy hasn't failed us, but we have failed democracy.

When the Cold War ended once and for all with the dissolution of the Soviet Union in 1991, the victory went not only to North Atlantic Treaty Organization, to the United States, or to any other outside entity, but to democracy, the free market, individual freedom, and the other guiding principles of the free world. The totalitarian socialism behind the Iron Curtain had never worked for anything other than systemic repression, and at last it had failed completely. The communism that had been held up as an alternative to free-market capitalism had been exposed forever as a fraud. This collapse would have taken even longer had the alternatives not been so successful—open societies that enjoyed unprecedented peace, growth, and contentment.

Representative democracy varied in the free world nearly as much as socialism and authoritarianism varied in the unfree world, with the common denominator being results as positive as those behind the Iron Curtain were negative. Parliamentary systems and federal republics, and combinations thereof, provided their citizens with roughly as much government as they desired. Local representatives conveyed their constituents' wants and needs to the regional and national level. Transparent elections, open debates, and an aggressive free press encouraged elected and appointed public officials to stick to their mandates.

Private citizens and corporations were largely content to carry on with their business without particular interest in politics, assuming—correctly for the most part—that public affairs would be conducted within acceptable, stable parameters, as they had for decades. Divisions over policy and priorities were overshadowed by shared goals and principles—and muted by the rotation of ruling parties and leaders as well as by endless bureaucratic wrangling. Fair rules and free markets rewarded the ambition and creativity of the people, who labored and innovated and created the wealthiest society in history.

This idealized description of the free world after World War II ignores many bumps and bruises, of course. The social upheaval of the 1960s, the dirty politics and corruption scandals, the unjust foreign interventions that darkened the perceptions of the just ones. But it has always been democracy's ability to correct course and to recover from its mistakes that distinguished it as superior. Democracy was far from perfect, to paraphrase Winston Churchill, but it was still far better than any known alternative.

The desirability of republican systems of government was also proved in a perverse way, as unfree regimes around the globe pantomimed democratic mechanisms. Fake elections and puppet parliaments with sham opposition groups became a common sight even in some of the world's most authoritarian states. These charades seek to distract the population with an illusion of agency and to provide scapegoats when things go poorly. "Democracy theater" also seeks to rebuff criticism from abroad on matters of human rights, although such criticism has become increasingly feeble in any case.

Democracy failed to take root in most former Soviet states when the USSR fell, and, in some places, like Russia, it failed to flourish despite initial success. Democracy requires numerous preconditions to thrive, and it is easily suppressed and subverted where those conditions do not exist or are not protected. Economic and social conditions are more important than any piece of paper. Many former Soviet citizens were disillusioned when their first meaningful elections failed to immediately produce the affluence they associated so closely with Western democracy. Communism was replaced with nonideological dictatorships of different types, nearly all of which are still in place today.

In the West, the isolation policies established in the 1950s to contain the USSR were abandoned as unnecessary with the disappearance of their principal target. The common understanding that the spread of democracy was a vital security interest for the free world was also discarded, even spoken of as condescending, or imperialistic, thinking. A new posture of unconditional engagement became the norm; trade agreements and foreign policy sidestepped matters of morality and human rights. It became unfashionable to criticize authoritarian regimes for how they treated their own citizens. Instead, the desire to find common ground was paramount, especially when mutually profitable. The free world held unprecedented advantages in military might, economic power, and social capital, but it lacked the will to press these advantages and to continue the hard work of spreading the rewards of democracy.

And so, the post–Cold War wave of democratization across liberated Eastern Europe failed to sweep across other parts of the globe. The authoritarian regimes of Asia, the Middle East, and Africa have seen little improvement. The global freedom index has declined for eleven consecutive years. The bedrock belief that greater commercial, financial, and political engagement with the free world would eventually liberalize places like Russia, China, and Saudi Arabia has been exposed as a myth.

Instead, the opposite happened. Engagement has allowed authoritarian regimes to profit from Western markets and technology while investing the returns in repression at home and consolidating power even more. Shunned no longer, the princes, oligarchs, and gangster elites have found that their riches are welcome in the banks, real estate, and stock markets of the free world. Nor do they simply move their money abroad; they invest it widely and often strategically—in media companies new and old, in partnerships with Western business leaders, and in political lobbying.

The international community has been fully co-opted into this moral wasteland. The United Nations places human-rights violators and terror sponsors on its Human Rights Council. Prominent organizations like the World Economic Forum invite authoritarian leaders to lecture their audiences, to warm applause. The torture chambers, the rigged elections, the murdered journalists—all are forgotten in the pursuit of a common ground that is as comforting as it is illusory. Even most global human-rights organizations focus on violations in the free world, where their complaints will not fall on deaf ears.

The stark differences between the free and unfree world have been blurred, a development that suits the authoritarians very well. These differences have not gone away, but they have become far easier to ignore than in the days of the Iron Curtain, when free people sympathized with those living under dictatorship and considered it a moral duty to extend the freedom they themselves enjoyed. This tells the billions of people living under dictatorship exactly what their oppressors have always told them—that no one cares about them and that democracy is just another sham.

This is not an abstract matter of good versus evil. There are very real consequences of this new balance in the world order. Tyranny causes or exacerbates nearly every one of the world's worst afflictions, from famine and poverty to terror and war. Liberal democracy may not be a perfect cure for these ills, but it is as close as we have yet come to finding one. Democratic nations do not wage war on one another, a fact that should make the spread of democracy a national and global security priority.

After the disappearance of the existential threat from Soviet Communism, the free world found it easy to ignore the smaller threats that were growing under the radar: the terror networks in failed states; cyberwarfare, disinformation, and other asymmetric tactics; the corrupting influence on institutions caused by a flood of cash emanating from wealthy dictatorships. As our weapons grow ever more powerful, so do the threats, with rogue actors capable of inflicting terrible harm. The trend will continue, making it even more important to address the root causes instead of waiting for the increasingly frequent outbreaks of violence.

The newly dominant principles of engagement and moral equivalence have also degraded the appreciation and practice of democracy in the free world. The benign political apathy that beset many democratic nations has turned into a pernicious complacency. If democracy is not important enough to worry about anywhere else, why should it be considered sacred at home? The sense of pride and purpose that many in the free world derived from upholding the principles of freedom and democracy has been lost. A vicious cycle has been created, with the loss of faith in democratic institutions leading more citizens to withdraw from political engagement and the duties of healthy citizenship.

Inevitably, this has led to the rise of competing value systems, and of those who champion them: nationalism, socialism, fascism, separatism—every toxic "-ism" that made the twentieth century the bloodiest in human history. The rule of law, the checks and balances of representative democracy, and the precepts of a free society are being pushed aside. The political extremes are increasingly dominating the stage, further driving the moderate middle away while radicalizing others. Hyperpartisanship has led to political tribalism that cares little for ideology or policy as long as one's side is winning. The quest for the common good has been abandoned for the raw pursuit of power.

The political pendulum once marked a relatively narrow divide as it swung between right and left, between conservative and liberal, between one coalition and another. Taxes, foreign policy, social issues—all the great responsibilities of nations great and small evolved over time. Today the pendulum is swinging faster and further as populists and demagogues find followers for whom things are not changing fast enough—or, in some cases, are changing far too quickly.

We know what works when it comes to deterring the global forces of dictatorship because we have done it before. Instead of lowering our standards to accommodate tyrannical regimes, we must raise our standards and vigorously maintain them. Instead of engaging with despots who exploit the openness of the free world for their own profit and power, we must isolate them before their corruption spreads further. The despots' free ride of enjoying the benefits and riches created by democracies while crushing any sign of liberalization at home must end.

Halting the rise of anti-democratic ideologies in the free world may be an even greater challenge. This transformation of the political landscape has been gradual, a slow cultural settling after the cataclysmic events of three decades ago. The first generation with no personal experience of the Cold War is coming of political age. Told that there are no great causes left, with no great enemy to confront, they may find that their parents' patriotic traditions sound quaint, especially in today's hyper-connected world. It is difficult to break through the political apathy and to remember that democracy and individual freedom still matter very much, and in concrete ways. Renewing the passion for these vital institutions and principles will be no easy task, but it is an essential one.

The Rise of Statist Great Power: China

★ ★ ★

MINXIN PEI

The future of liberal democracy depends, to a considerable extent, on the success or failure of its alternative—powerful autocracies that can outperform established Western democracies in providing better standards of living and governance and influencing world affairs. The most plausible contender that can realistically challenge the existing liberal order is, without any question, the People's Republic of China, the world's largest and strongest one-party state.

Minxin Pei is the Tom and Margot Pritzker '72 Professor of Government at Claremont McKenna College and author of *China's Crony Capitalism: The Dynamics of Regime Decay*.

Compared with other major powers ruled by autocratic regimes, China possesses a comprehensive set of advantages and capabilities denied to all the other major dictatorships, such as Russia, Saudi Arabia, Egypt, or North Korea. Unlike Russia or Saudi Arabia, both petro-states, China has a diversified manufacturing-based economy that is fast catching up with the liberal West in technological capabilities and competitiveness. If Russia and North Korea, two nuclear-armed dictatorships, are primarily security threats to the West, China has the military and economic means of undermining not only Western security with its rapid military modernization but also the foundations of Western liberal economic order.

In particular, the size of the Chinese economy, which is already the largest in the world in terms of purchasing power parity (a measure of the standard of living adjusted for the costs of goods and services in a given country) and will likely become the largest in dollar terms within a decade if China maintains moderately high growth, will allow Beijing to leverage the access to its vast market as an instrument of geopolitical influence, just as the United States did during the Cold War. If Beijing succeeds in achieving its objective of "becoming a great modern socialist country," as declared by China's new strongman Xi Jinping in his political report to the ruling Chinese Communist Party's (CCP) nineteenth congress in October 2017, the liberal world order as we know will face an existential threat. For the first time in modern history, a non-Western autocratic power will be the world's largest economy.

China's success is by no means a foregone conclusion. Historically, no autocratic regime outside petro-states so far has managed the difficult feat of achieving high-income status (defined as obtaining a level of per capita income at least half that of the most advanced country, the United States, where purchasing power parity is currently about $58,000, according to the World Bank). Given its predatory state, insecure private property, and privileges for inefficient state-owned enterprises, China is likely to encounter strongly adverse institutional barriers to sustainable economic development.

Structural factors vital to China's future growth are turning negative as well. Among other things, fast demographic aging, gender imbalances, environmental degradation, and stark income inequality will almost certainly drag down China's economic performance in the coming decades. Externally, the backlash against globalization and rising concerns about China's expansionism will also most likely result in a significant reduction of China's access to Western markets and technologies—developments that will undermine its economic growth.

The continuing political strength of China's one-party regime cannot be taken for granted, either. Ostensibly, the CCP appears to be a formidable one-party regime with more than 90 million members led by Xi Jinping. However, as the incessant purges conducted by Xi since coming to power in 2012 suggest, the party is fractured internally along factional lines. Xi's success in consolidating power and removing all constraints on his authority, including the two-term constitutional limit on the presidency, probably belies his insecurity more than it reveals his strength. Even if we assume that he now has fully centralized power in hand, the history of one-man rule in China is littered with political disasters such as the Cultural Revolution and the Great

Leap Forward. In an overcentralized regime, risks of calamitous policy mistakes are multiplied by tightly restricted channels of information, the prevalence of lies, few institutional checks, and complete dependence on the judgement of one ruler. Should history repeat itself, the revival of one-man rule under Xi could result in similar blunders, such as extravagant external commitments and ill-fated military adventures in the South China Sea or the Taiwan Strait.

However, even if China fails to become a high-income country with an economy larger than that of the United States, it will still be one of the two preeminent economies on the planet and will wield enormous influence in global affairs, playing a decisive role in determining the future of freedom in the world. As an economic peer competitor with the United States, China thus has numerous means and policy instruments to undermine the cause of liberty around the globe.

In the ideological realm, China's perceived economic success has already given rise to the growing appeal of a narrative referred to as the "China model," which credits the CCP's one-party rule with the country's four decades of fast economic growth. However intellectually questionable, the China model story line has gained considerable influence in the developing world because few countries in that category outside East Asia have achieved the same impressive growth record as China has. To be sure, there is no economic theory or empirical evidence behind the idea that a one-party state has single-handedly delivered China's economic miracle. Nevertheless, in the marketplace of ideas, propaganda backed by bogus claims and clever packaging can often be deceptively more attractive than truth. To the average person in developed democracies, the appearance of economic success in China has already raised doubts about the superiority and future of liberal democracy. For ordinary people in developing countries, the liberty-prosperity trade-off may increasingly appear worth making if they can be guaranteed China-like growth rates. For autocrats in developing countries, the China model is the best justification for holding onto power. Indeed, strongmen in countries such as Ethiopia and Rwanda have already begun to emulate the China model.

Besides challenging the liberal democratic ideology with an alternative model, China can also undermine the cause of liberty by developing and exporting repressive technologies and know-how that can help other autocracies construct and maintain the surveillance state, control their population, and increase the odds of their long-term survival. With its enormous investments in the technologies to monitor its people and control the flow of information in the digital age, China has already achieved a level of technological sophistication no other autocratic regime in the developing world is capable of. Autocratic regimes eager to apply China's technologies of political repression can easily do so by either importing them directly from China or learning how to operate them from open-source materials.

Dictatorships, especially those ruling strategically important or resource-rich countries, can count on China for support to prolong their survival. China's foreign policy is driven by three sets of interests: security, ideological competition with the West, and economic benefits. In most of the post-Mao era, Chinese foreign policy was pragmatic and made economic development a priority. However, this policy has been gradually replaced over the past decade with one that is more assertive and ideological. A notable change in China's foreign policy is its generous support for dictatorial regimes, particularly those in resource-rich countries. Chinese aid helped sustain Robert Mugabe's long rule in Zimbabwe, and it supports Nicolás Maduro in Venezuela as it did Hugo Chávez before him. Beijing's financial assistance to Moscow also enabled Vladimir Putin to weather Western sanctions following his annexation of Crimea and invasion of Ukraine in 2014.

A disturbing trend, which is likely to become even more pronounced in the coming years, is China's use of its economic muscle and proxies to gain political influence in Western democracies and extend its censorship abroad. Reports that rich ethnic Chinese business operators in Australia have been trying to buy influence with political donations and control of local Chinese media have already raised the specter that Beijing is attempting to steer the China policies of democracies that have close cultural and economic ties with China.

China's growing bargaining power has also been deployed to achieve undisguised political objectives. For instance, its censors in 2017 demanded that Cambridge University Press and Springer remove articles critical of the CCP from their online subscription services. (Cambridge University Press initially complied but later resisted, while Springer caved in to the demands.) Apple also cooperated with Chinese authorities in 2017 and removed hundreds of apps from its download store in China, including apps for the *New York Times* and Skype, that use virtual private networks (VPNs) and can circumvent censors. To get into the vast China market, Hollywood studios have apparently imposed strict self-censorship. Notably, while major Hollywood studios have collaborated with Chinese partners in producing mediocre movies, none has produced a single movie critical of China in recent years. These developments are just the start. It is almost a foregone conclusion that, as Chinese tycoons with close ties to the CCP start making large donations to prestigious Western education or cultural institutions, they will gradually gain the ability to muzzle these institutions.

The CCP will not be content to intimidate or silence just private-sector actors in the West. China has become even more aggressive in punishing democracies that dare to defy Beijing on human rights and security issues. Incensed by meetings between European leaders and the Tibetan spiritual leader the Dalai Lama over the past decade, China imposed diplomatic and economic sanctions on Germany, France, and Britain. Instructively but regrettably, China's intimidation tactics were effective—the leaders of these countries all backed down and implicitly promised not to meet with the Dalai Lama again. As a result, this widely revered champion of nonviolence is effectively barred from meeting with any Western European leaders. Another example that should raise worries among democracies is China's treatment of South Korea after Seoul agreed in 2015 to host the American missile-defense system Terminal High Altitude Area Defense, or THAAD. Beijing imposed economic sanctions on South Korea and launched a propaganda and diplomatic campaign to isolate the nation. China encountered no concerted pushback from South Korea's democratic allies and eventually succeeded in forcing Seoul to make critical concessions limiting its future cooperation with US-led defense efforts in the region.

At the heart of China's success in weakening the post–World War II liberal order is the CCP's mastery of the art of using capitalism against liberal democracy. Unlike the former Soviet Union, which attempted to intimidate the West with its nuclear arsenal, China is a far more sophisticated—and cynical— geopolitical adversary. It understands the existing liberal order's fatal weakness: the corrosive power of greed to undermine liberal values, norms, and institutions. Instead of using military aggression, China is relying on greed to entice Western elites, in particular its capitalist elites, into its orbit. So far, Beijing has every reason to believe that it has the right strategy and that it is working as intended.

Understanding the China challenge may be a useful intellectual exercise, but appreciation of it must lead to practical policy solutions if the West is to confront this test successfully. There are three steps Western democratic leaders must pursue in the coming years if they wish to sustain the dominance of the existing liberal order.

Their first priority must be the revitalization of liberal democracy at home. The appeal of China as a successful autocracy does not stem solely from the perception of Beijing's economic achievements. Dysfunction and stress in the world's leading democracies also play a role. As long as the West fails to address its internal problems, such as political polarization, socioeconomic dislocation caused by technological progress, globalization, cultural conflict, and money politics, it will not be able to confront the China challenge. Worrying signs of democratic deconsolidation, marked by the erosion of democratic values, the rise of right-wing populist movements, and the decline of political parties, should alert us to the danger that the greatest threat to liberal democracies lies not in Moscow or Beijing but inside their own borders.

The second critical step: conduct a comprehensive review of the West's China policy. After more than forty years of economic and political engagement with China that has enabled it to become an autocratic great power, the West must ask the tough question of whether this policy has achieved its desired objectives. As evidence of its failure becomes abundant, muscular alternatives, including those once deemed too costly to contemplate, must be put on the table. Although specifics—such as reducing economic interdependence with China in trade and investment, expanding the West's alliance network in the Asia Pacific, and strengthening military deterrence against aggression—will have to be decided over time, the major thrust of this policy should be clear: the West must be ready to confront the China challenge in a concerted and comprehensive way.

The last step that Western democracies must take is to launch an ideological counteroffensive. The ascendency of the China model owes as much to the West's complacency and negligence as to Beijing's aggressive (and successful) marketing. Yes, leading Western media organizations such as the *New York Times*, *Financial Times*, and the *Economist* have consistently exposed the flaws and failures of China's autocratic development model. But Western governments have been largely missing in action in this new ideological contest. In particular, Western leaders have been reluctant to confront China on issues of human-rights abuses, environmental degradation, and other socioeconomic failures. Instead, under the pretext of engagement, they have showered Chinese leaders with respect and praise. This is a self-defeating strategy and must stop. Western governments should also refrain from actions that may be construed as support for China's autocracy. They must invest more political capital and economic resources to counter China's soft-power offensive and regain the moral and ideological high ground in the world's renewed ideological contest between liberal democracy and dictatorship.

Confronting the China challenge will be one of the greatest tests of the political will and capacity of Western democracies in the coming decades. Given the sorry state in which Western democracies find themselves today, winning this new geopolitical and ideological contest will not be easy. But if Western democracies overcome their difficulties, revive their political institutions, and restore their economic vigor, they should have better-than-even odds, because modern autocracies, including the Chinese variant, are fundamentally unjust and flawed political systems maintained only with repression, corruption, and lies. Such dictatorships may flourish for a while, but ultimately, as the historical record shows, they will fail.

Putin and His Orchestrated Chaos Machine

★ ★ ★

ANNE APPLEBAUM

I n March 2014, just after street protests in Kiev persuaded the Ukrainian president to flee his country, "little green men," as they later came to be called, suddenly appeared on the Crimean Peninsula. They wore unmarked uniforms and drove unmarked military vehicles. With the help of local "politicians," some of whom had previously been leaders of criminal gangs, they occupied the major towns, police stations, and television towers.

Their assault was accompanied by a major disinformation campaign, one designed to confuse outsiders about the nature

Anne Applebaum, a *Washington Post* columnist and professor in practice at the London School of Economics, is the author, most recently, of *Red Famine: Stalin's War on Ukraine*. She was the recipient of the 2004 Pulitzer Prize in General Nonfiction for *Gulag: A History*.

of the operation. The men—all Russian soldiers, some of whom would later receive medals—were described as "Ukrainian separatists." Russian president Vladimir Putin, when asked where they might have obtained their military equipment, airily theorized that they might have picked it up in a shop. A major social media campaign sought to convince Russians and foreigners that the men on the peninsula had arrived in Crimea to fight "Nazis."

Although it was the first Russian disinformation campaign that made a real impression in the United States, the Crimean invasion was not the first instance of the Russian use of what has come to be called "hybrid warfare," a combination of military pressure, cyberattacks, corruption, and, above all, disinformation. Crimea was, rather, the culmination of a long investment: The Russian state propaganda and military apparatus had been reconfiguring itself to fight an ideological war against the West for at least the previous decade. Starting in the 2000s, the regime had been slowly reconstructing a state-run media machine far more sophisticated than anything the USSR ever invented. Dozens of Russian domestic news outlets, entertainment channels, and magazines had begun to offer an appearance of variety but a unity of messages. Among them: the United States is a threat; Europe is degenerate; Russia, unfairly deprived of its role in the world, is finally becoming a superpower again.

Abroad, Russian-funded media offers a unified set of messages as well. But these are very different from what they once were. Nowadays, the Kremlin is not trying to "sell" itself or its model, as it did during the Cold War. Instead of offering a Soviet vision, Russia seeks to confuse, disorient, and undermine its "opponents" in the West. It does so both overtly—through foreign-language television such as Russia Today, or RT, which now broadcasts in English and Spanish, and online with Sputnik International—and covertly, using notionally independent journalists, experts, and commentators as well as Internet trolls, bots, and both paid and unpaid propagandists on social media.

This system of journalists and pseudo-journalists, fake experts, and trolls operates in every Western country and every language, with varying degrees of success. Most often the system simply supports existing parties and movements on both the far left and on the far right, whether the National Front in France, the Freedom Party in Austria, the Alternative for Germany (AfD), or Syriza in Greece. These are real parties with real social bases; Russia's role is simply to enhance them, sometimes by amplifying their messages on social media, sometimes by supporting them financially. Not all of them are large: Russian money also assists extremist fringe groups, such as the small pro-Russian party, Zmiana, in Poland. Some of these parties are linked by a far-right ideology that advocates the resurrection of "traditional" society, fighting against feminism, racial integration, and secularism. But others have a far "left" extremist vision. It doesn't matter: Russia's goal in supporting them is simply to enhance extremism, to create deeper divisions and partisan divides.

But there are other forms of Russian influence too. There are quiet campaigns to approach business leaders and more centrist politicians, most notably in Germany, where they seek to appeal to "sensible" social democrats—or to businessmen who just want to make money with their Russian partners. Russian companies also use corruption more directly to shape politics and business abroad, and they often do so with the connivance of the offshore industry and international money launderers. Paul Manafort, who had one foot in Ukrainian politics, one foot in US politics, and a lot of shell companies in Cyprus, is an excellent example of the kind of person who promoted Russian interests around the world.

Russian influence operations have also long sought to shape foreign elections more directly. In several Eastern European countries, mysteriously leaked secret tapes or e-mails have played a large role in election campaigns. Subsequently, the material, sometimes quite banal, was spun into conspiracy theories by organized online campaigns. This was the same tactic deployed in the United States in 2016. Russian operatives organized the theft of personal e-mails and other material from the Hillary Clinton campaign; both Russian and alt-right online trolls and bots, many of which were using the same messages all the way through the campaign, then magnified the material into a series of scandals and conspiracy theories. By the time these tactics appeared in the United States, they were familiar elsewhere, even if they were new to Americans.

Although they take different forms, all these interventions do have a logic behind them. Certainly, Putin uses Russian foreign policy for domestic purposes. He wants to show his own people that he plays an important role on the world stage, to prove that he has "made Russia great again" after a period of supposedly lying prostrate. At a recent conference in the Middle East, a Russian participant explained with extraordinary cynicism that the Russian intervention in Syria had very little to do with Syria.

It was all about proving to the Americans—and of course to the Russians—that the Russian president matters. To put it differently: because Putin cannot hand out bread, he offers foreign circuses.

But there is a broader strategy too. Relative to the United States, China, or the European Union, Russia is a weak power. The Russian economy is very dependent on oil and gas prices; widespread corruption creates widespread discontent. The Russian president and his entourage trumpet their popularity, but in fact they fear their own public and are particularly afraid of street revolutions, which is why they reacted so harshly to the one in Ukraine.

Putin's desire to undermine Western democracy and Western institutions stems from this sentiment. It isn't Western tanks or missiles he fears but the language of "democracy," of transparency and of rule of law. To reduce the appeal of those ideas, he needs to undermine the institutions that promote them, to create chaos and discord in the democratic processes of the West and above all in Western institutions.

It is not an accident, for example, that Russian money, influence, and contacts flow to political parties and groups that oppose the European Union and NATO, from Marine Le Pen's National Front in France to the Ron Paul Institute in the United States. The EU is the only European institution that can push back against Russian gas monopolies and that can defend smaller and weaker European nations against the threat of trade boycotts. The EU also gives Europe the collective negotiating power that none of its members possess on their own. In Russia's bilateral economic relations, it is more powerful than, or at the very least the equal of, any individual country in Europe. By contrast, Russia is the weaker partner when it negotiates directly with the EU.

Russia's dislike of NATO stems from the same logic. No European country on its own is a match even for a Russia that is weaker than its Soviet predecessor. But NATO, backed by the United States, is far more powerful than Russia—which is precisely why, again, Putin seeks to undermine it. Because he can't confront the alliance outright, he has conducted a series of aggressive military exercises that rehearsed the invasion of the Baltic states and a nuclear attack on Poland. He has sought to undermine the region's faith in the NATO security guarantee by violating Scandinavian and Baltic airspace and launching a cyberattack in Tallinn, Estonia. After his seizure of Crimea in 2014, the transatlantic alliance was forced to take seriously the physical security of some of its members for the first time since 1991. NATO planners have still not discounted the possibility of a hybrid war—perhaps initially taking the form of a Russian minority "uprising" in one of the Baltic states—that Russia might launch to test NATO's willingness to fight back.

The long Russian cultivation of Donald Trump fit right into this strategy. Trump probably caught Russian attention very early on, as one of many ethically flexible businessmen who traveled to Moscow over the past couple of decades looking for "deals." Over many years, and long before he became president, Donald Trump repeatedly praised Russia and its president. In 2007, he declared that Putin is "doing a great job." In 2015, he described the Russian president as a "man so highly respected within his own country and beyond." But it was Trump's long-standing dislike of Western trade organizations as well as NATO itself that made him an ideal Russian candidate: because he doesn't understand that US power is projected through its ability to build coalitions and alliances, his interests and those of Russia coincided directly.

The extent of Russian help for Trump and his entourage doesn't need further review or examination here. The more important point is that if it was possible once, it will be possible again. If 2016 proved that hacked e-mails and conspiracy theories spread on social media were an effective form of electioneering, the period since then has proved that the bitter partisanship that divides Americans may have given Russian influence new openings in the United States. If nothing else, the spectacle of a US president in thrall to a foreign authoritarian has led to growing admiration for authoritarianism even inside the Republican Party. And if the Russians helped Trump, then that may persuade a part of the American electorate to support Russian aims in the United States and Europe too.

To repeat, Russia's use of social media and corruption to project power are a sign of weakness, not strength. Over the next two decades, Russia may not even prove to be the greatest challenge to American power or the global order. But, at the moment, Russia is the only world power whose foreign policy is aimed directly at US domestic politics, and at the domestic politics of America's allies. Even if Russia does not succeed in overthrowing NATO or undermining the EU, Russian disinformation has already done real damage, helping to destabilize democratic politics all across the West and helping extremist movements to grow.

Confronting the problem of Russian influence peddling will not be easy: it requires, first, a recognition of the nature and scale of the problem, as well as a response that reaches across borders. The US government and American organizations should be working with allies to analyze far right and far left networks, to present evidence of foreign social media interference to the general public. Digital literacy programs could teach young people to be aware of extremist disinformation and foreign influence campaigns. Critical thinking skills need to be not only taught in schools but also delivered via media and public awareness campaigns for adults. Tech companies should be brought into a common front with government and journalism to eliminate bots, trolls, and hidden political influence campaigns. Laws on transparency in advertising need to begin to apply to the Internet.

At the same time, the United States should work with allies to eliminate the shell companies and other legal loopholes that have allowed Russians and Russian companies—and indeed those of other nationalities—to launder money in the West, corruptly enriching themselves as well as Western partners like Paul Manafort and Donald Trump. The spread of oligarchic behavior and corrupt practices has damaged business and politics not only in Russia but also in Europe and North America. Foreign influence peddling in Washington now exists on an unprecedented scale and has already begun to skew American democracy in very fundamental ways.

Above all, the challenge posed by Russia—which is really a much broader challenge posed by globalized information and by a globalized financial system—needs to be understood. Until the

2016 presidential election, few in Washington took the threat of disinformation or foreign corruption seriously at all. Under a president who still does not acknowledge that either exists, it may still be impossible to change that mood inside the government. But outside the government there are opportunities to work on the problem—starting now.

Political Tribalism

★ ★ ★

JOHN AVLON

Throughout history, extreme voices have offered the false comfort of rigid certainties in a changing world. In recent years, we've seen a rising tide of ethno-nationalists attack liberal-democratic values as part of a broader backlash against globalization. Increasingly, these extreme voices have spurred a vicious cycle of hyper-partisanship that ultimately aids authoritarian regimes in their attempt to paint democracy as hopelessly divided, inefficient, and ineffective.

In the United States, Donald Trump is only a symptom of the problems the country faces. He did not create polarization; he

---

John Avlon is a senior political analyst and anchor at CNN. He was the editor-in-chief and managing director of the *Daily Beast* between 2013 and 2018. He served as chief speechwriter for New York City Mayor Rudy Giuliani and is the author of the books *Independent Nation*, *Wingnuts*, and *Washington's Farewell*.

exploited it. But, as president, he may have unwittingly begun to end it.

America is living through a stark departure from its best political traditions. Hyper-partisanship, by demonizing civic disagreement, paralyzes the political process. Polarization and the rigged system of redistricting has reduced the number of competitive swing districts in Congress by two-thirds in the past twenty years. Majorities of Republicans and Democrats now say that members of the opposing party make them feel angry and afraid, according to the Pew Research Center, while trust in civic institutions is in steep decline.

Democracies depend on an assumption of goodwill among fellow citizens. When trust erodes and political tribalism rises, liberal democracy suffers. Cynics will tell you that bitter political feuds are as American as apple pie, often as a way of excusing the extreme voices on their side of the aisle. But we should not be fooled into believing that today's hyper-partisan identity politics is normal or healthy.

It is worth remembering that the US Constitution doesn't mention political parties. This was not an oversight. The founding fathers initially hoped that members of Congress would represent their constituents and their conscience rather than falling in line behind any party agenda. As George Washington wrote to Thomas Jefferson, "I was no party man myself, and the first wish of my heart was, if parties did exist, to reconcile them."

The revolutionary generation called hyper-partisan special interest groups "factions," which James Madison helpfully defined in the *Federalist Papers* as "a number of citizens, whether amounting to a majority or a minority of the whole, who are united and actuated by some common impulse of passion, or of interest, adversed to the rights of other citizens, or to the permanent and aggregate interests of the community." In Washington's presidential farewell address in 1796, he warned against the appeals of a demagogue who "agitates the community with ill-founded jealousies and false alarms, kindles the animosity of one part against another." Sound familiar?

To the founding fathers, the fight against faction was best achieved by a wise and vigilant citizenry committed to forming a more perfect union, guided by the governing principle of moderation, which they viewed as not a position of weakness but a source of strength.

After all, the Constitutional Convention of 1787 was the product of principled compromise. In the words of political scientist Peter Berkowitz, "The framers' aim was to constitutionalize liberty by institutionalizing political moderation." This was a point of pride in the *Federalist Papers*, as in the first of those documents, where Alexander Hamilton praised "moderation" in opposition to the "intolerant spirit" of "those who are ever so much persuaded of their being in the right in any controversy."

If moderation and a nonpartisan vision of representative democracy were the founding fathers' heartfelt wishes, that ideal was never quite reality. Even before the political parties were formed, the heated debates over ratification of the Constitution were between advocates of national unity and a stronger central government, who largely came from urban areas, and rural populists, who passionately defended states' rights because they were afraid that the federal government would encroach upon their cultural and economic way of life. Both sides believed they

were fighting for freedom. The urban/rural clash was the original red state/blue state divide, with the partisan press stoking
conflict. These debates have been present since the nation's
early days, but they have rarely turned so toxic.

The middle of the American Century offers a compelling
counterpoint. When the Greatest Generation returned home
from military service in World War II and entered public service, the result was a Congress with voting patterns that resembled a bell curve, representing the moderate majority of
Americans across both political parties, with comparatively few
extremes on either end. It reflected an ideological diversity
within the two-party coalitions. Progressive Republicans over-
lapped and often allied with conservative Democrats, and, as a
result, even in times of divided government it was possible to
achieve ambitious goals through compromise, the art of reasoning together. The Marshall Plan, the National Highway System,
and civil rights legislation passed on this broad bipartisan basis.
The Reagan era's achievements were accomplished with divided
government, and even amid the bitter baby-boom grudge match
that was the Clinton-Gingrich era, Americans saw welfare reform and deficits turn to surpluses.

But the two parties' ideological and regional polarization was
already under way. Right-wing Barry Goldwater's defeat of centrist Republican Nelson Rockefeller for the 1964 nomination was
an early sign, but his general election massacre by Lyndon Johnson was seen as a cautionary tale. Republicans courted the South
and benefited from the left's cultural excesses amid domestic
unrest, including Vietnam War protests and urban riots, which
helped elect Richard Nixon and—save for the post-Watergate

interregnum of Jimmy Carter—secured the White House for the GOP from 1968 to 1992. The arrival of Bill Clinton, a centrist Southern governor who courted the "forgotten middle class," brought Democrats in from the electoral cold—and fired up a right-wing hostility to all things liberal, stoked by Fox News and talk radio, that remains intact.

On the congressional level, American politics have become polarized along ideological and geographic lines. The rise of partisan media and redistricting's systematic reduction of competitive seats have driven the parties further apart and empowered the extremes. Institutional changes brought by Newt Gingrich's 1994 conservative counterrevolution disrupted regular order and discouraged legislators from living in the District of Columbia, which hindered their ability to form personal friendships across partisan lines. These and other democratic deformations, described as "asymmetric polarization," are outlined by policy analysts Norm Ornstein and Thomas Mann in their 2012 book *It's Even Worse Than It Looks: How the American Constitutional System Collided with the New Politics of Extremism*. As the parties became more polarized over the past decade, the number of self-identified independent voters climbed as high as 43 percent of the electorate, and in 2017 more than 60 percent of Americans said there was a need for a third party, according to Gallup.

Barack Obama, in his 2008 presidential victory speech in Chicago, declared that "we have never been just a collection of individuals or a collection of red states and blue states. We are, and always will be, the United States of America." In the election, Obama had benefited from broad disenchantment with George W. Bush over the Iraq War and the fiscal crisis, but he also seemed to embody America's attempt to transcend the old black/white, left/right divides that had haunted US politics for decades. His ascension to the presidency offered an opportunity to defuse a partisanship that been growing in bitterness for decades.

It was an opportunity not so much missed as scorned. Republicans reflexively returned to the playbook that had worked well in the past, associating Obama with socialism and black nationalism while embracing a strategy of obstruction even on issues they had once supported, like public-private infrastructure reform. Conspiracy peddlers—including Donald Trump—made baseless claims about Obama's place of birth, feeding bigoted suspicions that, in addition to being anti-American, the president was literally un-American. In 2015, after he had been in office for six years, a CNN/ORC poll found that 43 percent of Republicans believed that President Obama was Muslim.

Democrats in Congress during Obama's first term took up a health-care reform inspired by a plan originally offered by Republicans; it passed on a strictly party-line vote with no Republican support. The nascent "Tea Party" wing of the GOP, livid about the Affordable Care Act and increased deficits from domestic stimulus spending, drove the wave election of 2010 that moved the party further right. Republicans gained the majority in Congress, but this radical wing crippled Republican congressional leaders' ability to corral their caucus. The internecine war between the GOP "establishment" and lawmakers tied to the Tea Party led to a two-week government shutdown in 2013.

An opportunity was ripening for a populist candidacy by a reality-TV star who ridiculed Democrats and Republicans alike as denizens of the Washington "swamp." Without a robust center-right wing providing ballast, the GOP was susceptible to a hostile takeover by an intentionally divisive, often fact-challenged candidate who disdained some of the party's most cherished priorities, from free trade to family values.

But on Election Day 2016, the fractured Republican coalition held together in opposition to Hillary Clinton and the Democratic Party's embrace of identity politics, another increasingly divisive force in America. This tide of negative partisanship and antiestablishment anger allowed Donald Trump to pull off a historic upset despite soundly losing the popular vote. Some Democrats took Trump's victory as evidence that they should, in an equal and opposite reaction, run hard to the left. In this political environment, reformers feel politically homeless, increasingly squeezed between radicals and reactionaries.

Since taking the oath of office, President Trump has assiduously played to his base, leading to the lowest first-term approval ratings on record, while attacking the press, the judiciary, and the law-enforcement community—the very civic institutions designed to instill accountability.

The problem does not simply lie with politicians. The rise of hyper-partisan media—hate news and fake news disseminated by social media, designed to enflame domestic divisions along tribal lines, sometimes with a Russian-fueled assist—has increased the bitterness in politics, creating an atmosphere of mutual incomprehension as people self-segregate into separate political realities, bolstered by confirmation-bias clickbait. In contrast to Senator Daniel Patrick Moynihan's wise warning that "everyone is entitled to his own opinion, but not to his own facts," people increasingly come to civic debates, online or in person, armed with their own "facts." That's a path to the Tower of Babel.

Given these toxic trends, why is there reason to believe that the tide could be turning against hyper-partisanship?

At the risk of elevating hope over recent experience, I see signs that the current political stress test will spur wider awareness that liberal democracy can't be taken for granted. Self-government requires vigorous citizenship. It can't simply be a spectator sport, dumbed down by rabid team-ism. In the fifteen months after Trump's inauguration, voter turnout surged in special elections and typically low-turnout state legislative races, with more than forty seats that Trump carried handily in 2016 flipping to Democrats.

Perhaps the most encouraging sign of progress is a long-overdue recognition that the rigged system of congressional redistricting is an incentive system for hyper-partisanship. Professional partisans have carved up districts to create "safe" seats while the number of swing districts has been cut from 103 in 1992 to just 35 twenty years later, according to the statistical-analysis website FiveThirty-Eight. As a result, incumbents are rewarded with 90 percent re-election rates, regardless of dismal congressional approval ratings routinely in the teens and low twenties. Because this segregation by political affiliation effectively ends competitive general elections, often the only real contests occur in closed partisan primaries, effectively disenfranchising independent voters. This forces parties to the margins—after all, in a typical 10 percent turnout primary, 5.1 percent of the electorate makes a majority.

The good news is that more state courts, including in the swing states of Florida, Pennsylvania, Virginia, and North

Carolina, have tossed out their gerrymandered districts after confronting partisan collusion as well as a stark disconnect between the popular vote and the number of congressional seats won by the parties. As of this writing, there are major legal cases pending in seven states in 2018, with some of them making their way to the US Supreme Court. Promising changes are in the air, with more cases likely to come, in advance of the 2020 census, when the next decade's congressional district lines will be drawn. Independent redistricting and competitive general elections are more likely to lead to more moderate and less hyper-partisan candidates. Likewise, opening up primaries would enfranchise independent voters by allowing them to vote for the candidate they most identify with in either party, giving an incentive to candidates to play beyond their base. Change the rules, change the game.

We're also witnessing the nascent creation of an alternative political architecture that can counteract hyper-partisan interests by uniting the center right and center left. Groups like No Labels, Unite America, and the Serve America Movement are working to form bipartisan policy coalitions in Congress or recruiting independent candidates to run statewide. Just a handful of independent US senators, working as a coalition, could break partisan deadlocks and move the balance of power back to the political center.

Political reforms are essential but not sufficient. There are cultural factors also driving today's political tribalism. George Washington said that "it is essential that public opinion be enlightened" in a self-governing society. But civic education has been cut from curricula, resulting in only a quarter of students in 2014 scoring "proficient" or better on a basic civics and American history exam, according to the National Assessment of Educational Progress. Improving civics education should be an area of bipartisan agreement, supported by patriotic philanthropy, defending liberal-democratic values while communicating a unifying national narrative that connects to the country's past, present, and future. Corporate citizens can also help combat hate news and fake news by consciously supporting sites that try to do it right. Supporting the free press in the disruptive digital era would also help maintain an "enlightened" electorate.

Companies could also play a role in reversing the long decline of regional economies that has fueled populist anger and hyperpartisanship. Public-private investment and incentives in these areas, particularly the rust belt, should be a bipartisan priority to help mend the frayed civic fabric through the glue of social mobility and economic opportunity.

Finally, not enough attention has been paid to a remarkable development during the electoral season of Brexit and Trump and its aftermath, as illiberalism flared around the globe. In the spring of 2017, France's Emmanuel Macron pulled off a successful counterrevolution: just fifteen months after founding the En Marche movement, he won the presidency, vanquishing the two parties that had ruled the country for decades. Macron channeled populist anger at the sclerotic status quo in a constructive rather than destructive direction, embracing liberal-democratic traditions and defending the European Union. He made the "radical centrist" case that the real political choice is not between the left and right but between bridge builders and wall builders, an open or closed vision of society.

Now a new movement in the United States is needed to unite reformers across the center right and center left, finding common ground and common purpose rooted in the forgotten wisdom of the founders, unapologetically defending the values of liberal democracy, armed with the understanding that the nation's independence is inseparable from the interdependence of its people.

The Digital Assault on Democracy

★ ★ ★

MASSIMO CALABRESI

Not long from now, a clever programmer will fully automate the dark art of propaganda. Digital influencers already can scan the data files of virtually every consumer in America in search of susceptible targets and can reach most of them, live, on Facebook, Twitter, and other social media. The technological breakthrough in this "age of mass customization of messaging, narrative, and persuasion," as the information scientist Rand Waltzman of RAND Corporation said in congressional testimony in April 2017, will bridge those two ends of the influence chain—targeting and delivery—by using algorithms and artificial intelligence to generate customized messages for millions of people in real time.

Massimo Calabresi is the Washington bureau chief of *Time* magazine.

And then a consequential moment will have arrived. Digitally sifting the billions of expressions of desire and conviction that we leave behind with every click of the mouse or tap of the smart phone, propagandists will be able to tailor information operations on a massive scale. Our online environment, at least, will monitor our fears and needs and respond to them, undetected, in ways designed to shape our behavior and beliefs.

For the world of democratic governance, this near future is worrying. As the public sphere has evolved over the course of modernity, propaganda has shown itself to be most disruptive when introduced into new media—whether that meant the printing press during the Reformation or film and radio with the rise of Nazism. The automation of propaganda in the age of big data and the iPhone has the potential to be just as disruptive.

Already, we have seen the danger posed by the introduction of propaganda into social media. It uses the core values of liberal democracies—free speech, assembly, and democratic debate— against them. Frustrated American information warriors are already seeking to relax constraints on domestic propaganda imposed during the Cold War. Although some adaptation is no doubt necessary in coping with new technology, past information- war abuses suggest that we must view as elements of the same problem both the threat itself and the danger of overreacting.

The pressing strategic question posed by this new and rapidly developing form of propaganda is whether liberal ideas, openly debated and discussed, can defeat it. It may be that, as it has in the past in combating hostile propaganda, Western liberalism will develop information antibodies to counteract illiberal cyber-propaganda. But America's policy response should be informed by the unsettling possibility that propaganda deployed in social media and elsewhere on the Internet poses a greater threat to the Constitution and to the Enlightenment values on which it is based, one that requires different strategies.

Propaganda and modernity share much the same time line. The word "propaganda" was coined by Pope Gregory XV in 1622 after a century of disruption unleashed by Protestant pamphleteers' innovative use of the new technology of printing. In creating the Congregation for the Propagation of the Faith four years into the Thirty Years' War, Gregory realized that force of arms alone could not answer the revolutionary challenge of Protestantism.

Propaganda in its current form is the product of "a peculiar combination of forces first appearing in nineteenth century industrial society," according to political scientist Terence H. Qualter in his seminal 1962 book *Propaganda and Psychological Warfare*. He continued:

The combined influence of Liberal and Rationalist philosophies, the extension of the franchise and the need to find methods of political persuasion to replace bribery and violence, the growth of population and its concentration in cities, a revolution in the technical means of communication commencing with the railways and culminating in radio and television, a rise in the general standard of living giving greater opportunities and incentives to take part in political activity, the spread of literacy, the beginnings of experimental psychology with its emphasis on the importance of unconscious and non-rational motivations, and the practical trial-and-error methods of commercial advertising, together produced a demand for large-scale persuasion, a technique of social control, the physical means of mass communication, and an audience equipped to absorb such appeals. Inevitably propaganda became a matter for the skilled professional rather than the inspired amateur.

The first strategic deployment of contemporary propaganda came during World War I. Allied governments aimed to hasten US involvement in the war, boost British support for it, and undermine German morale. The Bolsheviks embraced propaganda early and effectively in their revolution and thereafter as they sought to reunite Russia.

Technology then became an accelerant once again, particularly in the decade ahead of World War II. In their study "Radio and the Rise of the Nazis in Prewar Germany" (2015), social scientists Maja Adena, Ruben Enikolopov, and others found that "radio had a significant negative effect on the Nazi vote share between 1930 and 1933, when political news had an anti-Nazi slant." But "this negative effect was fully undone in just one month after Nazis got control over the radio in 1933 and initiated heavy radio propaganda." Soon after, Nazi propaganda minister Joseph Goebbels ordered the mass production of affordable radio receivers.

As propaganda became a central feature of the Cold War, the Western powers debated how best to respond to insidious and ingenious Soviet influence. From Stalin's use of the wealthy German communist Willi Münzenberg in seducing Britain's Bloomsbury set to the KGB's infiltration of peace movements in the 1960s and 1980s, democracies worldwide faced concerted, multifarious attempts to undermine constitutional government. Three responses predominated: doing nothing, allowing the free exchange of ideas organically to resist the lure of totalitarianism; actively pushing back against Russian influence operations by exposing them and advertising the truth via government and private entities; and promoting lies in addition to truth, especially in front-line countries around the world.

The West used all three approaches at different points but relied primarily on the first and second, in what ultimately proved to be a victorious information strategy. We appear to be reflexively taking the same approach to the new threat of propaganda in cyberspace. This default strategy may end up succeeding, but it is not clear that the Cold War is the right model to use in judging the challenge that liberalism now faces.

Much of what we know about the effectiveness of influence operations in social media comes from a short-lived and controversial program that was run from 2011 to 2014 out of the Defense Advanced Research Projects Agency, or DARPA, the Pentagon's in-house research arm. With a budget of $50 million, DARPA's Social Media in Strategic Communication program sought, among other things, to create computer algorithms that could detect and track the spread of disinformation and influence operations across social media sites. It also sought to figure out how to spot those behind the operations and to counter their efforts.

The DARPA researchers had realized earlier than most the significance of the new data wave that was crashing across the country. Google, Facebook, Twitter, and Reddit make money selling ads against the trillions of data points about users that the companies collect, store, and market to advertisers. Much of that information is either free or available inexpensively to anyone who is interested. And there's a lot of it: Twitter has more than 65 million American accounts generating more than a thousand tweets a second on average; Reddit has 135 million average monthly users voting on everything from politics to porn an average of two hundred times a second.

The DARPA researchers set about figuring out how to manipulate human behavior by meddling with social media, sponsoring companies and researchers to develop new tools tailored to the purpose. In the old days of marketing, advertisers would seek to influence behavior and beliefs by sorting people using census data such as age, sex, and political affiliation. Now you can sort tens of millions of people using thousands of data points—where they shop, what books they buy. The idea is to segment the population into groups likely to be susceptible to different kinds of manipulation.

Once the population had been segmented, the DARPA researchers found, you could search their social media data—what they liked or upvoted or followed—for each group's primary concerns: their hot-button issues. Automated tools based on mathematical formulas—algorithms—do that as well. Then, by monitoring the behavior of individuals in large groups in real time, DARPA found, you could identify "followers," or people who were particularly susceptible to messaging.

The final step was to craft a message designed to alter the behavior of targeted individuals by using the traditional techniques of propaganda—exploiting humans' intuitive love of rumor or playing on emotional triggers like fear, outrage, or sympathy.

One thing that made social media potentially so powerful, the researchers found, was the ability to do all of that in real time. Using mathematical formulas known as "graphs" that represent living, breathing communities in three dimensions, you could test which kinds of messages generated excitement or enthusiasm in conversation flows.

But perhaps the biggest new propaganda advantage provided by social media was scale. In the old days, influence operatives might distribute disinformation-laden newspapers to targeted political groups or insinuate an agent provocateur into a group of influential intellectuals. By harnessing computing power to segment and target millions of people with individually tailored pieces of propaganda in real time online, you could potentially change behavior on a national level. The challenge was figuring out how to reach all those people.

That was where the bots came in. Nongovernment researchers were busy doing their own studies of influence in social media at the time too. In one, a researcher named Tim Hwang launched a competition to see who could create socialbots so convincing that they could manipulate the behavior of Twitter users undetected. As he and his coauthors reported in the March/April 2012 issue of the journal *Interactions*, the project succeeded better than he had imagined. In just two weeks, three socialbots managed to insinuate themselves into a target group and got 250 unsuspecting followers, receiving more than 240 responses to the bots' tweets. One human member of the target group even formed a romantic attachment with one of the bots. Ultimately the bots were "able to heavily shape and distort the structure" of the community, Hwang concluded.

Hwang wrote afterward that he imagined "socialbots could be used to heal broken connections between infighting social groups and bridge existing social gaps. Socialbots could be deployed to leverage peer effects to promote more civic engagement and participation in elections." But he also sounded alarm bells: "It would be naïve not to consider that the technology may also enable novel malicious uses. The same bots that can be used to surgically bring together communities of users can also be used to shatter those social ties. The same socialbot algorithms that might improve the quality and fidelity of information circulated in social networks can be used to spread misinformation."

To be sure, the online world is only part of the equation when it comes to behavior and belief in liberal democracies. At home, at work, at places of worship, and at leisure, we are influenced in important ways that we can never be in the virtual world. But the rapid expansion of computational power and globally networked communication, and its steady and deep encroachment into our daily life, presents liberal democracy with a new kind of challenge as the Internet, social media, and the diffuse proliferation of news and video sources open up new venues for propagandists.

Moreover, this propaganda revolution is emerging at a precarious moment for liberal democracy. Americans and others around the world appear to be losing some faith in democratic processes. After steady declines from 2009 to 2015, Americans' faith in the honesty of elections is at an all-time low, with just 30 percent believing elections are honest, according to Gallup polling. Abroad, the hoped-for expansion of democracy in the post–Cold War era has yielded to retrenchment since the turn of the century, as political sociologist Larry Diamond reported in "Democracy in Decline" in the July/August 2016 issue of *Foreign Policy*. The drop has been variously attributed to failing support from the United States, the economic crisis of 2007–2008, and the rise of China. Whether and to what extent this loss of faith in democracy is related to technological developments is an open and complicated question.

And, at the same time that democracies are on their heels, those who oppose them are seizing on the opportunity presented by cyber-propaganda. Russia is rightly receiving much of the attention. While the West was focused on what the military calls the kinetic effects of cyberspace, like attacks on power grids, banking, or other physical disruptions, Russia, with its century of fascination with propaganda, seized on the psychological component of the new battlefield and developed weapons that we are only beginning to trace and understand.

Others like China, North Korea, and Iran are also active state players in the cyber-propaganda arena, but soon more forces will get in the game. Non-state actors can play as aggressively as governments in the cyber-propaganda realm, if they are rich enough and have access to the data. There is no reason to think that the rich and powerful at home would not see advantages to subverting traditional expressions of democratic will through the same tools that they or others might use abroad.

The information scientist Rand Waltzman, who ran DARPA's Social Media in Strategic Communication program, once told me that the likely result is a world where a few very wealthy state and non-state actors with access to massive data sets and the ability to exploit them in real time will engage in a "competition to manufacture reality" for large segments of the population. This,

MASSIMO CALABRESI

as much as any single element of the Russian 2016 operation against the US presidential election, explains the dire warning of former director of national intelligence James Clapper before Congress on May 8, 2017: "If there has ever been a clarion call for vigilance and action against a threat to the very foundation of our democratic political system, this episode is it."

If the threat is great, however, the solution is not straightforward. Cyber-propagandists are using the necessary openness of liberal-democratic societies to undermine them, turning our freedoms into weapons against liberty. There is already a nascent, and poorly enunciated, rush to respond to the threat. Capitol Hill has started throwing money at the problem: the 2017 National Defense Authorization Act included generous funding for unspecified efforts to counter cyber-propaganda at home and abroad. In May 2017, the Office of the Joint Chiefs of Staff moved to incorporate information operations as a "joint function" for US forces, elevating propaganda to the level of command and control, intelligence, and movement and maneuver within joint military doctrine.

Domestic information warriors are chafing as they struggle to defend against foreign and private influence operations, eager to get in the game themselves. Legal constraints protecting citizens from domestic propaganda, government electioneering, and privacy intrusions prevent much of what they would like to do. Already calls are going out to roll back Congress's mid-1970s Church Committee statutory reforms and other restrictions on domestic propaganda.

It is important to understand that Russia believes "modern warfare is based on the idea that the main battlespace is the mind," as military analyst Janis Berzins wrote in a study for the National Defence Academy of Latvia in 2014 following Russia's incursion in Ukraine. Over the past several years, Russia has developed weapons that it believes give the Kremlin a strategic advantage in the new conflict, and it is deploying them around the globe.

Some think the Russian propaganda threat is manageable. Clapper himself was deeply skeptical of the Russian operation in late July 2016, even as the first public indications of the Kremlin's active measures were coming into view. Some Russia experts, including former US diplomat Daniel Fried, argue that democracy will rapidly develop, on its own, information antibodies to counter the new challenge, as it did during the Cold War.

Recent experience shows, however, that we are not particularly skilled at countering social media propaganda. The efforts of the State Department, the traditional locus of the overt work of propaganda known as public diplomacy, were largely fruitless in the effort to undermine the recruitment of young people worldwide to the global terrorist movement envisioned by ISIS. Much of the US effort was moved, with resignation, to the covert realm, where assessing its effectiveness is much harder. Reporting suggests much of the success against ISIS's cyber-propagandists has come from old-fashioned military strikes—hardly a long-term solution.

This gets to the core of the problem. Comparing propaganda in democratic and nondemocratic societies amid the explosion of media outlets in the middle of the twentieth century, Terence Qualter concluded in *Propaganda and Psychological Warfare* that an increase in the volume of propaganda was not in itself bad for democracy. What was required was a sufficient engagement of democratic forces in the argument. "Within the democracies the actual effect of propaganda is to provide the stuff of political argument: the material for the formation of public opinion. The danger in our society is not that public opinion will be degraded by too much propaganda, but that, without the stimulating effect of genuinely rival propagandas, there might be established something approaching the closed society in which despotism flourishes."

Whether volume alone can counter the disruptive power of cyber-propaganda has yet to be tested in the age of "mass customization of messaging, narrative, and persuasion." The costly history of such tests shows that policy makers must move now to determine democracy's best defense.

The Islamist Extremism Challenge for Liberal Democracies

★ ★ ★

JOSEPH LIEBERMAN AND VANCE
SERCHUK

O f the challenges to liberal democracy and liberal international order that have arisen in the quarter century since
the demise of the Soviet Union, none has been as overt in its
aggression—or as deadly in its violence—as Islamist extremism.
Yet paradoxically, even as this threat has grown more explicit,
domestic consensus in the United States about its nature has
become more elusive. More than a decade and a half since the

Joseph Lieberman, a former four-term US senator from Connecticut, is senior
counsel at Kasowitz, Benson, Torres & Friedman. Vance Serchuk, former senior national security adviser to Senator Lieberman, is executive director of
the KKR Global Institute.

catastrophic attacks of September 11, 2001, basic questions about how to characterize this enemy—including the very name by which to call it—remain not only unsettled but the subject of intensified controversy. That the threat of Islamist extremism has itself become a source of polarization marks one of its most consequential victories against the liberal democracies.

In practice, the primary response of the United States and its allies to the problem of Islamist extremism has been to wage a series of counterterrorism campaigns, initially focused against al Qaeda, later expanded to its regional affiliates, and now directed most prominently at the so-called Islamic State, or ISIS. The goal has been to disrupt and degrade these terrorist networks—targeting their territory, finances, and membership to thwart their attack plotting, with the expectation that, over time, these networks can be reduced to the point they are no longer able to function coherently. Since 2001, the United States has invested enormous resources in the development of a counterterrorism enterprise that has become highly skilled in the prosecution of that mission.

This has been necessary and correct. It has also resulted in significant successes—foremost the prevention of another strike like 9/11 on American soil—while operating in ways that have largely respected the essential values of liberal democracy itself, despite functioning for the most part under the veil of secrecy.

However, this effort—for all its accomplishments—is also insufficient. That is because the center of gravity for the enemy is neither the terrain it controls nor the funding in its coffers nor the leadership at the top of its networks—all of which have been repeatedly decimated, only to regenerate. Rather, the enemy relies on the ability of Islamist extremist ideology to attract and mobilize followers, and on the political and security conditions that let it take root and flourish in various parts of the world. Unfortunately, the United States and other liberal democracies have yet to develop either the strategic doctrine or the institutional architecture to adequately address these core aspects of the Islamist extremist challenge.

Islamist extremism's ideology has several notable features. First, it is *totalitarian*—in its vision of the ideal society, every aspect of life is subject to the unchecked, coercive power of a self-appointed vanguard. In their fanatical pursuit of a kind of utopian purity and unity, Islamist extremists admit few if any limitations on what they consider permissible conduct; the extremists' capacity for bloodshed is constrained only by the tools at their disposal. If ISIS were to acquire a nuclear or biological weapon, there is every reason to believe that it would be used without hesitation or remorse.

Like past totalitarian movements that longed to impose on humanity their vision of heaven on earth, Islamist extremism also seeks to mobilize a mass following by exploiting the grievances of the disaffected and the marginalized. The Islamists offer a comprehensive worldview, a sense of sweeping historical purpose, and a feeling of personal empowerment and collective kinship to those who feel otherwise humiliated, inconsequential, and alienated.

Second, Islamist extremism is *rejectionist*—proposing, in its most extreme form, a comprehensive realignment of world order, with the erasure of existing borders, the dismissal of state and international structures as illegitimate, and the creation of entirely new geopolitical entities. Unlike revisionist powers such as Russia and China that equivocate about the extent of their challenge to the status quo—seeking to benefit from elements of the international system even as they work to undermine or overturn others—Islamist extremists like al Qaeda and ISIS are unique in their complete rejection of the modern world and in their mission to remake it through mass violence.

In this respect, while the challenge to the liberal democracies posed by resurgent authoritarian great powers carries echoes of the nineteenth century—when rival empires sought to carve the planet into competing spheres of influence and struggled for advantage in a fluctuating balance of power—the threat of Islamist extremism carries closer parallels to the unbridled totalitarian ideologies of the twentieth century.

Third, Islamist extremism is *resilient*—most notably in the sense that it is capable of governing territory and acquiring state-like characteristics when circumstances are favorable but can thrive equally in stateless form when necessary or advantageous. Unlike fascism, which perished in the rubble of the Third Reich, or communism, whose fortunes rose and fell alongside those of the Soviet Union, groups animated by Islamist extremism have captured, governed, and then lost large swaths of territory around the world several times, yet the ideology appears undiminished.

There are now multiple overlapping Islamist extremist networks that both compete and collaborate with each other, as well as a steady stream of radicalized individuals who seek to perpetrate attacks in their name, often without direction or control from any centralized leadership. Cyberspace has been a key enabler of this, yet technological factors alone provide only a partial explanation for Islamist extremism's ideological tenacity and organizational fluidity. The effect, regardless, is that the battlefield defeat of any single group does not doom or even necessarily weaken the overall project.

Not every person who drifts into the ranks of al Qaeda or sets out to murder under the ISIS banner is a hardened ideologue with a sophisticated worldview. One of the strengths of Islamist extremism is its ability to recruit individuals who have scant grasp of or interest in the intricacies of its ideology, or even of Islam itself, and are susceptible for psychological or interpersonal reasons to being drawn into the equivalent of a religious cult or a criminal gang.

It is true that Islamist extremism does not pose an "existential threat" to the United States in the literal sense of Russia's nuclear weapons arsenal, with its quantifiable power to obliterate civilization. Former president Barack Obama reportedly once noted, for instance, that more Americans die each year slipping in the bathtub than at the hands of terrorists. This has led some analysts to conclude that the United States suffers from an "obsession with terrorism" that has distorted America's understanding of its interests.

Such a statistical analysis misunderstands the nature of the danger that Islamist extremism poses to liberal democracy. The danger lies less in the actual or prospective body count than in its potential to collapse the basic sense of security and trust that is the prerequisite for a free, pluralistic society to function and thrive. On that score, the enemy in this conflict has done a better job of identifying and targeting our own center of gravity than we have of theirs.

As al Qaeda and Islamic State publications themselves explain, the acts of terrorism they advocate are informed by a deeper strategy than mere bloodlust. Their aim, rather, is to trigger a clash of civilizations not only between the West and the "Muslim world" but also within Muslim-majority and Western societies. In a statement published in February 2015, the Islamic State described this as eliminating "the gray space" of religious coexistence—committing atrocities that provoke anti-Muslim backlash across the West that in turn fuel Islamist radicalization and recruitment. The strategy has a twisted logic. Although Islamist extremism developed as a reaction against the failings of the ruling autocracies of the Middle East and hardened under repression, it is the succession of civil wars across the region that has been indispensable to the radicals' growth and empowerment.

It was Afghanistan's descent into internecine conflict in the 1990s, following the Soviet withdrawal from that country, that created the essential conditions for the rise of al Qaeda in its original form. Subsequently it was the post-2003 unraveling of Iraq—and, more specifically, the vicious contest for power that broke out among rival factions there in the vacuum that followed Saddam Hussein's overthrow—that opened the door for the group's expansion into the heart of the Middle East and the next stage in its evolution. A decade later, the even more brutal collapse of Syria, in parallel with renewed sectarian polarization in Iraq following the US military withdrawal, paved the way for the Islamic State's emergence. Much the same story has unfolded in Libya, Yemen, Mali, and Somalia, whose internal convulsions have similarly provided vital breathing space for al Qaeda and ISIS affiliates.

In none of these cases were Islamist extremists principally responsible for the outbreak of civil war, but in every instance, they were its primary beneficiaries. The extremists exploited and exacerbated these Hobbesian struggles with a ruthlessness and single-mindedness of purpose that their less fanatical rivals lacked. The staggering brutality of these conflicts has also helped inspire Islamist radicalization far beyond their front lines—what better proof the extremists are right about the bankruptcy of the existing order than the major powers' failure to stop the carnage? The conflicts have also provided precious sanctuaries where foreign fighters can swarm, train, and network with each other, before dispersing globally.

Much as the Bolsheviks stood little chance of seizing power but for the cataclysm of World War I and the collapse of the Russian state that the war precipitated, Islamist extremism's gains are inseparable from the geopolitical maelstrom that has turned almost every Middle Eastern country into either a battlefield or a combatant. Other regional trends have also nourished the extremists: Pakistan's decades-long sponsorship of radical groups as the demented outgrowth of its rivalry with India; the embrace and cultivation of a hard-line version of Islam by Saudi Arabia in a bid to preserve its own rule, at least until recently; and Iran's creeping hegemony over multiple Arab countries, which has enabled Sunni extremists to portray themselves as necessary defenders against Shiite dominion.

Yet just as Islamist extremism is the product of a discernable history—a set of identifiable decisions, processes, and personalities—so too can history result in its unmaking. There is nothing that predetermined its rise, and nothing that preordains its persistence on the world stage.

At present, however, the United States and other liberal democracies have eschewed any kind of grand strategy against Islamist extremism in favor of a narrower focus on smashing its manifestations. This approach is a consequence, in part, of our own disillusionment with earlier, more ambitious efforts that proved either ineffective, prohibitively expensive, or both.

The most prominent of these was the George W. Bush administration's Freedom Agenda, which envisioned the democratization of the Middle East as the key to dissolving the ideological underpinnings of Islamist extremism but subsequently became entangled in the rationale for the war in Iraq. Later, the Obama administration—despite its repudiation of the Iraq invasion and Bush-era democracy promotion—embraced the wave of 2011 popular uprisings known as the Arab Spring, predicting that they would prove a blow against al Qaeda's worldview. In neither case did the overthrow of despots deliver a decisive defeat to terrorism; on the contrary, Islamist extremists showed far greater ingenuity and resolve than did their opponents in turning these events to their advantage.

Likewise, while the United States eventually succeeded in quelling the sectarian civil war in Iraq through the 2007–2009 military surge, eviscerating al Qaeda's affiliate in the process, the undertaking was exhausting. It entailed nearly 200,000 troops at its peak, hundreds of American casualties, and billions of dollars of spending. This hard-won progress unraveled promptly after the US military exited. The idea of trying to impose peace in Syria or elsewhere in the Middle East with such a massive, unilateral American intervention is presently untenable.

The United States instead has relied increasingly on enabling local partners—the overwhelming majority of whom are themselves Muslim—as the "tip of the spear" against Islamist extremist networks. This approach has proven tactically effective against groups like al Qaeda and the Islamic State, but it has not resolved—and in many cases it has worsened—the underlying conflicts that sustain the radicals.

For the United States and other liberal democracies, then, the question is how to chart a path between unrealistic idealism—with its false promise of a rapid and irreversible victory against Islamist extremism, either through a military coup de grâce or the overnight transformation of the Middle East—and self-defeating fatalism, which effectively surrenders ideological initiative to the enemy and abandons any attempt to work toward an ultimate resolution of this conflict. While the former invites overextension and disillusionment, the latter is strategically and morally barren.

Two aspects of this challenge deserve special consideration. First, although the United States cannot and should not dispatch hundreds of thousands of its forces to the Middle East in a bid to end the region's interlocking wars, America can do much more to leverage the threat and use of its considerable military power to speed and shape their resolution. As Russia's intervention in Syria showed, the limited application of force can have profound effects. Doing so will require a much more deliberate integration of military and political lines of effort—a longstanding Achilles' heel in the structure and culture of US national security institutions—but this is a challenge that can be surmounted.

Second, targeted programs for countering radicalization—including inside the United States and other liberal democracies—hold considerable promise, but the institutional architecture for this remains woefully insufficient. There is no silver bullet to defeat Islamist extremism ideologically, but efforts to map, disrupt, and reverse the pathways by which individuals become radicalized ought to be pursued, particularly at the community level, with as much energy and ingenuity as the counterterrorism enterprise. Ultimately the United States should measure its success in this conflict less by the number of terrorists who are finished on the battlefields of the Middle East than by the number of would-be Islamist extremists who can be denied the enemy.

It is vital for the United States not to conflate Islamist extremism with the religion of Islam and its nearly 2 billion adherents. This is a question not of political correctness but of strategic self-interest. Muslim fighters, working in concert with US and allied forces, predominate today on the front lines of every major battle with Islamist extremists, from Libya and Iraq to Yemen and Afghanistan. In addition, it is Muslim civilians who have suffered the most casualties at the hands of Islamist extremists. Both militarily and ideologically, Muslims are indispensable allies in the fight against Islamist extremism.

It is likewise necessary to distinguish Islamist extremism from political Islam. The idea that the religion of Islam—its values, traditions, and laws—may play some role in informing the governance of Muslim-majority countries is neither intrinsically incompatible with liberal democracy nor a threat to international order. Just as the emergence of a democratic, anti-totalitarian left contributed to the defeat of Soviet Communism in Europe, an anti-totalitarian, anti-extremist Islamism can prove a valuable element in today's ideological struggle. Although Islamist extremists justify their fanaticism through a warped interpretation of the Muslim faith, what makes them and their ideology an enemy of liberal democracy is that they are totalitarian and violent—not that they are Islamist. The active cultivation of non-extremist interpretations of Islam by state and non-state actors—as the new leadership of Saudi Arabia has suggested it will now pursue—also holds tremendous promise.

Islamist extremism is not just a bid for power and territory, or a frenzy of mindless bloodlust; its power derives from its searing indictment of the present world, its intoxicating promise to build a better one, and its ability to captivate followers with this worldview. That is why fighting Islamist extremism requires more than conventional counterterrorism. The challenge is not just to capture or kill Islamist extremists but to erode their appeal and to prove them wrong. In this respect, Islamist extremism is above all a test of the purpose, cohesion, and self-confidence of liberal democracies themselves. It is a worthy challenge that we must rise to meet.

Failed States, Metastasizing

★ ★ ★

ROBERT D. KAPLAN

T he world has never been stable. A semi-island nation like the United States—geographically protected from upheavals in Afro-Eurasia to the extent of no other major power—sees global stability as the norm, but this is historically false. By contrast, a country like China, surrounded by hostile steppe peoples on three sides, has a far more realistic sense of history— instability is the norm, and partial solutions and accommodations are worked out only over years and decades. This mistaken American notion of history has ironically been amplified by the United States' own success: the construction of a liberal world

Robert D. Kaplan is the author, most recently, of *The Return of Marco Polo's World: War, Strategy, and American Interests in the Twenty-First Century.* He is a senior fellow at the Center for a New American Security and a senior adviser at Eurasia Group.

order in Europe and East Asia over the past three-quarters of a century. But the United States has lately showed an ambivalence over continuing along this path and, in fact, may even be retreating from it and contributing to more global disorder as a consequence. Failed states are the outriders of this disorder, and the death of civil liberty amid their chaos is a harbinger of what awaits other countries edging toward the abyss.

An American retreat would be both tragic as a moral proposition and wrong as an analytical one. After all, the world may never have been stable, but it is also true that instability can be alleviated by greater international cooperation.

Allow me to briefly provide the reasons for the current eruption of instability, describe one of its side effects, and propose a general path of action.

Globalization itself, although helping to unite the world in certain ways, is a direct cause of instability. This is because technology—jet airplanes, the information revolution, new roads and ports—has not negated geography. Rather, technology has shrunk geography, so that the world is more anxious and claustrophobic than ever. The more globalization, the more interactions there are, and the more one crisis zone can interact with other crisis zones. Integration itself thus becomes central to geopolitical instability. The very spread of populism, sectarianism, and extremism across continents is its own dark form of globalization, much as the proponents of these ideologies might strenuously deny it.

In addition to the disorder caused by globalization, there is now the particular disorder of a postimperial world. Take the Greater Middle East, ruled and stabilized, however badly, by successive imperial orders: the Ottoman Sultanate, European colonies and mandates, US and Soviet Cold War blocs, and a particular breed of strongmen (the Assads, Muammar Qaddafi, and Saddam Hussein) who emerged out of these imperial systems. It is the wreckage of imperialism, and the deformations it has wrought, that now leaves indigenous people to their own devices, with well-developed tribal and clan organizations but with much less developed traditions of state building. Sub-Saharan Africa, some peripheral areas of the former Soviet Union, and the former Byzantine and Ottoman parts of the Balkans have, to greater and lesser extents, also been examples of this pathology.

Add to all this the political and social distortion caused by the rapid growth of petroleum-based economies in such places as Nigeria and Venezuela, and we can see why the world today stands on the verge of chaos wrought not by age-old hatreds but by the very process of modernization itself. This, incidentally, was the real theme of the late Harvard political scientist Samuel P. Huntington's *The Clash of Civilizations and the Remaking of World Order* (1996), for those who bothered to read the whole book, rather than merely voice an opinion based on its provocative title.

Now we come to that familiar product of a world in disorder: failed states. Some were never really states to begin with, but places where colonial rule and postcolonial tyranny concealed a simmering anarchy awaiting breakout. This threat owed not to the inherent violence of their peoples but to the lack of indigenous political systems across communal lines that could function well in the industrial and postindustrial ages. Among these quasi-countries were Afghanistan, Yemen, Libya, Syria, Iraq, Sierra Leone, Liberia, Côte d'Ivoire, Somalia, and a few others that were not so much nations as vague geographical expressions, often organized by one outside power or another before departing the scene. These places are either currently in violent disorder or, in the case of the West African states, tentatively recovering from disorder while remaining wards of the international aid community, with little or no manufacturing bases that can provide for the middle-class stability so necessary in the twentieth and early twenty-first centuries.

Then, in addition, there are semi-failed states, very troubled states, and states simply going nowhere good. West African anarchy in the late 1990s and the collapse (or toppling) of suffocating tyrannies in the Middle East in the 2000s remain regional phenomena only. A more frightening prospect may be the slow-motion weakening of more populous pivot states such as Pakistan, Nigeria, South Africa, and Venezuela. Then there are the Balkans. Romania, Croatia, and Slovenia have performed relatively well since the end of the Yugoslav War and the collapse of the Berlin Wall, but the rest of the former Yugoslavia, as well as Albania, Bulgaria, and Greece, are in very different ways part of the category of states either partially failed or going nowhere good. In much of the former Yugoslavia, the wars of the 1990s have continued, except of course for the shooting. That is, ethnic rivalries still rob these places of the political energy required to truly rebuild. Albania and Bulgaria are undermined by weak bureaucratic systems and deeply embedded organized crime. And Greece has still to make the necessary financial reforms to recover from a devastating depression.

I specifically mention the Balkans because there is a solution available to them that is instructive in this age of creeping international disorder. The Balkans can find communal peace, and eventual economic prosperity, by coming more fully under the umbrella of what I call a *necessary empire*: the European Union.

The European Union, headquartered in Brussels, led by an often remote and only partially democratic bureaucracy, yet overseeing the daily economic reality of its member states, is another empire in all but name. Yet the EU promotes the rule of law over arbitrary fiat, legal states over ethnic nations, and the individual over the group. Only under the aegis of the EU can there be a true resolution, for example, to the territorial rivalry between Serbs and Albanians. Only within the EU is progress even imaginable for such troubled polities as Greece and Bulgaria.

The European Union, precisely by being an empire, albeit a good one, is also an example of multilateralism and globalization within the European continent. For empire and cosmopolitanism have been intertwined throughout history. Indeed, a principal definition of empire is the rule of different ethnicities and sects by a single organization, which, in turn, then becomes influenced by the many and varied cultures under its domain.

Just think about it for a moment. NATO, the EU, the International Court of Justice, the United Nations, the World Trade Organization, and so on are all, taken together, an attempt to replace the function of empire by more humane and less oppressive means. The fact that formal empires have dissolved and are not coming back does not remove the necessity of some form of supranational order and governance.

And this is not only true of the Balkans. The concept in general holds true for places as far-flung and as diverse as the Congo, Syria, and Ukraine. Any amelioration or solution for these trouble spots must ultimately entail an international response—that is, a response in which some of the international organizations named above will be involved. In many or even most cases, no one power will have either the capability or the naked self-interest to intervene alone, whether militarily or otherwise. The risk of taking action must be spread among a group of nations, most easily imaginable through an international organization. Indeed, the very definition of a humanitarian intervention is an intervention for reasons of humanity and not for reasons of state or strategy. Without such international cooperation, failed states will be forever doomed.

This is not about exporting democracy. In the early stages of any state recovery or state-building process, benign forms of autocracy may have to prevail. Order comes before freedom because without order there can be no freedom for anybody. This is a reality that I have lived vividly on the ground in Iraq and Sierra Leone in particular. As a foreign correspondent for more than three decades, I have learned to distinguish less between democracy and autocracy than among the various gray shades of enlightened authoritarianism and illiberal democracy that overlap both, when actually encountered face-to-face around the world. In truth, we should seek to expand civil society in all its manifestations, rather than legalistically obsess about elections.

So the answer to failed states is not anti-globalization, which can only lead to new blocs even more lethal than those of the Cold War, given today's advanced stages of technology and integration. The Cold War, despite its grievous small wars at the periphery, did not result in great-power warfare. But, in an age of cyber-weapons and new forms of nuclear proliferation, a retreat into amoral power politics may not be so kind.

In another, earlier book, *Political Order in Changing Societies*, published in 1968, Samuel Huntington (a liberal Democrat all his life, by the way) explained how greater economic and social development causes not political stability but new kinds of instability, and the solution to this new kind of instability is not a retreat into older forms of bureaucratic organization but a surge into even newer and more sophisticated forms of organization. Reform should never stop, in other words. To wit, the answer to the bad side effects of globalization must be even more globalization and integration, painstakingly applied, in order to fix or alleviate the problems.

A global *government* is impossible and wrong: that would mean a new kind of tyranny because the ways and means of political improvement will never be agreed upon. Yet more global *governance* is a necessity, and it provides the only practical way of dealing with failed and semi-failed states.

Critics will complain: But the United States is not the world's policeman! Agreed. That is why the United States must lead a community of nations to spread both the risk and the responsibility of dealing, however partially and imperfectly, with the anarchy of failed states. It is in America's self-interest to share the burden by operating within the context of a global community, and it is a matter of self-preservation not to retreat from this task. For precisely because new technology has shrunk geography, Americans can less and less escape the world.

Apocalypse in a Nuclear Warhead

★ ★ ★

WILLIAM J. PERRY

American politics today are in upheaval and confusion. So are the politics of the United Kingdom. Poland, for many years a vibrant democracy, now has an autocratic president. Hungary's autocratic president, Viktor Orbán, says he presides over an "illiberal democracy." Until 2017, Kenya for a decade had been a democratic model in Africa—then a presidential election was overturned, and the country descended into months of political chaos that may have irretrievably damaged its democratic future. In South Korea, the spectacle of the 2018 Winter Olympics

William J. Perry, former US secretary of defense, is the founder of the William J. Perry Project; its mission is to engage and educate the public about the dangers of nuclear weapons in the twenty-first century.

masked the political struggles of a nation that impeached and removed its president eleven months earlier.

Some dark voices suggest that all this turmoil reveals inherent weaknesses in the democratic form of government—that liberal democracy has had a good run but is rapidly losing steam. With the waning of global leadership provided by formal and informal democratic alliances, now anti-democratic, illiberal opportunists are rushing to fill the vacuum, raising tensions around the world. And the tensions often have a nuclear component: A nuclear-armed Russia sows discord wherever it can; a nuclear-armed China flexes its military muscles in the South China and East China seas; North Korea edges ever closer to becoming a full-fledged nuclear power; and Iran, possessing large amounts of enriched uranium, spreads its military influence deep into the Middle East.

I do not agree that liberal democracy is reaching the end of the road. It is certainly under siege in many places, and some of the wounds are self-inflicted. But the rising threats are real, and that is why democracies need new strength and new resolve. Restoring democratic leadership to the global stage is an urgent matter, because the world is more vulnerable to a nuclear catastrophe now than at any time since the height of the Cold War.

The danger comes in two forms. The first is what I call nuclear war by accident. The world got a sobering glimpse of how this could happen in January 2018 when a bungled emergency warning drill left Hawaiians terrified for more than half an hour that a ballistic missile attack was imminent. Hawaii is now within reach of North Korean missiles, so the "this is not a drill" message sent in error was plausible. Luckily, nothing came of the mistake—except a disquieting sense of how easily a disastrous scenario could unfold as retaliatory nuclear strikes are launched against a phantom threat. Maintaining constant vigilance and the highest standards of competence is essential.

The other danger is what I call nuclear war by miscalculation. We have to go back further in time for a cautionary tale about this threat, to the Cuban Missile Crisis in 1962. Like the confrontation that nearly brought the United States and Russia to the brink of disaster, a new military or geopolitical crisis could emerge from a sequence of miscalculations or misinterpretations.

The United States is rightly concerned about Russia, which is rebuilding its nuclear arsenal and playing a very aggressive game with an economically weak hand. Moscow's feints and saber rattling in the Baltics could—intentionally or not—spark a minor clash with US troops or those of a NATO ally and escalate into a nuclear war. There might even be instances when Russia and the United States both think they are pursuing reasonable political ends through minor military actions, without realizing that they are on a collision course that could end in calamity. Not likely, but not impossible. The current US administration needs to be more cognizant of the dangers posed by Russia under Vladimir Putin.

With China, the triggering event could occur in the South China Sea, where US military forces are in close proximity with theirs. A dispute is simmering over the right of free passage through what China considers its national waters. But I don't think China, or Russia, is seeking military conflict. Both believe strongly that they have certain rights and are working hard to assert them.

The potential for an accidental nuclear clash with Russia or China would be greatly reduced if the United States emphasized the deterrence power of nuclear-armed bombers and submarines and gradually eliminated its intercontinental ballistic missiles. If America ever mistakenly launches a retaliatory strike in response to a false alarm, it will be with ICBMs—they are fixed targets, and inviting ones, so they operate with a launch-on-warning policy. They are Cold War relics, their usefulness outstripped by advances in bomber and submarine technology.

What about other nuclear threats? Regional conflicts could spiral into nuclear war: India and Pakistan, both nuclear armed, have long-standing points of friction. The probability of all-out war is not what I would call "remote." China has a tense relationship with India and is an ally of Pakistan's, so the Chinese might also get involved, and possibly Russia. Such a war could involve an exchange of one hundred nuclear weapons, inflicting unimaginable horror on millions of people and pouring enough smoke and ash into the atmosphere to cause a "nuclear winter," with dire crop failures on a global scale.

The need for international diplomacy to prevent just such a scenario from happening should be obvious, but the recent struggles of democracies around the world have been accompanied by a trend toward isolationism and the fraying of long-standing alliances. A reinvigorated appreciation for liberal-democratic values would bring with it a stronger and much-needed emphasis on international cooperation.

Which brings us to North Korea. A US policy-by-Twitter of countering Kim Jong-un's bellicosity with more bellicosity is not a long-term solution and indeed could lead to disaster. The

North Korean government is not irrational—it isn't now, under Kim Jong-un, and it wasn't under his father, Kim Jong-il. The government has three priorities: to preserve the Kim dynasty, to gain international respect, and (a distant third) to improve the North Korean economy. I was aware of this in 1999 when I went to Pyongyang at the request of President Clinton, South Korean president Kim Dae Jung, and Japanese prime minister Keizō Obuchi to negotiate an agreement that would require North Korea to give up its programs to develop nuclear weapons and long-range missiles. In return, South Korea and Japan would provide economic assistance and the United States would provide security assurances.

The discussions were encouraging and were followed by Kim Jong-il's sending his senior military aide to Washington in October 2000 to discuss a formal agreement. We were quite close to reaching final terms, but time ran out on the Clinton administration before an agreement could be concluded. If we had been successful, the world would be very different, and certainly safer, than the one we have today.

When the Bush administration took office in 2001, it cut off all negotiations with North Korea. Two years later, at China's urging, the United States agreed to participate in so-called six-party talks. The negotiations began with great hope, but the results could not have been more disappointing. When the talks failed, North Korea focused on building a nuclear arsenal.

North Korean leaders believed, incorrectly, that the United States and South Korea were planning to overthrow their regime; they believed, correctly, that North Korea's large but poorly equipped conventional forces were significantly inferior to US and South Korean military forces. Developing nuclear weapons allowed the North Koreans to achieve their supreme goal: regime survival. A nuclear arsenal would deter such an attack. They also believed that it would gain them the international respect that they covet.

But the North Koreans did this at a terrible cost to their economy, from the diversion of resources and from economic sanctions. They were willing to sacrifice the goal of economic progress if it meant securing the regime's two top priorities. By the time the Obama administration arrived, the die was already cast. North Korea has steadily developed its missile capability in recent years and now may be able to strike the mainland United States. The situation is clearly dangerous and getting more dangerous every week.

But the danger is *not* that Pyongyang would launch a surprise nuclear attack. Preserving the Kim dynasty is paramount; suicide is not an option. Though the problem with North Korea seems unique, it is familiar: the danger comes from *blundering* into nuclear war. If Kim Jong-un, trying to increase international respect (or fear), attempts even riskier provocations than he has in the past, he could very well overplay his hand, provoking South Korea to take military action. A shooting war could quickly escalate, involving the United States. If the Kim dynasty perceived itself as on the verge of being overthrown, then North Korea might launch a last-resort nuclear attack.

I believe that it is still possible to negotiate an agreement with North Korea. Not the agreement we nearly reached in 2000 (before North Korea had nuclear weapons) but one that would considerably reduce the danger posed today. Negotiating with

North Korea requires understanding the regime's goals. To think that economic sanctions will break its will is to misunderstand the government's priorities. To base diplomacy on the assumption that North Korea is prepared to give up its nuclear weapons is also mistaken. But Pyongyang might accept significant limitations on its nuclear ambitions—while maintaining the ability to ensure the Kim dynasty's preservation—in exchange for economic gains. It is not beyond the diplomatic skills of America and its allies to formulate a workable new approach.

Iran is another potential nuclear threat—but not in the way many people think. The agreement negotiated by the Obama administration to restrict Iran's weapons program was a good one. It saved the world a lot of grief. The Trump administration's withdrawal from the deal was seriously misguided, and the uncertainty the decision introduced in the Middle East is potentially dangerous. But Iran already possesses large quantities of enriched uranium. What if a faction of the Iranian Revolutionary Guard decided to divert one hundred pounds of enriched uranium to a terror group? There are similar threats of proliferation from North Korea and Pakistan. And therein lies the menace of a nuclear attack that doesn't involve an accident or miscalculation.

Nuclear terrorism is a very real possibility today. All it involves is a terror group such as ISIS or al Qaeda getting its hands on fissile material from which it can produce a nuclear weapon. I have no doubt that these terrorists would use the weapon if they possessed it.

The result would not be as catastrophic as a full nuclear war, but millions could die if a nuclear weapon were detonated by terrorists in a major city. The likelihood of such an attack occurring is not high—but it is much higher than the other possibilities that I have mentioned. Preventing terrorists from obtaining fissile material is an essential component of fighting terror, and it is a campaign that must be prosecuted vigorously for years to come.

In the long term, I am optimistic that human intelligence and wisdom will prevail. Humanity will not destroy itself. In the short term, though, I am less sanguine, because leaders and governments are not taking the actions necessary to mitigate very real threats. During the Cold War, at least, people understood the nature of the dangers. I worry that powerful geopolitical forces are inexorably pushing the world toward catastrophe, and our leaders don't comprehend what is happening. The sooner that liberal-democratic governments, beginning with that of the United States, rededicate themselves to pursuing peace and co-operation as conditions that are essential for liberty's flourishing, the better it will be for the world.

The Anti-Press Crusade
Goes Global

★ ★ ★

MARK LASSWELL

When young English poet John Milton called on Italian astronomer and physicist Galileo Galilei in 1638, the man he found was old and ill and blind. Galileo had been living under house arrest for five years in the hills outside Florence, convicted of heresy by the Roman Catholic Church after publishing his Copernicus-echoing assertion that the earth revolves around the sun. Yet, during that same year, Galileo succeeded in defying the church's ban on his publishing new work. His final book, *Dialogues Concerning Two New Sciences*, was printed in Holland from a manuscript smuggled out of Italy.

Mark Lasswell is an op-ed editor at the *Washington Post* and the former editorial features editor, overseeing op-eds, at the *Wall Street Journal*.

Galileo's bleak predicament weighed on Milton. Six years later, he described it in a polemic that would become a lodestar in the history of the free press—one that shines a little brighter today, in an era when journalism is widely under attack.

Amid the religious and political tumult of the English Civil War, Parliament in 1643 passed the Ordinance for the Regulation of Printing, with restrictions on "Papers, Pamphlets, and Books" that included requiring printers to obtain a government license. Milton, who turned thirty-five that year, was a Puritan, and now he saw a Puritan-aligned Parliament moving to impose prepublication censorship. He responded with "Areopagitica; a Speech of Mr. John Milton for the Liberty of Unlicenc'd Printing to the Parlament of England." The nearly 18,000-word document argued that turning truth loose in the public square is essential to intellectual and moral development—and that attempting to eliminate falsehood, in addition to being a fool's errand, insults the power of truth.

Government-controlled printing reminded him of the Catholic Church's fear of new thinking. In lands where the Vatican ruled, Milton wrote, educated men "did nothing but bemoan the servil condition" of learning. He then described meeting Galileo, "a prisner to the Inquisition, for thinking in Astronomy otherwise then the Franciscan and Dominican thought." Milton was too early for the Enlightenment by half a century and can hardly be claimed as a forebear of classical liberalism, given that he held plenty of hidebound religious and political views. But in "Aeropagitica" Milton did observe that "hee who destroyes a good Booke, kills reason it selfe," and he asserted a large-hearted claim for individual freedom: "Give me the liberty to know, to utter, and to argue freely according to conscience, above all liberties."

Milton didn't actually deliver this "speech" to Parliament, and in any case the message went unheeded—the licensing law remained on the books until the 1690s. But his thinking echoed down the years, aided by the publication of an influential edition of "Areopagitica" by the Scottish poet James Thomson in 1738. The polemic and other Milton works "had no small influence on the Founding Fathers in America," Anna Beer wrote in *Milton: Poet, Pamphleteer, and Patriot* (2008). Milton's defense of press freedom and the "liberty to know, to utter, and to argue freely according to conscience" reverberates in the First Amendment of the US Constitution.

America's founding fathers knew that a free press, and an informed citizenry, is a cornerstone of democracy and that restricting what can be known is a cornerstone of tyranny. The autocratic urge to dictate what is considered the truth wasn't new when the first inquisitor asked Galileo to stop by for a chat, and it has proved resilient over centuries, even—or perhaps especially—into the modern era, when the means of distributing information burgeoned. Today's aspiring despots know that the first order of business in a coup is to seize the television stations; accomplished despots know that an essential tool for keeping a grip on power is jailing or killing reporters. And strangling the Internet.

Governments that dictate the news nowadays are, to varying degrees and with varying success, just practicing latter-day versions of the propaganda dark arts devised for the mass-media age by Joseph Goebbels in Nazi Germany and by Stalin's Soviet ministers. North Korea's near-total information control is the clearest contemporary homage to those noxious pioneers, followed by the news overlords in Turkmenistan and Uzbekistan. But Russia, China, Iran, Cuba, Venezuela, and their propagandistic brethren all do a creditable job of sculpting reality for their citizens.

Autocratic contempt for the concept of the free press may be immutable, but democratic respect for that right is similarly steadfast. Or it was until lately. As president, Donald Trump has merrily hacked away at one liberal-democratic value after another—the rule of law, free trade, immigration—but he has brought a particular relish to attacking press freedom. Trump made his intentions clear during the presidential campaign, disparaging and taunting journalists covering his rallies, even mocking one reporter's physical impairment. In August 2016, trailing in the polls, Trump went on Twitter and denounced the "disgusting and corrupt media," saying, "It is not 'freedom of the press' when newspapers and others are allowed to say and write whatever they want even if it is completely false!" That would be news to First Amendment lawyers.

Once he was in office, Trump's crusade against the press (whose good opinion he nonetheless craves) took on an added force. From his White House perch Trump could add a fillip of attempted presidential intimidation. Unhappy with an October 2017 NBC News report that said he was seeking a tenfold increase in the US nuclear arsenal, Trump tweeted that "network news has become so partisan, distorted and fake that licenses must be challenged and, if appropriate, revoked." Reporters noted that there is no national television network license that can be, if appropriate, revoked. The threat might have been empty, but the menacing intent was plain enough.

A few months into Trump's presidency, the Washington-based Freedom House issued its annual appraisal of global press freedom, reporting the lowest rating in thirteen years. The organization blamed "new threats to journalists and media outlets in major democracies" and "further crackdowns on independent media in authoritarian countries like Russia and China." The report added that Trump's "far-reaching attacks on the news media and their place in a democratic society... fuel predictions of further setbacks in years to come."

Trump may have broken new ground for the presidency in publicly reviling the press ("I have a running war with the media," he said the day after his inauguration. "They are among the most dishonest human beings on earth"), but he is unlikely to make much practical headway with reining in American journalists. Presidents are rarely fans of the coverage they receive—even the rose-colored glasses used by reporters during the Obama years weren't good enough for Trump's predecessor. The Obama administration's "war on leaks and other efforts to control information are the most aggressive I've seen since the Nixon administration," wrote former *Washington Post* executive editor Leonard Downie Jr. in a 2013 report for the Committee to Protect Journalists. But no matter how much they may vex presidents, journalists in America enjoy broad legal protections, with a historically sympathetic judiciary, and they work in an industry of robust competition that offers countless avenues for expression.

That is why the United States has long been a beacon of press freedom, one that prompted emulation by other democracies and offered a stirring alternative vision of life in liberty for those who lived under repressive regimes. And that is why

Trump's vilification of the news media is so pernicious. The aim is to delegitimize the press, not just to slander it. Where Obama and Nixon and other presidents hated seeing the truth get out and took steps to try to prevent it, none had the genius to try to corrupt the idea of truth itself. The message that America now sends to the world about press freedom: it is a tool for disseminating lies by those who are among the most dishonest human beings on earth. In that context, an administration's outright mendacity can be presented, in the immortal words of Trump adviser Kellyanne Conway, as "alternative facts." But the more insidious goal is to preemptively invalidate journalism itself.

The unsettling sight of democracies drifting toward populist nationalism and leaders who disdain liberal-democratic values like freedom of the press was well under way before Trump took office. His election was just the most prominent manifestation of the phenomenon. Hungarian prime minister Viktor Orbán, in office since 2010, has boasted of running an "illiberal democracy" as its independent media are gradually choked off, supplanted by pro-government owners. Poland's right-wing populist Law and Justice Party, governing with an outright parliamentary majority since 2015, has pursued similar tactics, according to the 2017 *World Press Freedom Index* issued by Reporters Without Borders. Law and Justice's anti-press measures include "bringing public radio and TV broadcasters under its control," the Paris-based organization said, "replacing their directors, and turning them into propaganda outlets. Several independent publications opposed to its reforms have been throttled economically."

With populist parties gaining ground in Austria, Germany, Italy, and elsewhere in Europe, journalists have plenty of reason to worry. A decline of press freedom anywhere is cause for concern, but its erosion in Europe—for so long a haven, with the United States, of liberal-democratic values—is especially disquieting. Freedom House's 2017 report attributed the slide in part to a weakened European Union, rattled by rising dissent among its members and chary of insisting on democratic standards. But the common thread detected by Freedom House and other monitors of press freedom has been the contempt for the news media stoked by Donald Trump.

The effect of Trump's campaign to delegitimize the press has been felt globally. In December 2017, *Politico* reported that "prominent leaders or state media" in at least fifteen countries had used the Trumpian term "fake news"—the president has unaccountably failed to trademark it—to attack news reports. Joel Simon, executive director of the Committee to Protect Journalists, told *Politico* that Trump "is providing a context and framework for all sorts of authoritarian leaders—or democratic leaders and others who are dissatisfied or upset by critical coverage—to undermine and discredit reporting." The list included Syrian president Bashar al-Assad dismissing a report that 13,000 people had been killed in a Syrian military prison ("You can forge anything these days, we are living in a fake news era"); Venezuelan president Nicolás Maduro griping about depictions of the socialist hell his country has become ("This is what we call 'fake news' today, isn't it?"); and Spanish foreign minister Alfonso Dastis, despite photos and video evidence to the contrary, claiming that reported police violence against voters in Catalonia's independence referendum was "fake news."

There was a time when the term "fake news" simply described phony online articles, like the clickbait baloney that seemed to enjoy a special currency among Trump's more-credulous supporters during the 2016 campaign. But eventually the world learned that Russia, a past master of information warfare, ran an elaborate online campaign to influence voters in Trump's favor and to stoke discord along the way. With the American media focusing on the Russian "fake news" offensive, Trump—ever quick to try to turn trouble to his advantage—made the phrase famously his own, repurposing "fake news" as a weapon against the press. The president deployed the phrase so often that he succeeded in largely effacing its former meaning, with its unflattering associations. Yet both Trump-friendly fake news and the president's rebranding of the phrase ultimately had the same effect: to shake belief in the reliability of reporting generally and to bulldoze openings that could be filled with ersatz facts, whether issuing from Russia Today or the podium in the White House press briefing room.

Four centuries ago, advocating for a free press in "Areopagitica," John Milton wrote about "Truth," saying, "Let her and Falshood grapple; who ever knew Truth put to the wors, in a free and open encounter." Truth is forever grappling with falsehood, but today the battle is less free and open than ever. Technology, especially social media, gives authoritarian regimes both remarkable targeting capabilities and unprecedented global reach, and soon the spread of disinformation may be aided by artificial intelligence used to produce "deepfake" video indistinguishable from genuine news footage. Truth's cause in this fight against falsehood is made all the more difficult when world leaders fill the ringside seats, heckling.

The Weakness in Democracy's Strength: Complacency

★ ★ ★

KARL-THEODOR ZU GUTTENBERG

I s democracy a permanent feature of the Western world or a transitory phenomenon? Alarmed by evidence like a 2017 World Bank report that average global voter turnout for legislative elections over the past twenty-five years plunged by more than 10 percent, many in academia and in think tanks focus on rising doubts about the democratic system, its institutions, achievements, and sustainability. The concern has only been heightened by the recent rise of nationalists and populists, some with clearly anti-democratic, autocratic leanings. These experts'

Karl-Theodor zu Guttenberg, chairman of Spitzberg Partners, is the former German minister of economics and technology and former minister of defense.

worries are not misplaced, but the decisive precondition that nurtured the flourishing of populist movements in the United States and Europe is often overlooked: a system weakened because its strength was not questioned, its resilience assumed.

Consider the case of Donald Trump and Hillary Clinton. Many factors go into voter turnout, but in the 2016 presidential election about 40 percent of voting-eligible citizens chose not to exercise their right. Partisans painted dire pictures of what would happen if the other side won, but tens of millions of Americans were sufficiently confident about democracy's resilience, and government's ability to meet their needs, that they stayed home. And the 2016 turnout was relatively good for a nation that chronically struggles to get 60 percent to the polls.

Trump benefited from the complacency of those tens of millions of stay-home Americans, just as he benefited from the complacency of many who voted for him. When citizens deem government incompetent or paralytic, more than a few will become willing to vote for candidates or parties that blatantly question democratic standards. (Recall that Trump refused to say whether he would accept the election result if he lost and suggested that he would claim the vote was "rigged.") Even if a candidate's interests don't align very well with their own, these voters still use the candidate as an amplifier to express their disappointment in the political establishment—while fully believing that the democratic system is strong enough to absorb their protest. They take its regenerative qualities for granted.

What about those citizens who suffer from voter fatigue, who tell themselves that their vote won't make a difference? Why would they draw that conclusion?

First, democracy is perceived as a self-perpetuating institution that, once set on track, will continue to run. There is a jaded view, widely shared, that regardless of one's vote, nothing will substantially change. The argument tends to be rooted in resentment toward the political class and the belief that elites cater for their own interests. At its core, this often-populist view regards the individual as incapable of influencing policy at the voting booth and believes that the effect one voter may have is, *qualitatively* speaking, infinitesimal.

Second, today democracy is a phenomenon of mass societies. Individuals may see their participation in the democratic process as inconsequential to the functioning of the apparatus. In an endless sea of voters, one may not recognize the origin of democracy, reflected in ancient Athens, where every adult male could make himself heard and meet his civic obligation to be a part of the chorus of those whose most noble endeavor was to uphold the res publica (or πολιτεία). The sense of being overwhelmed by the sheer number of voters is the *quantitative* aspect of voter fatigue.

This quantitative and qualitative disconnect is especially pronounced in the stratum of society that most needs the attention of the political democratic order: the economically disadvantaged. The poor, and those who feel themselves slipping toward poverty, are increasingly unmotivated to participate in elections—with the bitter result, over time, that policy makers shift their interest away from those who need it, further validating their belief that the system does not care about them. It is a vicious circle: the apathy mounts until it gives way to fury, fueling populist movements of resentment that seek to place blame on government, on immigrants, on minorities.

The wider disaffection from democracy has other origins. Karl Marx got plenty wrong, but he made a useful observation in the nineteenth century about the alienation of workers who labor on a tiny fraction of an end product, little knowing or caring about the final result. Other writers, such as Hannah Arendt and Theodor W. Adorno in the twentieth century, offered similar contemplations of the individual in mass society. These writers usually defined mass society as a consumer society, often warning that consumerism could have devastating consequences for democracy.

That was before the Internet. Today, digitally driven consumerism—of goods, of news, of popular culture, of seemingly life's every aspect—encourages people to identify themselves in terms of products rather than citizenship. The mechanisms of consumerism may suddenly overshadow liberal democracy—Facebook, after all, knows no boundaries (except when it comes to China, but that's another matter). Cultural phenomena are derived from consumerism, and social orders are formed as a result. To many, Instagram and Twitter are more powerful influences than the sense of belonging encouraged by democracy.

Maybe this new age of consumerism should be called "userism." Offering endless possibilities of engagement with and participation in systems, whether that means going to YouTube or shopping on Amazon, userism stirs feelings of immediate impact and response. Ubiquity and availability make consumption a quick and efficient adventure—as opposed to the traditionally slow mechanisms and consensus-seeking procedures of democracy. The understanding that some things take longer than clicking for an online purchase is in danger.

In the age of userism, voting may come to be regarded as a chore or inconvenience instead of a right. People may perceive that their online voices can be powerful—look how quickly that company apologized after I complained!—but that their voices as citizens are inconsequential and ignored. The flourishing of liberal democracy, and of the economic prosperity that came with it, helped pave the way for consumerism and userism, but there is obviously no reciprocal nurturing of democracy.

Will these developments gradually marginalize citizenship and, eventually, democracy? Will people regard democracy increasingly as a burdensome system or take it even more for granted than they already do? Yes, at least to a certain extent. For decades, we have seen millions of citizens in democracies declining their right to vote even while knowing that elsewhere in the world people forfeit their lives to gain that same right. Now many people are willing to sacrifice basic privacy rights for banal promises like more-privileged access to digital platforms and their services. Such a cavalier attitude doesn't bode well for an era when democracy is already suffering from the qualitative and quantitative sources of voter fatigue mentioned above.

Here we see a parallel with voters who, responding to demagogic candidates, send a message that they are willing to exchange liberties for more security. Security, however, is not a basic right in the sense that a human right is. To seek it at the risk of freedom of speech or religion is a naïve surrender to the facile promises offered by characters who are regarded (recklessly) as easily contained by democratic institutions.

The populists of our age take advantage of the divide between consumerism, or userism, and citizenship. And in a world where terrorism can strike seemingly anywhere at any time, they exploit the yearning for security. That every problem can be solved with the stroke of a pen is a compelling message to an electorate accustomed to instant gratification. These charlatans promote the idea that all problems are easily fixed and politicians who "don't get the job done" are either incompetent or corrupt. Though this message encourages the spread of conspiracy theories, its foremost aim is to shatter confidence in democratic institutions and to sell the idea of a strong, supremely competent leader. It is reminiscent of the messianic hopes that ancient people had when they dreamed of wise kings or philosophers on the throne.

Nowadays the opportunities available to the strongman (or strongwoman) are rather modest, compared with the visions of justice and righteousness in antiquity. Populists compensate by adding xenophobic ingredients to their platform, stoking a nativist hostility to minorities and foreigners. Attacking immigration and insulting Muslims competes with disparaging multinational institutions such as NATO or the European Union. These are just a few examples of how political profiteers delude a less-engaged public, a public that takes democracy—its values, institutions, and rights—as a given.

The question now is how to confront today's con artists and to revitalize the appreciation of democracy. The first step is for candidates and parties not to try to compete by offering simplistic solutions. The vast middle of the electorate will appreciate not being patronized and might even feel the fresh stirring of an ennobling democratic spirit.

Most citizens know that complex and often interrelated questions regarding matters such as migration, climate change, artificial intelligence, or violent extremism don't lend themselves to easy answers.

Most citizens recognize, and are repulsed by, that favorite technique of the autocratic populist: scapegoating. They know that blaming Mexicans in the United States, or Poles in England, or homosexuals in Russia, or Kurds in Turkey, or Muslims in India is utterly wrong.

The populists often camouflage their divisive politics with a call for governing efficiency that the current system, by design, does not possess. They bellow "drain the swamp" or "take our country back," or they denounce institutions like the US Congress or the European Union as ponderous burdens on the citizenry. The institutions themselves often seem cowed by the criticism, offering feeble defenses or none at all.

As a German citizen, I won't speak to matters involving the American legislative process, but I will gladly note that the European Union was never envisioned as a paragon of ruthless bureaucratic efficiency. The EU deservedly won the 2012 Nobel Peace Prize for bringing together the nations of the European continent that had been warring with one another, on and off, for centuries. The EU, like any institution, needs constant renewal and innovation as it strives to make the voices of its members equally heard, with the help of an armada of translators. This is not a sleek enterprise, and it was never intended to be. But as a liberal-democratic entity, the European Union is an unprecedented success. Pure efficiency wouldn't ensure this kind of security, regardless of what consumerist impatience might demand. Liberal democracy does. It starts with the right to vote.

Democracy itself is an institution that similarly strives to let everyone be heard. And if those who govern must consult their citizens, and if the governed vote to sanction their authority every four or five years, democracy can seem to operate with an outdated, frustrating sluggishness. But that is what the responsible, judicious conduct of human affairs looks like. Populist demagogues are irresponsible and injudicious, and their glorification of efficiency is the pandering that masks the lust for power, as mankind's ghastly experience in the twentieth century attests.

Instead of taking for granted the strength of liberal democracy to resist assaults on its values, those who see the threat must join the fray—and rally the indifferent or distracted to its defense. When free speech or the free press or the rule of law comes under attack, the attacks must be resisted and called out for what they are: firefights in a larger campaign to damage and discredit democracy itself. Citizen by citizen, group by group, the allies of liberal democracy must shake off the complacency that this marvelous invention inspires. Even if the anti-democratic forces now loose in the world don't succeed, they may be preparing the way for something worse. The moment has come to ensure that it is today's illiberalism, and not democracy, that is a transitory phenomenon.

Illiberals of the World, Unite!

★ ★ ★

JAMES KIRCHICK

The Russian government is thoroughly corrupt. It seeks to obtain excellence only in the arts of war—for that there is no sum they will not pay. Russia lives on the intrigues of agents and on the reports of highly paid spies. Rather than govern its own country well, it disturbs countries better governed than its own and strives to reduce them to their own level of debasement.

—Harry Verney,
Our Quarrel with Russia, 1855

It is especially important to introduce geopolitical disorder into internal American activity, encouraging all kinds of separatism and ethnic, social and racial conflicts, actively supporting all dissident movements—extremist, racist, and sectarian groups, thus destabilizing internal

---

James Kirchick, a visiting fellow at the Brookings Institution, is the author of *The End of Europe: Dictators, Demagogues and the Coming Dark Age*.

political processes in the U.S. It would also make sense simultaneously to support isolationist tendencies in American politics.

—Alexander Dugin,
The Foundation of Geopolitics, 1997

When Russian foreign minister Sergei Lavrov took the stage at the Munich Security Conference in 2015, he did not intend for his speech to prompt peals of laughter. The annual forum—a high-level confab bringing together presidents, prime ministers, defense chiefs, think tank denizens, and other grandees from Europe and beyond—is an opportunity for earnest chin-stroking about international problems. Yet when Lavrov delivered Moscow's view of the ongoing crisis in Ukraine, whose territory it had invaded and annexed just a year before, the VIPs who filled the room at the elegant Bayerischer Hof hotel could only guffaw in response.

"What happened in Crimea was the people invoking the right of self-determination," Lavrov said, referring to the sham referendum in which 97 percent of ballots were reported as favoring unification with the motherland, a referendum that took place under the watchful eye of Russian soldiers. "You've got to read the U.N. Charter," Lavrov insisted, to more laughter. "Territorial integrity and sovereignty must be respected."

Appeals to "sovereignty," international law, and "territorial integrity" from the foreign minister of almost any other country would be unremarkable. Yet Russia had committed the first armed annexation of territory on the European continent since World War II and had perpetrated it with the same blood-and-soil pretext that Adolf Hitler had used in conquering the Sudetenland. That the Russians are living "in another world" than their Western interlocutors (an observation made of Lavrov's boss, President Vladimir Putin, by German chancellor Angela Merkel) became evident with his next remark, which, given the setting, was clearly calculated to shock. "Germany's reunification was conducted without any referendum, and we actively supported this," Lavrov said, appearing to challenge the very legal basis of the country in which he was speaking. "As you remember," he continued, "after the end of World War II the Soviet Union spoke against the division of Germany." Protest the Russians did, though their construction of an Iron Curtain that divided not just Germany but all of Europe spoke more to their sincerity.

It's easier to mock the silliness of official Russian assertions than grapple with the mind-set that produces them—a mind-set finding more adherents, alas, including in Western democracies. None of those startled dignitaries in the audience could claim that Russia's recent behavior had come as a surprise. For it was on that very same Munich stage in 2007 that Putin unleashed a portentous tirade against the American-led liberal world order. Countries that had once lived under the Soviet heel voluntarily joining the North Atlantic Treaty Organization (NATO), he declared, amounted to "a stunning provocation." The West had turned the Organization for Security and Cooperation in Europe, a multilateral institution of which Russia is itself a member, "into a vulgar instrument of ensuring the foreign policy interests of one country." And that country under indictment, the United States, resembled no less tyrannical a regime than the "Third

Reich" in its "contempt for human life and the same claims of exceptionality and diktat in the world." Putin ended ominously: "Political solutions," he warned, "are becoming impossible."

The following year, Putin made good on that reflection by invading Russia's tiny neighbor Georgia, over 20 percent of whose territory Moscow continues to occupy. Six years later came the annexation of Crimea. In 2016, Russia launched an unprecedented assault on American democracy, a multifaceted influence operation that combined hacking, strategically timed leaks, propaganda, and manipulation of social media networks, all designed to sow chaos and assist the campaign of Donald J. Trump. The most pro-Russian presidential candidate since the communist fellow traveler Henry Wallace ran on the Progressive Party ticket in 1948, Trump had repudiated some of his postwar predecessors' most foundational, bipartisan foreign-policy commitments, chief among them the importance of alliances.

Following World War II, American statesmen of both parties constructed an international constellation of alliances, agreements, institutions, values, and norms ensuring a period of unprecedented peace and prosperity for the United States and its allies. That liberal order—encapsulated in the 1941 Atlantic Charter and encompassing such institutions and agreements as the United Nations, NATO, the Genocide Convention, the Bretton Woods financial system, and the European Union—successfully weathered a decades-long Cold War against a totalitarian adversary. Free markets and the free movement of labor were also crucial to this order. "Anglo-American capitalism can be harsh in many ways," Ian Buruma reflected in the *New York Times* in 2016, "but because free markets are receptive to new talent and cheap labor, they have spawned the kind of societies, pragmatic and relatively open, where immigrants can thrive, the very kind that rulers of more closed, communitarian, autocratic societies tend to despise."

Following the Soviet Union's collapse, there was every indication this liberal order should endure, in some form or another, as the basis of international relations in the oncoming era of "globalization."

In those early years of the post–Cold War respite from geopolitical competition, "convergence" was the bipartisan buzzword. Addressing the challenges posed by a rising China and democratizing Russia, President Bill Clinton's National Security Strategy optimistically described the United States "seizing on the desire of both countries to participate in the global economy and global institutions, insisting that both accept the obligations as well as the benefits of integration." Robert Zoellick, deputy secretary of state for Clinton's Republican successor, George W. Bush, often spoke of China becoming a "responsible stakeholder" in the liberal international order. These sunny forecasts were predicated on the assumption that both nations roughly shared the geopolitical outlook of Sweden and that their preoccupation with retrograde things like martial glory and national pride had been relegated to the twentieth century.

Unfortunately, leaders in Beijing and Moscow did not fulfill the constructive roles that starry-eyed idealists in Washington and Brussels had planned for them. Instead, they reverted to the sort of aggressive nationalism associated with the nineteenth century. Trends in the more developed and democratic regions of the world have not been encouraging either. According to

Freedom House, 2017 marked the twelfth consecutive year of global democratic decline. If the 1990s and early 2000s represented an era of Western integration, we are now experiencing a period of Western *disintegration*. In Europe, momentum has reversed from growing the European Union to persuading present members not to leave. Nor is it just the composition of supranational institutions that's at risk but nations themselves. Independence movements have roiled Catalonia, Scotland, and elsewhere, and regional differences within nations—as evidenced by the sharp, urban/rural divide of the American presidential election and Brexit referendum—are becoming more profound.

"The story of the past quarter century is the rise and fall of this idea of convergence," Brookings Institution senior fellow Tom Wright has observed about the return of geopolitical rivalry, this time between those states seeking to uphold the liberal order and those seeking to overturn it. Although geostrategists have been writing about the return of great power conflict for at least the past decade, unanticipated was the rise of opposition to this order from *within* the West: for the first time in history, the de facto guardian of that order—the United States—elected as leader a man who ran on a platform explicitly rejecting his country's singular role in maintaining it.

Arrayed against the liberal world order is what might be termed the Illiberal International, an ideologically and geographically disparate confederation of governments and political movements seeking to undermine the concept of universal human rights, overturn the rules-based international order, and replace it with one in which might makes right. As the Communist

International of yore committed itself to the "overthrow of the international bourgeoisie," this global alliance propagates the virtues of majoritarian-backed strongman rule, xenophobia, and other reactionary values. The Kremlin's appeals to "traditional values" as an alternative to classical liberalism (which Moscow portrays as little more than a mélange of sexual licentiousness and rootless multiculturalism) have found sympathizers across the West, not least in the Trump administration. Governments in Poland, Hungary, and increasingly the Czech Republic—all once extolled as the heart and soul of "New Europe" and all members of the EU and NATO—are slowly abandoning some of the liberal, democratic values they struggled so heroically to win under Communist rule. Meanwhile the rising democracies of Brazil, India, and South Africa have shown a tendency to side with the major authoritarian powers on key normative questions—for instance, joining China in abstaining from the 2014 UN General Assembly vote criticizing Russia's illegal referendum in Crimea.

Part of the motivation for this assault on liberal norms is specific to Russia: Putin's revanchism in Eastern Europe and interference in Western democracies are payback for the twenty-five years of democracy promotion and "color" revolutions in the former Soviet space that he believes to be the work of the CIA. Yet Russia's aggressive actions and rhetorical broadsides have struck a chord with other authoritarian powers and political movements around the world.

As China seeks to become the dominant military power in Asia, it is employing what Patrick Cronin of the Center for a New American Security calls "incremental salami slicing tactics"

against freedom of navigation in the seas and skies, construct-
ing artificial islands to buttress its maritime claims, and uni-
laterally declaring an Air Defense Identification Zone to exert
control over flight traffic. Through the establishment of multilateral groups like the Bolivarian Alliance for the Peoples of Our
Americas (founded in 2004 by the Venezuelan regime of Hugo
Chávez), the Russian-led Eurasian Union, and the Chinese-
dominated Shanghai Cooperation Organization (which masks
its disregard for basic human rights in rhetoric of "respect for
civilizational diversity"), illiberal regimes have institutionalized
their assault on the liberal world order. This "authoritarian re-
gionalism," in the words of political science scholar Alexander
Cooley, is set to counter the postwar alliance structures created
and led by the United States and its democratic allies. Preach-
ing absolute state sovereignty, the Illiberal International aims to
undermine American global leadership, the international order
the United States upholds, and the very ability to distinguish fact
from fiction.

This latest challenge to the liberal world order does not possess
the ideological coherence of its communist predecessor, which
had a supranational narrative (dialectical Marxist Leninism) that
could unite Russian Bolsheviks with French intellectuals and
Central American revolutionaries. Yet that lack of political dog-
matism has not served as an impediment to the fortunes of the
Illiberal International; on the contrary, it has brought a disparate collection of forces together in common purpose. Across
the West, voices railing against the liberal status quo include
the free-market fundamentalist former president of the Czech
Republic Vaclav Klaus, the neo-Marxists of Greece's Syriza, the

aspiring authoritarian Hungarian prime minister Viktor Orbán, and French National Front leader Marine Le Pen. Strange bedfellows, indeed.

At its essence, the Illiberal International is composed of nationalists, who, although perhaps sharing some prejudices and momentary tactical interests, will inevitably clash. It was equally parts puzzling and amusing to watch Marine Le Pen join supporters of the Polish Law and Justice Party in cheering Alternative for Deutschland, which won a startling 13 percent of the vote in the September 2017 German federal election. Sure, all these groups share a xenophobia toward Muslims and antipathy for the liberal norms of the European Union. But has German nationalism historically been good for France, never mind Poland?

Constituents of the Illiberal International are defined more by what they stand against than by what they have in common. "We need to unite all the forces that are opposed to Western norms and its economic system," Alexander Dugin, the Rasputin-esque Russian philosopher who serves as the International's bard, bluntly admitted in 2012. "What we are against will unite us, while what we are for divides us. Therefore, we should emphasize what we oppose." To be more specific, "All those who oppose liberal hegemony are our friends for the moment."

It is in light of this full-on ideological assault against the norms and precepts of the liberal world order that the approach of the current US administration is so worrying. Attempting to provide fuller substance to the president's "America First" rhetoric, National Security Adviser H. R. McMaster and National Economic Council Director Gary Cohn (who have both since left the administration) wrote a widely cited op-ed for the *Wall*

Street Journal in May 2017. "The president embarked on his first foreign trip with a clear-eyed outlook that the world is not a 'global community' but an arena where nations, nongovernmental actors, and businesses engage and compete for advantage." Though this sentence was widely assailed for its alleged jingoism, the coauthors should be praised for rejecting one of the more banal phrases beloved of international affairs analysts, "global community." No group of countries that includes North Korea, the United States, Venezuela, and Belgium can be described as a "community." Where the authors erred, however, was in their lack of recognition that, although it is indeed naïve, if not foolish, to speak of all two hundred countries as belonging to the same "community," nations do not "compete for advantage" against one another individually but rather *alongside* other states that share their interests and values. What Cohn and McMaster elided was the vital importance of alliances.

Which brings us to how that not antique concept of "the free world" can stem the growing tide of illiberalism. The surest way for the community of liberal democracies to counter the illiberal axis is to strengthen and expand their alliances. What distinguishes the postwar American-led liberal order from every other global empire that preceded it is its vast network of alliances, centered in Europe and Asia but spanning most of the world. Not only have these alliances ensured American global primacy, they also prevented war, laid the groundwork for unprecedented economic prosperity, and allowed for the spread and consolidation of democracy worldwide.

No global power in human history has enjoyed more allies than has the United States, and it is only through these alliances that America will be able to resist and defend the liberal world order from its predators. America's postwar policy of internationalism, embodied in initiatives like the Marshall Plan and institutions like NATO and maintained by a system of free trade and immigration, has been the epitome of enlightened geopolitical self-interest. "The great lesson of my lifetime is that all difficult problems and challenges are best addressed with partners and allies," Sir Michael Howard, the great British military historian and strategist, told the *New York Review of Books* in 2017. The point seems obvious (what problem, whether grandiosely complex or routinely mundane, *is not* more readily solved with the help of others?) yet bears repeating.

The Illiberal International emerges at a perilous moment. For, just as authoritarian powers like Russia, China, Iran, and North Korea increasingly assert themselves as enemies of liberal order, the world's democracies are exhausted and unwilling to defend it. Yet now more than ever in the past twenty-five years, that order needs defending—from without *and* within.

PART THREE

Solutions

Democratic values are under heavy siege, but the forces of illiberalism cannot triumph if the millions of those who count themselves in the center left and center right rally to its defense. Clarity about the specific values and policies that promote freedom—and are bulwarks against authoritarianism, nationalism, and other anti-democratic ideologies—is essential. The past century attests to the importance of US leadership on the world stage; isolationism leaves a vacuum that bad actors will gladly fill. A similar spirit of American engagement animates the belief in free trade and free markets as pillars of individual liberty. Welcoming immigrants is a democratic tradition, but unfortunately so is periodically reviling them—responsible immigration reform is the confident, optimistic alternative to wall building. Sometimes sticking up for democracy is as simple as championing the US Constitution: advocating for constitutional order, for religious freedom, for muscular free-speech rights, for the rule of law. The news media can do their part in shoring up press freedom by shunning the partisanship that undermines their authority. Everyone with an interest in combating illiberalism has a potential role to play, from members of the transatlantic alliance rededicating themselves to this partnership to universities firmly embracing their duty to nurture reason and debate. In America, a foreign policy predicated on time-honored values, not short-term interests, would go far in fortifying the liberal order. Disquieting trends are loose in the world, but the tools for defending democracy are numerous, time-tested, and effective.

What the World Needs Now: US Leadership

★ ★ ★

MAX BOOT

America's legacy of global leadership—under assault to-day from within and without—has historical antecedents stretching back to the early days of the Republic. The founders believed that in battling for independence they were fighting not just for their own freedom but also for, in Benjamin Franklin's words, "the cause of all mankind." And, indeed, the American victory in the War of Independence had far-flung reverberations, encouraging revolutionaries from France to Latin America to fight for their own freedom.

Max Boot, a senior fellow at the Council on Foreign Relations, is the author, most recently, of *The Road Not Taken: Edward Lansdale and the American Tragedy in Vietnam.*

It was because America stood for "certain unalienable rights" that it was seen as a subversive influence—"a very dangerous member of the society of nations," as John Quincy Adams put it in 1817. Abraham Lincoln's issuance in 1863 of the Emancipation Proclamation, which turned the Civil War from a fight over the future of the Union to a fight over the future of slavery, further bolstered America's reputation as a "city on a hill" that invited emulation and admiration from liberals around the world—and fear and hostility from authoritarians.

Contrary to myth, the new Republic was never truly isolationist. Even in the early nineteenth century, when American presidents heeded the admonitions of George Washington ("steer clear of permanent alliances"), Thomas Jefferson ("peace, commerce, and honest friendship with all nations—entangling alliances with none"), and John Quincy Adams ("she goes not abroad, in search of monsters to destroy"), America was still sending clipper ships to trade with China and warships to the Mediterranean to fight Barbary pirates. The nation was also proclaiming the Monroe Doctrine to stop the spread of European empires in the Western Hemisphere and providing moral and financial support to battlers for freedom, including the Greeks fighting the Ottoman Empire in the 1820s and the Hungarians fighting the Ottoman Empire in 1848–1849.

But, until the turn of the twentieth century, Americans did not become involved in major conflicts or territorial expansion overseas. They had no need to. Their energies were consumed by expansion across the North American continent, and America did not have to worry overmuch about foreign threats. It was protected by two oceans and, indirectly, by the British Empire, which ruled the waves. The United States greatly benefited from the international free-trade system policed by the Royal Navy.

With the process of continental expansion complete by 1890—the year that the Census Bureau proclaimed the end of the Western frontier—Americans' energies turned abroad. And so it was that in 1898 the United States went to war against Spain in two far-flung theaters: Cuba and the Philippines. The casus belli was the explosion of the armored cruiser USS *Maine* in Havana Harbor, a calamity that the sensationalistic "yellow press" blamed on the Spanish. But the underlying reason for conflict was Americans' outrage at Spanish mistreatment of their Cuban subjects. President William McKinley announced that he had no choice but to declare war "to protest against the uncivilized and inhuman conduct of the campaign in the island of Cuba."

A direct result of this "splendid little war," as Theodore Roosevelt called it, was America's acquisition of its first overseas colonies, including the Philippines, Guam, and Puerto Rico, and a larger role in the world. As president (1901–1909), Roosevelt proclaimed his own corollary to the Monroe Doctrine ("If we intend to say 'hands off' to the powers of Europe, then sooner or later we must keep order ourselves"), thus committing the United States to an active policing role in the Western Hemisphere. He was awarded the Nobel Peace Prize for mediating an end to the Russo-Japanese War of 1905.

America stepped further into world affairs in 1917 when the United States entered the Great War as an Associated Power fighting the Triple Entente. The United States was provoked to fight by Germany's attempts to bring Mexico into the war (via the Zimmerman Telegram, intercepted by British intelligence) and by its unrestricted submarine warfare against American merchant ships. But President Woodrow Wilson asked Congress for a declaration of war, committing America to its first conflict on European soil, on loftier grounds that evoked America's idealistic mission in the world: "The right is more precious than peace, and we shall fight for the things which we have always carried nearest our hearts—for democracy, for the right of those who submit to authority to have a voice in their own governments, for the rights and liberties of small nations, for a universal dominion of right by such a concert of free peoples as shall bring peace and safety to all nations and make the world itself at last free."

Wilson showed that he was sincere in his devotion to these ideals, if inconsistent and not entirely successful in their application, by pushing at the Paris Peace Conference in 1919 to forge new nations such as Czechoslovakia, Iraq, and the Baltic Republics out of the ruins of old empires and to create a League of Nations to enforce international law. But the Senate broke Wilson's heart by refusing to ratify the League of Nations covenant. America's failure to police the peace—its retreat into isolationism in the 1920s and especially the 1930s—effectively squandered the military victory that 116,000 US soldiers had given their lives to achieve in 1917–1918 and made inevitable another world war.

President Franklin D. Roosevelt understood from an early stage that America would have to oppose Nazi and Japanese militarists, and in 1941 he managed to enact the lend-lease program to provide an embattled Britain with badly needed military materiel. But it was not until the Japanese attack on Pearl Harbor on December 7, 1941, that Congress belatedly recognized that

America would have to mobilize against the Axis powers of Germany, Italy, and Japan. It is sobering to reflect how history might have been different if the United States had joined with Britain and France to enforce the 1919 Treaty of Versailles and prevent Axis aggression. Hitler, in particular, remained weak throughout much of the 1930s and might have been stopped and even overthrown if the Western powers had acted. But they did not awaken to the danger until too late and then paid a high price to end fascist and Nazi tyranny.

America lost 405,000 soldiers to win World War II, the contribution of its armed forces proving pivotal in East Asia, North Africa, the North Atlantic, and Western Europe, even if the Soviet Union did the bulk of the fighting against Germany's land forces. Once Germany and Japan finally surrendered in 1945, the Greatest Generation was determined that this sacrifice not be in vain. Harry Truman, thrust into the presidency by the caprice of fate, set about with his aides—George Kennan, George Marshall, and Dean Acheson were particularly important—and prominent Republicans such as Senator Arthur Vandenberg in a bipartisan effort to construct a better world out of the ruins of war.

Their commitment led to the creation of a plethora of international institutions—the United Nations, the International Monetary Fund, the World Bank, the General Agreement on Tariffs and Trade (GATT, which eventually morphed into the World Trade Organization), NATO—to serve as pillars of peace and prosperity. It also led to the wise decision not to impose a Carthaginian peace on the Axis states—an option favored by, among others, Secretary of the Treasury Henry Morgenthau—but, rather, to rebuild their shattered societies, turning foes into friends. This was a singularly far-sighted policy borne of the recognition that America had to help others in order to help itself.

Having sacrificed heavily to win World War II—albeit not as much as most of the other combatants—America now sacrificed again by garrisoning troops in Europe and Asia and sending forces into combat on the Korean Peninsula. After the Soviets acquired the atomic bomb in 1949, the United States was prepared to risk nuclear annihilation to defend its overseas allies. Truman explained the thinking behind what came to be known as the "containment" strategy in his 1947 speech asking Congress to aid Greece and Turkey in their battles against Communist subversion. "The seeds of totalitarian regimes are nurtured by misery and want," the president said. "They spread and grow in the evil soil of poverty and strife. They reach their full growth when the hope of a people for a better life has died. We must keep that hope alive. The free peoples of the world look to us for support in maintaining their freedoms. If we falter in our leadership, we may endanger the peace of the world—and we shall surely endanger the welfare of our own nation."

The American commitment to resist the spread of Communist encroachment was not cost- or error-free. It led directly to the deaths of 94,000 American troops in Korea and Vietnam—both conflicts that, in hindsight, might have been avoided. (The United States should have more clearly signaled prior to 1950 that it would defend South Korea, and it should not have sponsored a coup in 1963 that overthrew the president of South Vietnam, Ngo Dinh Diem, thus destabilizing that country and leading to the introduction of American combat troops within two years.) The Cold War also led the United States to align itself with illiberal regimes, from Mobuto Sese Seko's in Zaire to Anastasio Somoza's in Nicaragua, all in the name of fighting communism. But the United States also promoted democracy and championed dissidents behind the Iron Curtain. And ultimately its generational, bipartisan commitment led to the fall of the Berlin Wall in 1989 and the collapse of the Soviet Union in 1991.

In the wake of the Cold War's end, there were calls in the 1990s for a "peace dividend," and indeed US armed forces were cut by roughly a third, but events soon showed that history had not ended and the need for America's global leadership had not declined. If anything, the United States, as the sole remaining superpower, had the responsibility of shouldering an even heavier burden in an increasingly disorderly world. In 1989, President George H. W. Bush toppled Panama's dictator, Manuel Noriega, and the next year assembled an international coalition to roll back the Iraqi invasion of Kuwait. He then committed the United States to protecting the Kurds, patrolling Iraq from the air, and feeding the people of Somalia. His successor, Bill Clinton, committed US forces in smaller numbers in the Balkans to stamp out civil wars and in Haiti to restore democracy.

In the meantime, hiding in plain sight, a new threat was emerging—that of Islamist extremism. Al Qaeda, founded in Pakistan in 1988 by a Saudi exile, carried out a series of atrocities in the 1990s culminating in 2001 with the worst terrorist attack in history. This, in turn, led America directly into Afghanistan and indirectly into Iraq. The United States succeeded in overthrowing the old regimes—the Taliban and Saddam Hussein—in surprisingly short order, but building new governments proved to be a more arduous task, one that remains incomplete to this day.

The US experience in the post-9/11 world showed, for neither the first nor the last time, the limits of American power. It is understandable that, after the costly setbacks in Iraq from 2003 to 2007, the American public grew wary of foreign interventions. But when Barack Obama, elected in no small part because of his opposition to the Iraq War, removed US troops from Iraq and refused to intervene in the Syrian civil war that broke out in 2011, the world soon discovered what happens when America leaves a vacuum behind. By 2014 large swathes of Iraq and Syria had fallen to the fanatics of the Islamic State, and President Obama was forced, however reluctantly, to commit US forces to help Syrians and Iraqis to battle back.

Donald Trump won the presidency in 2016 on a foreign policy platform that was incoherent but generally hostile to the exercise of American global leadership. He assailed nation building, vowed to avoid long-term military entanglements, bitterly criticized trade treaties as "bad deals," and demanded that American allies pay a far greater cost of their defense. Yet he also vowed to "bomb the shit" out of terrorists, to torture them and their relatives, and to commandeer Iraq's oil to pay for the US war effort. Sometimes Trump sounded isolationist; at other times interventionist. Calling his approach Jacksonian may confer greater coherence than actually exists.

In practice President Trump's foreign policy has been as confused and inconsistent as expected. For the most part he has not changed America's long-term commitments around the world. US troops remain stationed in Germany and South Korea, in Eastern Europe and Japan, and throughout the Middle East. Trump, with evident reluctance, reaffirmed NATO's Article V mutual-defense provision, and he did not lift sanctions on Russia—indeed Congress, to his evident displeasure, toughened those sanctions. After claiming that the United States had no stake in Syria, he bombed Syria—twice—in retaliation for Bashar al-Assad's use of chemical weapons, while still signaling his determination to pull all US forces out, thereby handing the eastern third of the country to Assad and Iran. He pulled out of the Trans-Pacific Partnership and renegotiated NAFTA and the US–South Korea Free Trade Agreement. He imposed hefty steel and aluminum tariffs but offered plenty of exemptions to US allies. He threatened steep tariffs on China and, when China threatened to retaliate, claimed that a "trade war is good, and easy to win." He left the Paris climate accords but vowed to re-enter if the treaty could be renegotiated—without saying what changes to this nonbinding agreement would satisfy him. He refused to criticize human-rights abuses in Russia, China, Saudi Arabia, Egypt, or Turkey; he did denounce abuses in Cuba, Venezuela, North Korea, and Iran.

While acting more moderately, by and large, than his campaign rhetoric would suggest, Trump has consistently expressed scorn for America's global leadership, insisting that he would pursue an America First policy and urging all other nations to look after their own self-interest. "Our government's first duty is to its people, to our citizens, to serve their needs, to ensure their safety, to preserve their rights and to defend their values," Trump said at the United Nations on September 19, 2017. "As president of the United States, I will always put America first, just like you, as the leaders of your countries, will always and should always put your countries first." His concern for sovereignty did not extend, however, to calling out Vladimir Putin for interfering in America's presidential election in 2016, to his benefit.

Trump's rhetoric has alarmed US allies and delighted its enemies. Russia and China, in particular, have sought to move into the vacuum that America may leave behind. China has postured unconvincingly as a champion of free trade, environmentalism, and the international order, while seeking to displace America as the hegemon of East Asia. Russia has increased its activities from Syria to North Korea, consistently attempting to stymie American designs. Allies from South Korea to Germany fear they can no longer count on America and must look after their own interests as best they can. "We Europeans must take our destiny into our own hands," German chancellor Angela Merkel said in May 2017.

America's post–Cold War international dominance was eroding anyway, given the growing economic and military might of China in particular. But Trump may well be accelerating the process, raising the risks of a leaderless world engulfed in chaos. He shows scant appreciation for the hard-won achievements of the Greatest Generation—the men and women who, in the wake of the most devastating war in history, created an American-led, liberal international order to prevent the outbreak of another, even more horrific world war. English historian John Robert Seeley observed in 1883 that the British Empire was acquired "in a fit of absence of mind." It would be a historic tragedy of untold proportions if America loses its international predominance in its own fit of absentmindedness.

The British could comfortably give up their hegemony after 1942 because they knew that another liberal superpower stood waiting in the wings. But there is no other democratic state that can do what America does. No one else will police sea lanes, defend democracies, promote free trade, champion human rights, and battle the enemies of all mankind—terrorists, criminal networks, weapons proliferators, war criminals. No one else can or will respond so effectively to natural disasters and the spread of contagious diseases. The post-American world would be one where dictators, terrorists, and criminals hold sway and democracy is on the defensive—and where American security will no longer be protected by two oceans. It will not be easy, but the nation must do all it can to make the twenty-first century another American century. That will only happen, however, if it displays moral as well as military leadership and maintains the confidence of badly needed allies.

In Defense of Free Trade

★ ★ ★

RICHARD HUROWITZ

S ince the end of World War II, the vital role played by free trade in fostering peace and prosperity has been widely accepted. But in the 2016 US presidential election, free trade became a target of Donald Trump and of Hillary Clinton and her challenger for the Democratic nomination, Bernie Sanders. They vociferously opposed American entry into the Trans-Pacific Partnership and lambasted US participation in trade agreements generally.

Since then, President Trump has continued his attacks on free trade—making good on his threat to abandon negotiations for the Trans-Pacific Partnership and doubling down on his complaints about the North American Free Trade Agreement. In

Richard Hurowitz is the chief executive officer of Octavian Group Holdings and publisher of *The Octavian Report*.

January 2018, he imposed steep tariffs on imported solar panels and washing machines, followed shortly by even more sweeping duties on steel and aluminum. His hostility to free trade is about his only position that doesn't spark Democratic outrage.

The longstanding bipartisan US consensus favoring free trade is eroding. Instead, we are more likely to hear the sort of criticism more typically used by crony capitalists and labor unions. Trade makes an inviting target for demagogues because its massive benefits are diffuse and often hard to measure, its complex mechanisms can be difficult to understand, and yet its dislocations are readily apparent. But the consequences of abandoning free trade can be catastrophic.

The economic theory of free trade lies at the roots of classical economics. In 1776, Adam Smith argued in *The Wealth of Nations* for the power of free markets in commerce not only among individuals but among nations. A nation, and its citizens, would be better off when the invisible hand of the markets worked most efficiently, with the fewest constraints. It was self-evidently in the interests of consumers to have access to the highest-quality goods at the best price regardless of origin. Heretically, Smith even critiqued the system of imperial preference that kept a monopoly on trade with Britain's colonies, questioning the benefits even to the mother country itself. Such a monopoly, he wrote, "like all other means and malignant expedients of the mercantile system depresses the industry of all other countries, but chiefly that of the colonies, without, in the least, increasing, but on the contrary diminishing, that of the country in whose favor it is established."

Smith's protégé David Ricardo is the most celebrated economist on free trade. In his 1817 magnum opus, *The Principles of*

Political Economy and Taxation, Ricardo explained the benefits of international commerce:

> Under a system of perfectly free commerce, each country naturally devotes its capital and labour to such employments as are more beneficial to each. This pursuit of individual advantage is admirably connected with the universal good of the whole. By stimulating industry, by regarding ingenuity, and by using most efficaciously the peculiar powers bestowed by nature, it distributes labour most effective and most economically: while, by increasing the general mass of productions, it diffuses general benefit, and binds together by one common tie of interest and intercourse, the universal society of nations throughout the civilized world. It is this principle which determines that wine shall be made in France and Portugal, that corn shall be grown in America and Poland, and that hardware and other goods shall be manufactured in England.

This mechanism of "comparative advantage" makes sure that all are better off because of trade, that free commerce between nations is a win-win and not a zero-sum game.

Two hundred years after Ricardo's book was first published, few serious economists would dispute its thesis. Progressives like Bernie Sanders and Elizabeth Warren certainly don't subscribe to it, yet once upon a time free trade was a liberal cause. Consider William Jennings Bryan, the three-time presidential candidate known as the "Great Commoner." Bryan was a staunch free trader precisely because he knew trade benefited the country in general and its poorer citizens in particular. It was the robber baron industrialists, anxious to protect their manufacturing concerns from competition, who were most in favor of the tariffs. "A protective tariff is simply a system by which the Government taxes all of the people for the benefit of a portion of the people," Bryan said on the floor of Congress in 1894, "and justifies the language of the Democratic platform, which denounces Republican protection 'as a fraud, a robbery of the great majority of the American people for the benefit of the few.'"

Then as now tariffs are not only a tax but a regressive one that hits poorer consumers far harder than the wealthy. The goods that dominate lower-income expenditures such as food, clothing, and footwear are globally traded; they become more expensive when trade is restricted. "Instead of preventing foreign countries from deluging us with something which they can sell us cheaper than we can produce it, we had better let the flood come, and pay them with something which we can produce cheaper than they can," Bryan said, "and that is the principle upon which commercial freedom stands." In today's world this is even more the case. Within hours of the announcement of the Trump administration's tariffs on washing machines, several manufacturers announced price increases of up to 8 percent, a direct burden on American consumers.

The positive economic effects of free trade for business and consumers are self-evident, or ought to be. Take for example a recent punching bag of anti-globalization activists: the North American Free Trade Agreement, or NAFTA. Negotiated by Republican George H. W. Bush and signed into law by Democrat Bill Clinton, the agreement has offered significant benefits that until recently were generally recognized. One-third of total

US exports goes to Canada and Mexico, and trade among the three partners has increased by almost five times since the pact's inception. About 14 million US jobs depend on trade with Mexico and Canada, and an additional 200,000 are created each year, paying significantly higher than average wages. Some manufacturing jobs have indeed moved to Mexico, as critics complain, but about 40 percent of Mexican exports' value comes from parts that were manufactured in the United States. The geopolitical benefit must also be noted. A more prosperous Mexican economy, with the improved labor and environmental standards that NAFTA stipulated, enhances the stability of America's southern neighbor and thus benefits US security.

Viewed through this lens, the rejection of the Trans-Pacific Partnership is alarming. A rising China poses a significant challenge to the United States, and the TPP was an extraordinary opportunity to use economic might to reinforce American leadership in the region. The agreement might one day have even included China itself. The TPP negotiations continue without US involvement, during a period when Beijing is increasingly assertive in the East and South China Seas—conduits for 90 percent of global trade. While the United States disengages economically from the Pacific region, China has increased its outreach. The Chinese-sponsored Asian Infrastructure Development Bank, opened in January 2016, now has fifty-six member states, including Canada, the UK, and Australia, who joined despite US objections. And China's One Belt, One Road Initiative proposes several trillions of dollars of investment in the region.

Given that many military conflicts are economic in origin, despite being cloaked in ideological and political differences, the US retreat from the Pacific is unsettling. Reduced American leadership increases the likelihood of regional clashes. And there is nothing more expensive than war.

It was out of this understanding, a lesson learned at terrible cost, that the post–World War II system of free trade arose. The infamous Smoot-Hawley Act instituted by the United States in 1930 following the stock market crash had increased nearly nine hundred duties in a misguided attempt to fight domestic unemployment. Critics ranged from progressive senator Robert La Follette to the Wall Street banker Thomas Lamont of J. P. Morgan, who recalled that he "almost went down on my knees to beg Herbert Hoover to veto the asinine Hawley-Smoot Tariff. That Act intensified nationalism all over the world." More than a thousand economists, led by Irving Fisher at Yale, signed a protest letter outlining the potential consequences with startling precision, warning that Smoot-Hawley "would operate in general, to increase the prices which domestic consumers would have to pay" and "raise the cost of living and injure the great majority of our citizens. Few people could hope to gain from such a change."

Miners, professionals, bankers, newspaper publishers, hoteliers, wholesalers and retailers, farmers, export manufacturers, as well as construction, transportation and public utility workers would all be crushed by retaliatory tariffs. And the economists presciently warned against the "bitterness which a policy of higher tariffs would inevitably inject into our international relations."

The result was disaster as country after country erected barriers in retaliation. World trade plummeted. Upon assuming office, Franklin Roosevelt compounded Herbert Hoover's mistakes, adding within the first one hundred days additional trade restrictions in the form of the Agricultural Adjustment Act and National Industrial Recovery Act. Against the backdrop of the Depression, exacerbated and prolonged by the rise of economic nationalism, the 1930s saw the world descend into violence, extremism, and totalitarianism.

Postwar Western leaders were determined to never see such a catastrophe repeated. Secretary of State Cordell Hull, the architect of the United Nations, had for decades argued that the pernicious effect of protectionism was one of the key contributors to global conflict and noted "unhampered trade dovetailed with peace; high tariffs, trade barriers and unfair economic competition with war." The United States pressed its allies to end colonialism, and the Atlantic Charter itself called for the end of protectionism. A variety of institutions, including the World Bank, the International Monetary Fund, and the General Agreement on Tariffs and Trade (later the World Trade Organization) were founded to ensure global economic stability.

At the same time, visionary European statesmen, led by the Frenchmen Jean Monnet and Robert Schumann, established the European Coal and Steel Community, a common market that evolved over time to the present-day European Union. Schumann declared that the trade community's purpose was "to make war not only unthinkable but materially impossible."

The results of these multilateral efforts speak for themselves: decades of prosperity, previously unimagined in history, lifting countless millions from poverty.

Donald Trump's assertion that "trade wars are good, and easy to win" is unconscionable. Almost 11 million American jobs depend on exports, according to the US Commerce Department. As the world's biggest economy, America has the most to lose. Critics talk about "fair trade" and opening foreign markets for US companies. But this is the rationale for free trade itself. What *is* needed: better US enforcement of its existing rights. Ronald Reagan called for an enforcement mechanism to ensure a level playing field *against* protectionist intervention by others that violated international rules and treaties. The result was the Uruguay Round of negotiations that in 1995 created the World Trade Organization, whose 164 members are bound to the rules-based order. This American project to prevent "unfair trade" is now the very system under assault.

Free-trade advocates also need to do a better job of explaining statistics from the global supply chain, which is often measured in confusing ways. For example, an iPhone will be accounted as an import for purposes of calculating the US trade balance with China, yet most of its components come from outside of China, from countries as disparate as Germany and Japan. The iPhone's most valuable components, its intellectual property and brand, are wholly American. According to the Asian Development Bank, only about ten dollars of the total value of an iPhone actually benefits China, which largely does the assembly work. This American export is thus oddly accounted for as an import.

The ebb and flow of goods and services does cause dislocation. The Chinese economic juggernaut certainly has driven down labor costs, for example. But far more impactful on US workers have been the relentless improvements in automation and productivity in recent decades. More must be done to help retrain and reemploy dislocated workers, but trying to halt the march of progress and the benefits to society as a whole isn't a plausible option. Tariffs may provide short-term political benefits in certain regions, but they do broad economic harm and delay needed structural changes. The Obama administration's 2009 tire subsidies to protect 1,200 jobs are estimated to have cost consumers $1.2 billion, and the Bush administration's steel tariffs protected a far smaller number of jobs than it harmed in steel-consuming industries such as automotive and appliance manufacturers.

Liberal democracy is the most successful political system in world history, and its championing of liberty in all matters—free speech, freedom of religion, free trade—has been a boon to civilization. Free trade is not exclusively responsible for the prosperity that has characterized liberal democracy, because a myriad of factors affects the rise and fall of economies, but it has inarguably raised living standards, created jobs, and added to international comity and the respect for the free movement of people and goods. And one thing is certain: protectionist policies restricting free trade will make a struggling economy worse, they will blunt the gains of a healthy one, and they will raise tensions in an unstable world. Politicians genuinely searching for economic answers wouldn't attack free trade, they would embrace it.

Immigration for the Twenty-First Century

★ ★ ★

LINDA CHAVEZ

More than almost any nation in the world, the United States has been defined by its openness to immigration. For much of the country's history, anyone with the will and the heart to get to America, to use Ronald Reagan's formulation, could do so. The European colonists who came during the seventeenth century encountered a vast territory with a widely scattered, relatively modest indigenous population; navigable waters throughout the interior; fertile land; and abundant forests. Without the arrival of millions of newcomers, including not just immigrants but also Africans forcibly brought as slaves, America's

---

Linda Chavez is a syndicated columnist and chairman of the Center for Equal Opportunity.

vast resources would have remained largely untapped. And yet, to describe America as an immigrant-loving nation would be misleading. Many Americans from colonial times to the present have regarded new arrivals with distrust and the fear that they would not measure up to those who had come before them.

Ben Franklin set the tone for this inhospitable theme when he famously complained in 1751, "Why should the *Palatine Boors* be suffered to swarm into our Settlements and, by herding together, establish their Language and Manners, to the Exclusion of ours? Why should *Pennsylvania*, founded by the *English*, become a Colony of *Aliens*, who will shortly be so numerous as to Germanize us instead of our Anglifying them, and will never adopt our Language or Customs any more than they can acquire our Complexion?"

Whether they came from Northern Europe, as the Germans, Irish, and Scandinavians did throughout the nineteenth century, or from Central, Southern, and Eastern Europe, as immigrants did in the twentieth century, each crop of new arrivals faced the prejudice—sometimes from people whose families had arrived just one generation earlier—that they would never become fully American. It should come as no surprise, then, that immigrants in recent years, the overwhelming majority of whom have come from Latin America and Asia, should be met with suspicion and resistance.

Such hostility to outsiders is an unfortunately common human trait, and America has no monopoly on anti-immigrant rhetoric. In an increasingly mobile world, with illiberal, often nativist sentiments rising in many countries, including other liberal democracies, heated debates about immigrants can be found almost anywhere people seeking a better life have arrived in numbers. But to better understand how matters reached this fractious point, we would do well to look at America and its history as a nation of immigrants. Doing so will help in seeking public-policy solutions that not only serve American interests but also honor the nation's founding principles.

The first anti-immigrant legislation in the United States came early with the Alien and Sedition Acts of 1798, signed into law by the second American president, John Adams. The group of four laws gave the president power to imprison or remove aliens deemed at any time to be "dangerous to the peace and safety of the United States"; to remove, during times of war, any male above the age of fourteen who came from a hostile nation; to restrict speech critical of the government; and to increase the residency requirements for naturalization from five to fourteen years.

The laws were highly controversial, and Adams used them during the 1800 presidential campaign to shut down newspapers that favored his opponent and then–vice president, Thomas Jefferson. Congress repealed three of the four acts after Jefferson won the election; but one of the laws, the Alien Enemies Act, remained in effect long after, with some provisions surviving to the present day. Most notoriously, the Alien Enemies Act provided the justification for President Truman's executive order directing the internment of more than 100,000 Japanese living on the West Coast during World War II and was explicitly used to imprison some Germans living in the United States during the war.

But, for the most part during the United States' first century, the need for labor and population to settle the country as it expanded west attracted millions of immigrants without restrictions. The first real efforts to exclude any class of immigrants came near the end of the nineteenth century and was aimed primarily at the Chinese. Laborers from China had come to the United States in large numbers from 1850 to 1880 to work on railroad construction, mining, and agriculture in the West, but the Chinese Exclusion Act of 1882 barred further entry for ten years and imposed heavy restrictions on Chinese immigrants already in the United States. The law's harsh provisions were not repealed fully until 1943.

Even American-born children of Chinese immigrants, citizens by birth under the Fourteenth Amendment, faced bars to reentry if they left the United States, until an 1898 Supreme Court decision found the practice unconstitutional. Although prejudice against immigrants from other nations was widespread in the nineteenth century, the Chinese Exclusion Acts and, later, broader restrictions on Asian immigration and citizenship were the first laws to codify *racial* qualifications for immigration. But they were not the last—for more than a century, racial, ethnic, and cultural fears have largely driven the push to restrict the flow of people into America.

With the arrival of millions of immigrants from Southern and Eastern Europe in the early twentieth century, anti-immigration forces gained popular momentum by arguing that Italians, Poles, Jews, and other non–Northern Europeans would never fully assimilate as Americans. The Dillingham Commission, established by the US Senate in 1907, compiled forty volumes of testimony, studies, and recommendations concerning this new wave of immigrants. The commission's final report reflected prevailing opinion, saying the "new immigration as a class is far less intelligent than the old," and "racially they are for the most part essentially unlike the British, German, and other peoples who came during the period prior to 1880, and generally speaking they are actuated in coming by different ideals, for the old immigration came to be a part of this country, while the new, in a large measure, comes with the intention of profiting in a pecuniary way, by the superior advantages of the New World and then returning to the old country."

Following the Dillingham Commission's recommendation, Congress passed (over President Woodrow Wilson's veto) the first broad limits on immigration in the country's history, the Immigration Act of 1917, which imposed literacy requirements for *all* adults, regardless of their country of origin, and prohibited immigration from a so-called Asiatic Barred Zone that included nearly the entirety of Asia. Congress widened these restrictions and imposed more draconian limits with passage of the Immigration Act of 1924, which for the first time capped the number of immigrants admitted each year (at 150,000) and established national origin quotas limited to 2 percent of those nationalities present in the population in 1880.

The effect was to virtually exclude immigrants from countries that made up the lion's share of those who arrived between 1900 and 1924: Italians, Russians, Poles (mostly Jews), and other groups that restrictionists deemed unfit. Madison Grant, a Yale-educated eugenicist and author in 1922 of *The Passing of the Great Race*, argued for such restrictions to prevent what he called the "mongrelization" of the long-established Americans: "These immigrants adopt the language of the native American, they wear his clothes, they steal his name, and they are beginning to take his women, but they seldom adopt his religion or understand his ideals."

If the rhetoric sounds familiar, it should. Though they usually employ less inflammatory terms, modern immigration restrictionists make similar claims about newcomers from Latin America and Asia, who have made up an increasingly large share of the immigration population since the enactment, and subsequent revisions, of the 1965 Immigration and Nationality Act. Like their predecessors, contemporary critics—some of them, like writers Michelle Malkin, Ramesh Ponnuru, and Reihan Salam, with immigrant parents of their own—worry that the changing racial and ethnic profile of the most recent immigrants makes their successful assimilation difficult if not impossible. But all available evidence suggests that, despite the ethnic and racial differences between this wave of newcomers and past immigrants, assimilation is proceeding apace: they are learning English; improving their education; climbing the economic ladder; and, most significantly, intermarrying as rapidly as previous immigrant cohorts.

Perhaps more remarkable, even those immigrants who have come illegally or overstayed the terms of their original, legal visas—a population of some 11 million persons currently—two-thirds have been in the United States more than a decade, setting down roots, working, paying taxes, and filling niches in the labor market that Americans have shunned. Contrary to the ugly caricature, illegal immigrants are *less* likely to commit crimes than the general US population.

As with Germans in the nineteenth century and Italians and Jews in the early twentieth century, the true test of whether America will succeed in absorbing so many Asians and Latinos in the early twenty-first century largely depends not on immigrants but their children. Here, too, the signs are positive. Second-generation Americans are thriving, according to Pew Research and census data. By measures of education and income, Asian Americans are more successful than their immigrant parents and Americans generally, and the children of Latino immigrants are surpassing Latinos whose families have been here three generations or longer.

Yet opposition to immigration—legal as well as illegal—has grown dramatically in recent years. Candidate Donald Trump rode the issue all the way to the Oval Office, beginning with his June 16, 2015, speech announcing his candidacy: "When Mexico sends its people, they're not sending their best.... They're sending people that have lots of problems, and they're bringing those problems with us [*sic*]. They're bringing drugs. They're bringing crime. They're rapists. And some, I assume, are good people."

Since then, in speeches, position papers, executive orders, and proposed legislation, President Trump has offered the most restrictive immigration policy of any president in more than a hundred years. Though he sometimes vacillates and contradicts himself, as is his custom on policy matters, he has promised to build a wall along the US border with Mexico, asked for $4.5 billion in additional funding for more border agents and other security measures, stepped up domestic enforcement, and expanded the grounds on which illegal immigrants may be arrested and removed. He has also supported legislation that would cut the current level of legal immigration by half over the next decade.

Trump's coarse comments during a January 2018 White House immigration policy meeting—disparaging Haiti and some African nations while extolling the idea of Norwegian immigrants, according to attendees—were startling, but they reflected the outlook of an administration that wants to radically restrict family preferences (allowing only spouses and minor children, and cutting off parents, siblings, and adult children) and to establish a points system that favors young, English-speaking immigrants who hold advanced degrees and already have lucrative job offers. The countries that most rely on family-based visas, according to the Migration Policy Institute, are Mexico, the Dominican Republic, the Philippines, China, India, and Vietnam. The long-ago restrictionist prejudice against "undesirables" lives on, under the guise of more anodyne concerns about "unskilled labor." If restrictionists get their way, limiting immigration to the well-educated and affluent, it will be a victory for the xenophobic strain that runs through US history and a repudiation of the America that has welcomed "your tired, your poor / Your huddled masses yearning to breathe free," as Emma Lazarus's poem on the Statue of Liberty promises.

Every sovereign nation has the right to determine whom to admit, for how long, and under what rules and regulations, just as every nation has the right to decide who may or may not become a permanent resident or a citizen. But how each nation exercises those rights says something important, indeed fundamental, about the nation and its society. For more than two hundred years, the United States has struggled to live up to the ideals of its founding, not always perfectly but making progress over time to guarantee "life, liberty and the pursuit of happiness" for ever-expanding groups within its boundaries.

The naturalization process to gain citizenship was a relatively relaxed one during much of the nation's history. Little more than a waiting period, a character witness, and an oath administered by a judge, even a local justice of the peace, was required through much of the nineteenth century. Not until 1906, with the passage of the Basic Naturalization Act, did the process become more standardized, with the responsibility for naturalizing new citizens eventually falling to federal judges after federal naturalization officers established that applicants were qualified to become citizens based on lengths of residency and other mandated qualifications, including knowledge of English and, at a later point, US history.

So, who should be admitted to America permanently and allowed to become citizens today? Opening the borders to all comers is unrealistic. The country is no longer sparsely populated, and there are many current US citizens who still have not achieved the American dream. But how the nation makes choices, both in the qualifications it seeks and the numbers it admits, must be guided by principles that reflect the Constitution and other laws.

First, immigration policy should never be based on race, ethnicity, or religion. No one should be denied permission to immigrate—or granted preference—based on skin color or religious belief. Whether it was the Chinese Exclusion Acts of the nineteenth century, the national-origins quotas of the twentieth century, or proposed changes to US law, endorsed by the Trump administration, that thinly veil a preference for English-speaking and European immigrants, racial, ethnic, and religious prejudices make for bad policy. And they dishonor the Constitution.

Second, the best immigration policy would be one that is flexible and market driven. It is nearly impossible to predict what the ideal level of immigration will be years down the road—the US economy is too complex. Yet legislators and government bureaucrats and immigration laws consistently try to set such limits. We do know that the United States, like most of the developed world, has an aging native-born population. Just when millions of elderly Americans expect Social Security and Medicare to take care of their needs, fewer workers will be contributing to the taxes that pay for those benefits, unless immigration increases the working-age population. Barring unprecedented, dramatic improvements in productivity, gross domestic product will also fall, leaving all Americans poorer.

Third, assimilating immigrants is important both to their ultimate success in their adopted country and to Americans' continued openness to newcomers. Disproving restrictionists' fears, every group of immigrants to the United States throughout its history has ultimately assimilated. But assimilation in the American model has always been balanced by a tradition of pluralism: the recognition that immigrants add to American culture, they don't simply conform to what constitutes that culture at a given historical moment. English is the de facto national language, and if immigrants don't always become fully fluent in English, their children do—and the language and culture are enriched along the way. Americans send their children to *kindergarten*, eat *matzo* ball soup at *delicatessens*, dip *tortilla* chips in *salsa*, marvel at the *chutzpah* of certain politicians and their *gung-ho* followers.

Fourth, America must remain open to refugees and asylum seekers fleeing persecution in their homelands. Today's efforts to limit the number of refugees admitted both by number and by country of origin make a mockery of America's history as a beacon of hope to the persecuted. Clearly, national security concerns play a role in deciding whom to admit, but the United States already has a vigorous and lengthy vetting system to ensure that those seeking entry are not a threat; the average wait time for admittance is two years. Unlike Europe, which has faced an enormous crisis in recent years as hundreds of thousands of refugees and asylum seekers have crossed land borders or arrived by sea, the United States has a well-established system to interview refugees abroad and gather information, including biometric data, before they may enter the country. As the world's preeminent liberal democracy, America has a special obligation to continue showing liberality in welcoming those anxious for its embrace.

Contrary to the views of extremists who want to wall off America, immigration has been at the heart of what made America great. The United States was built by poor people escaping lives of drudgery, oppressed religious minorities seeking freedom to worship, idealists pursuing the promise of a better life for themselves and their children. These people came from every continent, in all colors, and from all faiths or no faith at all. We have not always lived up to these ideals, and those comfortably here haven't always welcomed those wanting to come. But America has fought that impulse before, and it must do so again. The way forward is to embrace the immigration challenge in ways that honor freedom, not to pull up the drawbridge and retreat into an imagined past.

The Courts as Bulwarks Against Tyranny

★ ★ ★

MICHAEL C. DORF

The framers of the US Constitution knew from their study of classical antiquity that republics do not necessarily last forever, and so they bequeathed to the nation a government structure designed to resist devolution into tyranny. Conversely, modern-day would-be tyrants have learned that courts committed to the rule of law will stand in the way of realizing their will to power. Thus, in recent years authoritarians in Hungary, Poland, Turkey, and Venezuela have sought to render once proudly independent courts subservient to political authority as a means of consolidating their own rule.

Regimes go about undermining the rule of law—and consolidating their own power—by a variety of means. After coming

---

Michael C. Dorf is Robert S. Stevens Professor of Law at Cornell University.

to power in 2010, the authoritarian Fidesz Party of Hungarian prime minister Viktor Orbán moved in tandem to pass hundreds of new laws and neuter the judiciary as a potential brake. Before the Constitutional Court was packed to ensure a Fidesz-friendly majority, the justices ruled that some of the new laws were unconstitutional—and so the Fidesz-dominated Parliament wrote the laws into the Hungarian Constitution. In the summer of 2016, Poland's populist, right-wing government brought the judiciary under state control, giving the justice minister the right to fire judges—a move that exacerbated Poland's already deteriorating relations with the European Union. Turkish president Recep Tayyip Erdogan used a failed coup in 2016 as an excuse to purge more than 4,000 judges and prosecutors for their supposed connection to an exiled cleric blamed by the government for plotting the overthrow attempt. Meanwhile, the socialist government of Nicolás Maduro, which already dominates Venezuela's Supreme Court, uses it as a weapon for state control: in March 2017 the court effectively dissolved the nation's opposition-controlled congress, with the justices assuming legislative functions for themselves.

Could it happen in the United States? Certainly not yet, but we should not fool ourselves into thinking that, as the poet James Russell Lowell said in 1888, the Constitution is "a machine that would go of itself." It requires tending by a vigilant people standing in opposition to those who would throw sand in its gears.

From one perspective, Donald Trump is an unlikely sand thrower. In 2016, a team of reporters for *USA Today* discovered that he or his businesses had been involved in roughly 3,500 lawsuits—many more than people with comparable business interests and orders of magnitude more than any prior major-party presidential candidate. No one likes to be sued, so one might think that the repeated experience soured Trump on courts and judges. Apparently, it did not, though, because Trump often does the suing. He is a frequent filer, not just a repeat defendant. Nor was Trump's role as a party in these legal matters his only pre-presidential exposure to the courts. His sister is a respected federal appeals court judge. Unlike his immediate predecessor in the White House, Trump never taught constitutional law, but, given his background, he ought to have come to the office of the presidency with a healthy appreciation for the role of courts as impartial guardians of life, liberty, and property.

And yet Trump has repeatedly attacked the judiciary. During the presidential campaign, he asserted that a US-born federal judge could not impartially adjudicate a lawsuit against the erstwhile Trump University because the judge's parents were immigrants from Mexico. When another federal judge enjoined the first version of Trump's executive order barring travel from various mostly Muslim countries, Trump dismissed the ruling as emanating from a "so-called judge."

Admittedly, the criticisms of Judge Gonzalo Curiel (in the Trump University case) and Judge James Robart (in the travel ban case) were not uniquely Trumpian. Judge Curiel ostensibly had a bias due to Trump's immigration and border security policies, while Judge Robart was criticized for overstepping the proper role of courts in matters of national security. Presidents and other politicians whose policies the courts block have long complained that the operative judicial decisions are not only wrong but fundamentally illegitimate.

The complaints have been bipartisan. Conservatives say that liberal judges and justices impose their subjective values to require legal same-sex marriage. Liberals say that conservative judges and justices impose their subjective values to restrict gun control. Seen in this light, Trump's attacks on the judiciary fit within a familiar pattern.

There is nonetheless something distinctly worrying about Trump's attacks on the judiciary. He poses a threat not posed by other politicians who have brought charges of judicial activism.

The difference is not simply a matter of tone, although Trump's charges against judges, like his charges against rival politicians, celebrities, and athletes, certainly use more colorful and coarser language than one typically encounters even in the rough-and-tumble of public debate. Beyond their tone, Trump's attacks on judges are worrisome because they are of a piece with his other actions and statements that aim to delegitimize institutions that could challenge him.

Trump has repeatedly attacked the free press. During his campaign rallies, which have continued into his presidency, he points to the press box and riles up the crowds against the reporters corralled there. He has called the press the "enemy of the people." He dismisses accurate reportage that casts him or his administration in a negative light as "fake news." He even raised the possibility of revoking NBC's broadcast license because of coverage he disliked. The threat is idle, as FCC broadcast licenses are local, not national, and none of these actions clearly crosses the line into illegality; yet collectively they treat criticism and even honest reporting as unpatriotic. Such attacks on the press enable authoritarians to consolidate power. They facilitate strongman rule.

The rule of a strongman is, more or less by definition, contrary to the rule of law.

A liberal democracy needs a free press to hold government accountable. It also needs institutions *within* the government that answer to the rule of law. The principle that no man (or woman) is above the law operates effectively only if people within the government are free to follow the law rather than the unlawful orders of the leader (or those who ultimately answer to the leader).

President Trump has also sought to undermine that principle. He fired FBI director James Comey because he was irked by Comey's investigation into Russian meddling in the election and possible collusion in that meddling by the Trump campaign. He then publicly criticized his own attorney general for having (quite properly) recused himself from the Russia investigation rather than killing it. He has reportedly speculated about pardoning members of his campaign and White House staff—and even himself—should special counsel Robert Mueller's Russia investigation strike too close to home.

The best that can be said in defense of Trump's approach to the Russia investigation is that the Constitution vests all executive power, and the pardon power specifically, in the president. Such a defense would draw on the theory of the so-called unitary executive. Justice Antonin Scalia argued that allowing prosecution by government officials not answerable to the president poses too great a risk that a special prosecutor will run amok.

But Scalia, who died in 2016, made that argument as the lone dissenter from an otherwise unanimous Supreme Court ruling in 1988 that upheld a law authorizing the appointment and political insulation of an independent counsel. All the other justices in that case thought that Congress had sufficient grounds to believe that the risk of self-dealing justified insulating prosecutors investigating wrongdoing by high-ranking executive officials.

Although rejected by his colleagues in the independent counsel case, Scalia's argument had a plausible basis in the text of the Constitution. Yet that suggests only that our Constitution may be flawed in this respect. One might think that a well-designed constitution would expressly take investigation and prosecution of crimes by high-ranking executive officials out of the hands of the highest-ranking executive official. Indeed, one could go much further. In the overwhelming majority of US states, the attorney general is elected by the people rather than appointed by the governor. If, as Scalia argued, a president has the constitutional prerogative to fire prosecutors who investigate him and his aides, that should be regarded not so much as a feature of the US Constitution but as a bug.

Whatever one concludes about the president's power over prosecutors, the Constitution makes clear that he has no power over how members of the judiciary do their job. The president, with the advice and consent of the Senate, appoints Supreme Court justices and lower court judges, but, once confirmed, they serve until they die, choose to retire, or are impeached. In 1804, the House of Representatives impeached Justice Samuel Chase on charges of having conducted trials (while serving double duty as a trial court judge, which was common at the time) in a biased manner. Even though Chase had departed from the ideal of judicial impartiality, he was nonetheless acquitted by the Senate on the ground that the charges themselves were politically motivated. Ever since, it has been well accepted that mere disagreement with judicial rulings—even very strong disagreement—is not a proper basis for impeachment and removal.

Judicial independence has sometimes been controversial in the United States because state and federal courts exercise the power of judicial review—that is, the power to set aside laws passed by Congress or a state legislature as unconstitutional. That power can be used for good—as it was when the Supreme Court in 1943 held that the First Amendment does not permit school authorities to compel children to recite the Pledge of Allegiance and when in 1954 it ruled that state laws mandating racially segregated schools violated the Fourteenth Amendment's Equal Protection Clause. The power of judicial review can also be used for ill—as it was in 1857, when the court ruled that African Americans could not be citizens and in 1918 when it said that Congress lacked the power to forbid the interstate transportation of goods made by child labor. And then there are cases that were and remain divisive, like those protecting a right to abortion (criticized by conservatives) and those striking down campaign finance regulation (criticized by liberals).

Assessing whether judicial review does more harm than good requires a complex calculus. Which poses the greater danger:

the likelihood that, using the power of judicial review, the courts will strike down laws that the legislature should be permitted to enact; or the likelihood that, in the absence of judicial review, the legislature will enact harmful, unconstitutional laws? No one can answer that question with great confidence, although it is notable that over time more and more constitutional democracies have adopted judicial review. Even the United Kingdom, in which it was traditionally said that the king or queen in Parliament can make any law, now has a form of judicial review under the Human Rights Act of 1998 and the European Convention on Human Rights (which was unaffected by the 2016 vote to exit the European Union).

Despite its spread, judicial review remains controversial, because people who find themselves on the losing side of constitutional cases understandably believe that adverse rulings are not merely wrong but, if they invalidate state or federal laws, illegitimate. Introductory classes in constitutional law still typically begin with *Marbury v. Madison*, the landmark case that in 1803 established judicial review—or that "deviant institution" of democracy, as legal scholar Alexander Bickel famously described it in 1962. Perhaps a justified institution, all things considered, but deviant nonetheless.

Critics of judicial review in the United States often charge that politically unaccountable judges should not be displacing the policy judgments of politically accountable officials. The charge has a certain logic to it in the context of judicial review but not beyond. In a properly designed and functioning constitutional democracy, judges should not be politically accountable.

To be sure, in many US states, judges stand for election, a practice that has attracted criticism from many quarters, especially retired Supreme Court justice Sandra Day O'Connor. But even elected judges must follow strict codes of judicial ethics forbidding them from favoring their political allies or campaign donors. Despite the problematic incentives that judicial elections create, elected judges are at least supposed to strive for independence from the other branches in adjudicating cases.

Meanwhile, review of executive action by independent judges is not, strictly speaking, essential to good government. In many circumstances, internal grievance procedures can produce satisfactory results. If you believe that the Internal Revenue Service has incorrectly found that you owe more in taxes, you may contest its findings before the agency itself, and you may succeed. But you will not always succeed, and, even when you do, it may be chiefly because agency personnel know that their own decisions will be subject to judicial scrutiny.

Judicial independence safeguards the rule of law in two ways. In ordinary times, when the president and other executive officials are trying their best to conform to the law, judicial independence acts as a backstop. It prevents the government from acting on subtle biases in its own favor.

In extraordinary times—when the government is led by people who do not care what the law says but care only about what they can get away with—judicial independence is no backstop but the first line of defense against self-dealing or worse. In my opinion, we now live in extraordinary times, with a president who shows little regard for basic norms of civility, much less the norms of constitutional democracy.

In an insightful 1985 article in the *Columbia Law Review*, Vincent Blasi explained that in generating principles by which to evaluate First Amendment cases, courts would do well to adopt what he called the "pathological perspective." In other words, rules and standards should be formulated to provide maximum protection in those periods when "intolerance of unorthodox ideas is most prevalent and when governments are most able and most likely to stifle dissent systematically."

Blasi's proposal is sound but incomplete in two ways. It is institutionally incomplete, because First Amendment principles do not enforce themselves. They require organs that will resist the censorial impulses of government in periods of intolerance. Blasi's proposal is also substantively incomplete. It ought to apply to nearly the whole of the law. During times of crisis, government tests not only our commitment to dissent but other basic commitments, including, especially, to equality and fairness.

The most shameful Supreme Court performance in the past century did not involve the court using the power of judicial review to override the will of Congress. It involved the court's failure to stand up to the executive branch when the latter invoked a bogus national security justification as the basis for driving thousands of Americans of Japanese ancestry from their West Coast homes. The *Korematsu* case was a sin of cowardice, not temerity.

An independent judiciary is not sufficient to protect constitutional democracy, but then, nothing is. "A dependence on the people is, no doubt, the primary control on the government," James Madison wrote in *Federalist 51*, and he was surely right.

However, he was also right when he added that "experience has taught mankind the necessity of auxiliary precautions," including an independent judiciary as a check on the other branches of government. The additional experience of twenty-three decades confirms the wisdom of that observation.

Reform for Islam

★ ★ ★

MAAJID NAWAZ

Public debate is a cornerstone of any liberal, democratic society, yet free discussion of the Islamic faith has been all but
crippled. On the left, misplaced fear of offending all Muslims
has deformed public debate. On the right, the urge to stigmatize
every believer in Islam has done further harm.

This impediment has touched even the highest platforms of
democratic speech. President Obama was infamously unwilling
to call the Islamist ideology by its proper name; President Trump
repeats "radical Islamic terrorism" ad nauseam, as if by calling
out "Rumpelstiltskin" enough times he can magically break extremism's malevolent grip.

The result has been mass confusion sometimes verging on
public hysteria. By way of example, this writer—for having

Maajid Nawaz is an author, broadcaster, and founder of the counter-extremism
organization Quilliam.

encouraged public debate about Islam—has received the dubious honor of being labeled with a Muslim terrorism designation in the United Kingdom by the Thompson Reuters World Check database, while being simultaneously listed as an "anti-Muslim extremist" in the United States by the Southern Poverty Law Center. Thompson Reuters World Check has since recognized its error and paid significant compensation. The Southern Poverty Law Center is yet to follow suit.

Few other topics today are in as much need of discussion as the Islamic faith, and yet few other topics are as confusing and polarizing. First, a clear definition of terms is needed. Islam is a religion, and, just like many other faiths, it is internally diverse. The followers of Islam are Muslims, whether of Sunni, Shiite, or some other variety. *Islamism*, by contrast, is a political ideology, with a desire to impose a single version of Islam on the world. In other words, Islamism is a call for a global Muslim theocracy. Its adherents are *Islamists*; they too can be of the Sunni or Shiite variety. Islamist doctrine has taken the traditional notion of jihad in Islam—meaning to struggle or strive on behalf of the faith— and turned it to violent ends. Jihadism is thus the use of force to spread Islamism. Arabs have long referred to *Islamawiyya* as the noun for Islamism, with *Islamiyiin* and *jihadiyiin* referring to Islamists and jihadists respectively.

By definition, Islamists and jihadists view their ideology as Islam itself—as do many populist anti-Islam critics who have arisen in the West. Further complicating matters: many ordinary Muslims, disturbed by being stuck between these two warring ideological factions, have joined allies on the left in proclaiming that jihadism has "nothing to do with Islam." But it is as intellectually unhelpful to claim that jihadism has "nothing to do" with Islam as it is to insist that jihadism is the embodiment of Islam. For although Islamism and jihadism do not define Islam, they are certainly offshoots of the faith. Islamism and jihadism have *something* to do with Islam.

Even among many non-devout Muslims, general ignorance of Islamist ideology—and confusion over the terms involved and the distinct concepts they seek to describe—has led them to mistake any criticism of *Islamism* to be a criticism of Islam itself, and even of Muslims. This misunderstanding is especially unfortunate because Islam today, drifting toward a modern fundamentalism, does indeed require scrutiny. But criticizing contemporary Islam would be best served by the strategic aim of encouraging Islamic reform, while the goal of challenging Islamism must be to fully discredit this theocratic ideology. Islam today needs reform; the ideology of Islamism must be intellectually terminated.

Many from the left, in a faction I call the regressive left, have taken to defending any and every belief, action, or stance taken by Muslims. This is often done in the name of multiculturalism and tolerance. The relativist confusion has been seized upon by Islamists themselves, who deliberately conflate their ideological stances with the religion of Islam. They want to insinuate themselves within broader Muslim communities, where they are protected and even vocally defended by Muslims and the regressive left.

Regressive leftists might seem like natural allies of reform-minded liberal Muslims, but they typically shout down liberal Muslim voices seeking to chart a course through this fog, labeling them "Islamophobes." The accusation is not just misguided and misinformed—it also runs dangerously parallel with the treacherous road to blasphemy laws. Anti-Muslim bigotry is real, but the right to disagreement—and to heresy and to blasphemy—must necessarily be embedded within the human right to free speech. If our hard-earned liberties had to be reduced to one basic and indispensable right, it would be the right to free speech. Our freedom to speak represents our freedom to think, and our freedom to think represents our ability to create, to innovate, and to progress. No idea is above scrutiny, just as no person is beneath dignity.

The pressure to silence voices for reform from within Islam casts doubt on society's commitment to these fundamental freedoms. It also does immeasurable damage to the communities that are most in need of support: the minorities within minorities. Among these are gay Muslims, feminist Muslims, secular Muslims, and ex-Muslims. In the name of supposed cultural authenticity, dissenting voices from within Muslim communities have been dismissed as "native informers" or, worse, apostates deserving of death. These delegitimizing efforts amount to religious policing and have the effect of sabotaging what is likely the best hope of significant, long-term solutions.

The misguided desire to be politically and culturally correct in liberal-democratic societies has meant the toleration of disturbing practices among some Muslims, such as female genital mutilation (apologists prefer the term "cutting"), and of abhorrent attitudes toward homosexuals. In Britain, according to statistics cited by the government's Department for International Development, more than 20,000 girls under the age of fifteen are still at risk of FGM annually. As of 2018, Britain is yet to witness one successful prosecution for this reprehensible practice. In fact, the West Midlands police force said in February 2017 that parents caught practicing FGM on their daughters should not be prosecuted and that the best course of action is to "educate parents." The police explained their opposition to "prosecuting/jailing" parents who had carried out FGM because doing so would be "unlikely to benefit" the victimized children.

A similar squeamishness marked the response to the over-representation of British South Asian Muslim men in child-grooming rape gangs that targeted underage white girls a decade ago. It took British-Pakistani prosecutor Nazir Afzal to finally bring the now-infamous Rochdale child sex-abuse ring to justice in 2012. Afzal readily admitted that "my Pakistani heritage helped cut through barriers within the black and minority ethnic communities." He added that "white professionals' oversensitivity to political correctness and fear of appearing racist may well have contributed to justice being stalled."

Such reluctance in addressing these very real problems have allowed Islamism and Muslim fundamentalism to flourish within many Muslim communities. It is no wonder that Islamist views, and a corresponding anti-Muslim response in the broader public, have become entrenched in much of the West. I have seen this firsthand in Britain. On the subject of gender and sexuality, a large-scale study of British Muslims commissioned by the television network Channel 4 found in 2016 that 52 percent of British Muslims agreed that homosexuality (not gay marriage, but merely being gay) should be criminalized; 47 percent deemed it unacceptable for a gay person to hold a teaching position; 39

percent said that a wife should always obey her husband; and 31 percent said it is acceptable for a British Muslim man to have more than one wife.

And yet liberal outrage was directed instead at the former head of the Equality and Human Rights Commission Trevor Phillips, who presented the poll results in a documentary called *What Muslims Really Think*, and said of the findings, "We are more nervous about Muslims because we feel people will be offended. But my view is that looking at the results of this survey, which have surprised me, that we have gone beyond the situation where we can say, 'OK, don't worry; they will come round in time,' because that is not going to happen. We have to make things change now."

In survey after survey in the West over the past decade, Muslims have shown an alarming toleration of even more dangerous beliefs. A 2011 Pew Research poll found that 7 percent of American Muslims thought "suicide bombings and other forms of violence against civilian targets" are "sometimes justified" to protect Islam. Pew estimated the population of American Muslim adults in 2011 at 1.8 million; that translates to 126,000 Muslims in the United States who think protecting Islam by hitting civilian targets with suicide bombers and other violence is sometimes all right. Surveys in Britain have been even more dispiriting: a 2008 YouGov poll found that a third of Muslim students believe that killing for religion can be justified, and 40 percent wanted the introduction of Shariah as law in the UK.

After an onslaught of terror attacks in Paris in November 2015 killed more than 125 people, Pope Francis declared that we are in the midst of a "piecemeal" World War III. It is more accurate to say that we face a global jihadist insurgency. The Islamic State, or ISIS, is the latest brutal incarnation, but the insurgency has been brewing for decades, spurred on by Islamist social movements that have filled the void left by far too many weak Muslim-majority governments. Characterizing ISIS as part of an insurgency is important. As experience from the Vietnam War shows, confronting insurgency is not like waging a conventional war.

Counterinsurgency efforts rest on the assumption that the enemy has gained significant support for its basic ideological aims from within the communities it targets. The aim of counterinsurgency must therefore include denying the enemy propaganda victories that can fuel recruitment. Insurgents must be isolated from their targeted host communities. This requires a combination of physical, psychological, and economic warfare, all with the aim of undermining the insurgents' ideological, operational, and financial capabilities.

This struggle against Islamist attitudes will not be easy, but *it can be won*. For victory even to be possible, though, the regressive left must permit the critical discussion of contemporary Muslim fundamentalism and of the Islamist ideology. As for the populist right, it must distinguish between Muslims, with their various interpretations of the religion, and Islamism.

Messaging is an essential part of such a strategy. In fighting the Islamist ideology and its jihadist manifestation, we must avoid using language that promotes its own worldview. The Islamists' ideology is Islam, their people are Muslims, their law is Sharia, and their state is a caliphate. Islamists see Muslims around the world not only as a religious community but also as a political one. As such, they view the "Muslim world" just as Leninists viewed the International Proletariat, seeking to unite this "Muslim world" under one global caliphate just as Lenin sought to expand his Soviet Union. President Obama's 2009 Cairo speech addressing "the Muslim world" merely reinforced the Islamist notion that Muslims identify as one bloc, politically. Imagine a Middle Eastern head of state addressing the "Christian world" from London, to picture just how archaic this is. Such unwitting echoing of the enemy was known during the Cold War as "semantic infiltration."

At the same time, we must provide more compelling counter- and alternative narratives. A counternarrative would challenge the legitimacy of a piece of Islamist propaganda—such as the notion that Shariah has been enforced throughout history as law among Muslims—by undermining it intellectually, scripturally, and historically. An alternative narrative would present a more positive ideational framework for Muslims to adopt, such as the idea of freedom of, and from, religion.

Islamists and jihadists use community-based organizations and online messaging to portray themselves to mainstream Muslims as their sole representatives and to attack dissenters as anti-Muslim. These toxic efforts must be curtailed by proactive initiatives that seek out and promote a religiously and politically diverse range of Muslims and ex-Muslims.

This effort could be hampered by Muslims and non-Muslims alike who seek to obfuscate or deny that Islamist extremism poses an ideological threat; they are as counterproductive as the populists who would demonize all Muslims, even in a reformed manifestation of the faith. Both factions increase the polarization and mistrust that is relished by extremists of all sorts, but this especially appeals to ISIS, which has vowed to eliminate the "gray zone," or the middle ground between Islamist theocrats and anti-Muslim bigots, so that everyone is forced to pick sides in a polarized debate.

To resist the reform of Islam today is to regard Islamism as a problem intrinsic to Islam itself and therefore intrinsic to every Muslim. That will in turn aid the rise of xenophobia and bigotry in both Europe and the United States, prompting the further spread of Islamism, in a vicious cycle.

There is no easy fix. Reversing Islamist propaganda will require decades of work by Muslims and non-Muslims alike, but the endgame *must* be to render the ideology intellectually and socially obsolete. We cannot even begin to do this until we recognize the problem for what it is. Affirming and revitalizing the secular Enlightenment values that formed the basis of liberal-democratic societies is the only path to winning this ideological struggle.

The Free Market Remains Essential

★ ★ ★

TYLER COWEN

The concept of a capitalist market economy is a vital element of liberal-democratic order, but recent polls of young people in America—the flagship for liberal democracy—have found a rising sympathy for socialism. That unsettling trend has occurred in an era when the United States also faltered in global rankings of economic freedom. Donald Trump sometimes sounds "pro-business," but neither major party talks much about economic freedom, a very different concept. Yet the case for markets remains robust. I'd like to consider three of the traditional defenses of a market economy and why they not only still apply but are likely to gain in urgency.

Tyler Cowen is Holbert L. Harris Chair of Economics at George Mason University, where he is chairman and general director of the Mercatus Center.

First, market economies encourage the efficient use of dispersed and decentralized information. Communist central planning in both the Soviet Union and China, by contrast, resulted in anemic economic performance and a paucity of consumer goods. Central planners just don't have enough information at their fingertips to allocate resources effectively, and so Russia and China gradually moved toward decentralized systems, albeit ones with dysfunctional incentives, price controls, systematic shortages, and sometimes even famine.

But it was not only the goods side of the economy that was distorted under Communist central planning. Career ambitions were thwarted, or they never were developed in the first place, because labor markets were not in general available to allocate labor on the basis of voluntary decisions between businesses and workers. The resulting frustrations on the consumer side and on the career side made life intolerable for many people in these societies. Even for those who didn't run afoul of the totalitarian regimes—and millions did, facing death or imprisonment—their days were plagued by endless queues, privation, and dependence on the arbitrary whims of Communist bureaucrats.

Sadder yet, this history, widely known in the West in the second half of the twentieth century, now seems to have fallen down a memory hole. Communism's central-planning cousin, socialism, has become a cool idea once again, with many young people embracing the term when it is championed by politicians like Bernie Sanders in the United States or Jeremy Corbyn in the UK.

Unlike central planning, markets rely on price signals to direct resources to the ends that consumers value most. Those price signals are highly imperfect, especially when externalities are present (e.g., pollution), but in most cases the use of prices as an allocative mechanism outperforms the central planner. Prices bring together supply and demand, and more generally that means a meeting of the minds of some kind—an agreement resulting from the steady dialogue between businesses and consumers. Businesses are competing to create at low cost the consumer goods that people desire the most and to offer the career opportunities that will help the businesses attract the most productive workers. On all sides of the market, the core incentive is for quality and convenience to be ratcheted up, and indeed wealthy capitalist economies produce both better consumer goods and more satisfying and safer jobs. What makes this all work is that if you don't like what one business is offering, usually you can go elsewhere or simply not purchase at all. The market will take the hint.

Decentralized business production also does the most to mobilize different skills to serve the consumer. For instance, the knowledge of how to best make a ventilation system for kitchens is held by those companies that actually do the work. A more centralized institution would simply be incapable of recording, transmitting, implementing, and continuously improving upon this knowledge. Governments can succeed in some limited projects when they make the projects priorities and the objectives are fairly well defined. The military lends itself to this approach. But it is almost impossible to imagine a government building, running, and improving upon decentralized knowledge for an entire complex economy. History is replete with failed attempts;

the most recent example can found in the mounting misery of Venezuela.

Government can aid in the transmission of market price signals by supplying valuable infrastructure, by enforcing property rights and rule of law, and by subsidizing basic science to encourage the public good of innovation. But the actual assembling of a supply chain, and the use of profit and loss to weed out inefficient companies, projects, and products, is best done through decentralized markets. Governments have a long-standing history of not shutting down failing projects and, when bureaucrats are in charge, not letting dysfunctional firms fail.

As economies have grown larger and more complex, the case for decentralization through markets has become stronger. Sometimes you hear it argued that advances in computers and software have made central planning easier, but more likely the opposite is true. The use of technology in the private sector has far outpaced the use of technology in government. It is not unusual to see a US government agency operating with what is still largely the information technology of the 1990s (the military operations of the Pentagon being a notable exception). This technological backwardness again illustrates the importance of decentralization. The most efficient private business firms can adopt or develop new technologies rapidly without having to ask for permission; successful adoption boosts their profits and thereby encourages additional good decisions in the future. The same is not true for government agencies, where approval is hard to come by and does not directly benefit the agencies' leaders.

What does government do reasonably well? The list is not long. Most prominently, the US government is adept at sending out checks, to Social Security recipients and other beneficiaries. Often the check mailing has been replaced by direct deposit, but for the most part the technology behind this activity has stayed relatively constant, and so the United States and other governments do not find the task too challenging even on a large scale. The most successful countries in the world therefore have settled on infrastructure and social welfare spending as basic government activities, while leaving the production of most goods and services to the private sector. Government planning has never come close to producing the assemblage of goods found in a Walmart, much less at such low cost.

The second argument for markets has to do with incentives. The basic incentive in markets is to serve consumers so that businesses may earn profit. This helps supply everything from our food and manufactured goods to our information technology and recreation. As early economists Adam Smith and Frédéric Bastiat famously noted, we are fed because of the self-interest of the farmer, baker, and shopkeeper, not out of altruism. Capitalist democracies simply do not experience famine because all their incentives are geared in the opposite direction, plus there is the safety net of social welfare spending. Nowadays in capitalist countries, obesity is a much bigger problem than hunger.

Market incentives do sometimes require steering or backup support from government. Unscrupulous business operators can take advantage of ignorant consumers and defraud them, so strong anti-fraud laws from government are a good idea. (That said, most of the actual protection against fraud still stems from marketplace reputation and consumer vigilance.) In some other cases, consumer purchases may involve what economists call negative externalities—if a certain kind of automobile releases too many pollutants, regulation in the form of limiting lead emissions can benefit society more broadly.

Political incentives don't have the diversity or responsiveness of most market incentives. The fundamental incentive for politicians is to seek election or reelection or, in the case of autocracies, to hold on to power. In addition to serving those desires, politicians often seek to use their positions to promote particular ideologies and policies, but that too requires being in power, perhaps with a popular mandate. These political incentives can work reasonably well for producing broad-based public goods where most of the citizenry is in agreement and the quality of the output is relatively easy to observe. Safe public spaces, national defense, and clean air are products of the public sector, and the incentives of politicians are often sufficiently close to those of the citizenry for the incentives to work acceptably well, especially in democracies with a reasonable degree of electoral accountability.

But political incentives don't translate into good outcomes for most of the economy. Maximizing the number of votes is not the same as maximum benefit for society. Workers and capitalists who are already entrenched in a sector, for instance, tend to have more political clout than do entrepreneurs working on innovations. Politics therefore tends to favor established interests, which are visible and easier to organize. This limits dynamism, as economies tend to end up with too much protectionism, labor unions entrenched by political privilege, and crony-like regulations that favor incumbents.

By contrast, consider the tech entrepreneurs who founded Google or Amazon. It was far from clear that their companies would succeed; they didn't have much money, and they certainly didn't have much if any political clout. Note also that entrepreneurs are immigrants at a much higher rate than average, which also limits their initial influence in Washington. Politics does far too little to stimulate dynamism, because the entrepreneurs who make the new goods and services are not yet a significant political constituency. If we rely too heavily on politics, the result will be insufficient innovation, weaker job creation, and living standards below what should otherwise be possible.

In the United States, Western Europe, and Japan, government policies are also warped by the outsize political clout wielded by the elderly. Older people tend to be more likely to vote—and to vote to keep or extend transfer benefits, such as Social Security, to themselves. The result too often is out-of-control pension spending; growing deficits; fiscal inflexibility; crowding out of more dynamic investments; and, in some extreme cases, such as Greece, an explosive financial crisis. Yet politicians continue to compete against each other to funnel more and more money to the elderly.

The third argument for markets has to do with trust. Markets, for all their imperfections, are more productive of trust and trustworthiness overall than is government. And the trustworthiness of markets has improved considerably with the onset of the Internet. You can consult reviews for just about any product to figure out what to buy and where to buy it. Purchases made in error usually mean somebody didn't do enough homework. If I want to go to a restaurant, even an obscure one, I can consult Yelp.com and food blogs and Twitter. If I am considering buying music, usually I can listen to it in advance, at no charge. If I need to buy a new refrigerator or car, I have access to mountains of relevant information, and the best postings are sorted for me by Google. I could also post a query on Facebook and hear from those who have real experience with the product.

These new communications options have been one of the biggest improvements in modern life, and they have made our budgets more efficient and greatly reduced everyday frustrations. Unlike in the recent past, almost every product purchased today is the result of an informed choice. Overall that means more trust in markets, and trust tends to create a virtuous circle involving more long-range planning, more cooperation, lower transaction costs, and a greater interchange of ideas across markets, leading to more efficient discovery and innovation.

Now consider Americans' trust in government: the numbers are shockingly low. Sometimes the approval ratings for Congress scrape below 10 percent. It is widely understood that President Trump is a serial liar, and possibly corrupt, but this doesn't discourage his core supporters because they view the alternatives to Trump as no better and maybe worse. That in turn leads to a downward spiral in trust. If Americans expect corrupt and dishonest behavior from politicians, the politicians will know they can get away with it—and that is exactly what the country will get. Expectations on all sides will sink and standards will fall too. I believe the American Republic is currently in this kind of bad equilibrium, and it is not obvious how we will get out of it.

Given the simple math—markets increase trust, government decreases trust—a positive first step would be a renewed appreciation for the essential role of market economies in the flourishing of liberal democracies. Luckily, the case for markets is stronger than ever.

Facts and the Free Press

★ ★ ★

TED KOPPEL

Freedom of the press in the United States is at a fragile stage, suffering, ironically, from an overdose of freedom and the exuberant high that often precedes an imminent crash. We have, as an industry, fallen victim to the opioid that is Donald Trump. He has been very good for the business of journalism and very dangerous for the profession. But he deserves neither all the credit nor even most of the blame. The circumstances that are undermining freedom of the press have evolved over a period of decades. They are the product of an eighteenth-century process being overwhelmed by twentieth- and twenty-first-century technology. It has been a gradual process but has evolved to a point

---

Ted Koppel, the anchor of ABC News's *Nightline* from 1980 to 2005, is a senior contributor for CBS News's *Sunday Morning* and the author, most recently, of *Lights Out: A Cyberattack, a Nation Unprepared, Surviving the Aftermath*.

that it now enables the actual democratization of journalism. The means to communicate instantaneously with large numbers of people, over vast distances, are now essentially available to anyone with access to the Internet. Anyone! It is, simultaneously, an enhancement of the professional journalist's reach and capabilities and a stunningly powerful tool recently bestowed on everyone else. The First Amendment has always gifted Americans with the right to be journalists, neither license nor entrance exam required. But, without access to a printing press or a radio or television station, the privilege of actual journalism was largely theoretical. The Internet has closed that gap. Anyone can now reach everyone.

Simply because we *can* do something, however, does not mean that we should.

What might the consequences be, for example, were we to apply the potential of the Internet to the realization of a pure political democracy? It no longer takes a great deal of imagination to envision an Internet app that would enable each and every legitimate voter to cast his or her ballot through a portable device employing a retinal scanner as a means of identification. We could vote multiple times a day on as many or as few issues and legislative proposals as we chose. One issue, one vote. It might be uninformed. It could be bought or traded. Not too dissimilar, in other words, from the system now in place but vastly more democratic. Town and city councils, state legislatures, the House and Senate would become superfluous. In time, this new technology could totally eliminate the need for representational government.

A truly horrific idea that, one hopes, would be rejected on even a moment's reflection. As flawed as our political process may be, it recognizes the value of elected representatives with time and staff to weigh and consider important issues—and the understanding that they will periodically be held to account. There remains a modicum of discipline within the process. Pure democracy would border on chaos.

And yet.

We seem enchanted by the democratization of journalism.

Let us recall the wisdom of Martin J. Dooley, a fictional Irish bartender, created in the 1890s by the journalist Finley Peter Dunne. Mr. Dooley's description of the newspaper as an agency "that comforts th' afflicted and afflicts the comfortable" is actually a squishy and truncated version of the significantly more caustic original: "Th' newspaper," opined the sage, Dooley, "does iverything f'r us. It runs th' polis foorce an' the banks, commands th' milishy, controls th' ligislachure, baptizes th' young, marries th' foolish, comforts th' afflicted, afflicts th' comfortable, buries th' dead an' roasts thim aftherward."

The newspaper was an agency of such unmatched power and influence that no equivalent or countervailing force existed. To be a Hearst or a Pulitzer at the dawn of the twentieth century, in other words, was to wield almost limitless power. It was only as each technological advance displaced or diluted the influence of a previous power center that freedom of the press was bestowed on an ever-increasing body of practitioners. Over the course of the next hundred years, newspaper chains and national magazines had their moments in the sun, to be superseded in short order by radio and then television. The body of news consumers doubled and redoubled. What all these media had in common, though, was that they operated in a unidirectional fashion.

Each gathered and processed information in its own way, but all of them spoke *to* their consumers, making merely the shallowest pretense of listening to how their audiences might be reacting.

The late Wilbur Schramm coined a term to describe the role played by media in filtering the flow of information: gatekeepers. At the apogee of network television news influence, CBS anchorman Walter Cronkite was the national personification of the breed—authoritative but avuncular. Known to tens of millions, widely trusted, Cronkite was the cohesive agent who gave Americans of disparate backgrounds a sense of common identity. His counterparts on NBC News and ABC News played similar, if less influential, roles. Each brought a slightly different flavor to the role, but the function remained largely the same: electronic paterfamilias—disseminators of essentially undisputed facts.

The audiences for these broadcasts existed for the most part in isolation. Ratings services numbered them in their tens of millions, but they watched and listened in solitary or family units, only vaguely aware of one another's existence. The fact that the FCC's so-called Fairness Doctrine required licensed broadcasters to treat controversial issues in an "honest, equitable and balanced" fashion added to an impression of national harmony. Insofar as media had any influence on Congress and the drafting of legislation, it encouraged moderation and compromise. It was a bland but relatively orderly process. The democratization of journalism had not yet begun.

Then, in 1987, the Fairness Doctrine was abolished, and by the next year the unabashedly conservative viewpoints of Rush Limbaugh were broadcast on a nationally syndicated radio program. That is worthy of particular note. Limbaugh made no pretense of impartiality. His approach has been partisan, his style bombastic and utterly lacking in humility. If network news anchors wrapped themselves in an aura of rigid neutrality, Limbaugh mockingly insisted that his is "a talent on loan from God," which he promptly put to use creating the "Limbaugh Institute for Advanced Conservative Studies."

During the almost thirty years that Limbaugh has served as a national radio host, his success has spawned a small army of (mostly conservative) imitators. Limbaugh alone claims a weekly audience of 20 million listeners; other estimates of his weekly audience are less generous but still hover in the 14 million to 15 million range. Indisputably, he has given his radio audience, the "ditto-heads" as they call themselves, a striking sense of ideological identity. Even as Rush Limbaugh attained national prominence, the World Wide Web, making its initial appearance in 1991, provided public access to the Internet. For the first time in recorded history, millions of people had direct access to a medium of mass communication. The notion of a web, countless connective strands linking previously isolated audiences into ever-expanding units of common interests, political inclinations, sympathies, and prejudices, laid the foundation for a social revolution waiting to happen. Mass communication, which traditionally flowed in only one direction, now opened infinite lines of contact available to anyone with access to the Internet. As readers and listeners and viewers grew accustomed to having voices of their own, and with the growing awareness that their voices had been granted access to audiences of their own, the democratization of journalism was truly underway.

More or less simultaneous with the rise of the Internet, cable and satellite television offered fresh alternatives to broadcast news. The presentation of news on CNN, for example, was a twenty-four-hour operation. No longer did the news consumer have to wait until such time as the networks deigned to program an update. Ted Turner's contribution to the spiraling evolution of coverage was to promise news whenever it suited the viewer. If Turner and CNN promised greater convenience and accessibility, Rupert Murdoch and Roger Ailes, creators of Fox News, offered an alternative ideology. The existing outlets tended toward liberalism and the left. Fox skewed right. It may have been intended, from the first, to serve a political purpose, but it was also a hugely successful business plan. Financially and ideologically Fox News duplicated on television what Rush Limbaugh had achieved on radio. And it was done according to a new set of rules. A modest amount of journalism was committed during the day, but in the evening, when advertising rates were highest, objectivity was largely discarded. Subjective opinions stoked controversy and built audience. Furthermore, bloviating is cheap. Panel discussions are cheap. The traditional building blocks of journalism—reporting, editorial supervision, fact-checking— were largely ignored. Whereas network radio and television had traditionally served a cohesive role, drawing audiences of disparate backgrounds together, the fragmentation of media, frequently along narrow, ideological lines, has led to the creation of opinion silos, offering radically different worldviews.

The success of Fox News, with its heavy reliance on loud, opinionated hosts touting the virtues of conservatism, encouraged the corporate owners of MSNBC to double down on the liberal or progressive side of the political agenda. An endless stream of panel discussions, hosted by journalists unencumbered by any apparent commitment to objectivity, flooded the highest-rated and therefore most profitable evening hours of Fox News and MSNBC. CNN, struggling to retain at least a semblance of objectivity, nevertheless succumbed to the economic imperative of garrulous, opinionated panels—dubious "experts" expressing themselves with largely unsubstantiated certainty on the hot-button issues of the day. Whatever else we may think of them, let the record show that panels are easy and cheap, while the actual gathering of news is neither.

The voices of the people reinforced the trend. Twitter, Face-book, and social media in general established the avenues by which audiences, in real time and in vast numbers, were able to communicate directly with the communicators. Their message was clear: more ideology, more controversy, more red meat.

The implied authority that once gave broadcast network producers and anchors the latitude to determine what was im-portant and what needed coverage waned. Losing audience and therefore advertising revenue, the networks looked for cost-saving measures. The ranks of foreign correspondents, who once numbered in the dozens at each network, were sharply reduced, as was the coverage of foreign news. The preeminence of the evening news anchor, emblematic of the network's commitment to "hard" news, was displaced by the rise of folksier hosts of the morning shows, where the emphasis on soft news and banal chatter generated literally hundreds of millions of dollars a year. The marketplace dictated a diminished role for network news operations.

It was not, however, until the 2016 presidential campaign (what must be called the beginning of the "age of Trump"), that the news business and the business of news became indistinguishable from one another. Without providing hard evidence, the *New York Times* contended, toward the end of that campaign, that television had provided Trump with two billion dollars' worth of free publicity. It would be churlish to quibble.

Mr. Trump had merely to suggest a willingness to appear, and producers and anchors would set aside all customary conditions. Previously, the Sunday morning talk shows had required that guests be in attendance, on the set. Trump was permitted to appear by phone. There was a day when the occurrence of a major news event was a prerequisite to live coverage. The cable networks, however, thought nothing of devoting live coverage to an empty tarmac, awaiting the arrival of Trump's plane. What he might actually say, on arrival, was of little or no concern. Trump was a ratings magnet.

Taken in isolation, these are relatively trivial developments. Collectively, they amount to a lowering of standards that cannot easily be recovered.

Undeniably, the Trump presidency has also revitalized tough, investigative journalism. The *New York Times* and the *Washington Post* have done some brilliant reporting, but it has been hard to escape the sense of a prosecutorial mission—a determination to bring Trump down. The blizzard of presidential tweets, enabling Trump to communicate directly and immediately with tens of millions of mostly supporters, has incessantly hammered home the theme of "the lying media" and "fake news." It does not help that so many of the reporters incurring the president's wrath have become regular spear carriers on cable television.

Legend has it that, back in the 1980s, a *New York Times* reporter asked Abe Rosenthal, the paper's executive editor at the time, for permission to appear as a guest on a television news program. "Of course," Rosenthal is reported to have said. "Only don't then come back to the *Times*."

These days, cable news programs could barely exist without the platoons of reporters from the *New York Times* and the *Washington Post* dropping the latest nuggets from their inquiries into President Trump's possible collusion with the Russians, his mental state, or his likely interference with special counsel Robert Mueller's investigation. These journalists' reporting may be meticulous and beyond reproach, but their regular appearance on panels that all but salivate at the prospect of bringing Trump down contribute to the perception that they subscribe to the same agenda.

The democratization of media, the accessibility of the Internet to so many who lack any journalistic training or discipline whatsoever, suggests a loosening of standards that must inevitably infect journalism overall. To the contrary, it demands a greater discipline than ever before from the ranks of professionals.

A blunt warning against the danger of publicly engaging unscrupulous rivals has made its way down through generations of political observers: *You get down in the mud and start wrasslin' with a hog, you're both gonna get dirty and the hog loves it.*

It will certainly not be easy. Traditional news organizations are struggling, in the face of mounting skepticism, to maintain discipline and objectivity, while an army of undisciplined and wholly subjective amateurs undermines the very notion of freedom of the press. In truth, there is no real equivalence between the failings of the establishment media and the stark propaganda of Breitbart News and its right-wing radio echo chambers. But we are sailing in uncharted waters.

Donald Trump and the establishment media are locked in a toxic embrace that may ultimately serve neither. The president caters to the lowest common denominator among his supporters by vilifying the press as enemies of the people. Whether the Trump presidency survives or not, tens of millions of Americans have had their confidence in the concepts of objective reality, indisputable facts, and good journalism perhaps irretrievably undermined. Freedom of the press was never intended to convey an absolute democratization of the process. Freedom unrestrained by rules, boundaries, discipline is merely anarchy. Freedom of the press that lowers its standards, on the one hand, and abolishes them altogether, on the other, disparages the very term.

The Internet, originally designed to survive even nuclear war, has produced a democratization of journalism that can never be entirely reversed. We have been propelled into an era of "fake news" and "alternative facts." Although the media have surely changed over the past fifty years, the antidote to lies and propaganda has not.

Facts.

World Order and the American Constitutional Order

★ ★ ★

PHILIP BOBBITT

W orld order is on many people's minds these days, perhaps because it seems to be coming apart. For the first
time since World War II—that is, since the founding of the
institutions of the current world order—a European state has
invaded another state and annexed its territory. Yet another
state has admitted to deceiving its treaty partners by developing
nuclear weapons and testing them in defiance of UN Security
Council resolutions. A leading state has defected from the European Union, and there are secessionist movements in several

Philip Bobbitt is the Herbert Wechsler Professor of Federal Jurisprudence and
director of the Center for National Security at Columbia Law School.

other member states. The American president has renounced a crucial climate-change treaty negotiated by his predecessor and accused some of the country's closest allies of exploiting their alliance relationships with the United States.

I believe we cannot understand what is going wrong in the international order without first understanding what is going wrong in America. Moreover, I believe that if we can success-fully address America's crisis, we will be able to cope with the threatening dissolution of the world order. So let me begin at home.

Have you ever asked yourself why the Americans were the first people to have a written constitution? Every society has a constitution and many societies in the late eighteenth century—clubs, religious orders, merchant corporations, households and their domestics, bankers and their clients—had written sets of rules meant to govern their behavior. But not states. The reason the United States wrote down its constitution was because the Americans had put the state under law. As long as the state was sovereign, there was no point in writing down rules to govern it—the state could always simply amend those rules. But the US Constitution reflects the idea that the state is a limited sover-eign: there are certain inalienable powers that are reserved to the people and cannot be vested in the state.

The liberal consensus in America around property rights, so-cial mobility, individual freedom, and popular democracy arose from shared commitments to the decisive role of the conscience in determining the individual's fate, a role that is incompatible with insecure property rights and promises, rigid class bound-aries that are inherited, coercive rules that suppress individual expression, and the derivation of legitimate governmental authority from constitutional processes that privilege the few while denying equality before the law to the many.

What we are conserving when we enforce the provisions of the Constitution is the American constitutional ethos—the liberal ethos of tolerance, social mobility based on merit and effort, a pluralist society with power based on consent. This ethos is given republican form by the system of federalism, checks and balances, and shared and linked powers, including an independent judiciary.

But the American constitutional ethos has lately been under attack both for its internal and external history. That attack will be familiar. It denies that America's values, political system, and history are really worthy of admiration. Although conceding that the United States possesses certain unique qualities—from high levels of religiosity to a political culture that privileges the individual conscience—this critique asserts that American action abroad has nothing to do with this ethos and has been determined primarily by power and the competitive nature of international politics. Let me give some of the historical examples marshaled by these critics.

The United States has been one of the most expansionist powers in modern history, spreading across the North American continent, seizing territory from Mexico and the Native American population, which it eliminated with a genocidal campaign. The conquest of the Philippines at the end of the nineteenth century killed some 200,000–400,000 Filipinos, most of them civilians, and the United States and its allies killed another 300,000 Germans and 330,000 Japanese civilians through a deliberate campaign of bombing enemy cities. The United States dropped more than 6 million tons of bombs during the Indochina war and should be held responsible for the roughly 1 million civilians who died in that conflict. More recently the US-backed Contras in Nicaragua killed some 30,000 Nicaraguans. US military action has led directly or indirectly to the deaths of 250,000 Muslims over the past three decades, not counting the deaths resulting from the sanctions against Iraq in the 1990s and including the more than 100,000 people who died following the invasion of Iraq in 2003. US drones and Special Forces, seeking to destroy terrorists in at least five countries, have killed an unknown number of innocent civilians in the process.

One way of answering this indictment is to imagine what the international order would be like if the United States had never come into being in the first place.

It is true that by purchasing the Louisiana Territory, by fighting countless wars against the native population, and by spreading the American political culture westward, the United States created the empire of its island continent. But would that continent have fared better if Texas had remained under the dictator Santa Anna? Or if the bucolic but ruthless cultures of the Native American tribes had fought their own internecine campaigns of ethnic cleansing against each other as they had done for centuries before the European colonists came? The strategic bombing campaign against Germany and Japan played a crucial role in the defeat of those fascist dictatorships—dictatorships, it should be remembered, that declared war on the United States before American soldiers took the field. Would those wars have been won without American participation in those campaigns, which destroyed the German war machine and discredited Japanese fascism in the eyes of its own people? Is there a military strategist or historian alive who believes that the Soviet Union could have successfully resisted Germany without American aid, without a second front, without American strategic bombing? Of course the United States did not win the Cold War by itself; America's strategy was to build alliances to achieve victory. But rather than ask the critics who decried the US policy of containment at the time, why not ask the dissidents themselves in the states they liberated—do they believe that without the American presence in Germany the wall would have come crashing down?

One often hears of the clumsy US interventions in Central America or the Philippines, but shouldn't we also be reminded that the Americans liberated France and Italy? That it was the American bombing campaign against Japan that led to the liberation of China and Korea? The US occupation of Iraq was a fiasco, but would the world really be safer if Saddam Hussein and his psychopathic sons were still in power in Baghdad? Is it even conceivable that Iran would have agreed to cease production of nuclear weapons if Saddam were still in power and were to seek nuclear weapons, as his own scientists testified he would, at the earliest possible moment? US drones and Special Forces may inadvertently kill civilians, but more French civilians died in the invasion of Normandy than British and American forces. Aren't the number of civilian casualties dramatically reduced by the use of drones and Special Forces instead of high-altitude bombing—or would the countries that suffer from the predations of terrorists be better off if the United States ceased trying to cripple those malevolent networks?

The theory of American history that today seems to be on the march claims that the national narrative is born in original sin—three sins, actually: slavery, the theft of land from its owners, and genocide. In this telling, the United States has grown great through monstrous crimes. Americans can have no common morality; no common heroes; no common national anthem or song; no common etiquette where national symbols, like the American flag, are concerned, because to make common cause with these cultural artifacts is to consume the poison that has contaminated US history from the founding.

The original, unamended Constitution protected slavery. It was written within a particular worldview about the way of life that was shared by the European societies—and most others—that colonized the Americas. That worldview was patriarchal, racist, and imperialistic; we live with its consequences and, for some, even its ideology. What made the Constitution unique among modern states was not its patriarchy, racism, and imperialism but rather the decisive role it gives to law and, in constitutional law, to the individual conscience.

For the present purposes, the question is not whether American history is unblemished but whether that history would have been better in some other country's hands and what efforts the United States has made to overcome its negative legacies, because that overcoming is also part of the ethos I have been describing.

It hasn't been a good couple of years for the informal constitutional norms that support the American constitutional ethos. A president who vows to incarcerate his political opponents; who, as a candidate, refused to commit to accepting the verdict of the election; whose staff attempted to conspire with a hostile foreign power in cyber-burglaries and cyber-propaganda campaigns; and who encourages violence against the press embodies a troubling historical change. A president who asserts the power to pardon himself, who may have attempted to bribe the head of the FBI to shelve an investigation into his aides, who exhorts naval officers to commit themselves to partisan declarations, who demeans judges on the basis of their ethnicity, who invents and persists in telling the now proven lie that his predecessor was wiretapping him, who engages in a studied campaign to delegitimate the electoral process itself by falsely claiming that millions of votes have been stolen, and who uses the office of the presidency to enrich himself and his family strikes at constitutional norms that are not codified but dwell in the consciences of the men who have held that office.

Sometimes a pretty accurate view of one's vulnerabilities can be obtained by interrogating one's adversaries. Russia has clearly identified America's domestic division as the nation's international Achilles' heel. This is why Russian trolls set up the Blacktivist website pretending to be an affiliate of the Black Lives Matter movement; it's why Russia set up the secessionist and Islamophobic Heart of Texas Facebook accounts. It ought to be obvious that Vladimir Putin's regime has no interest per se in US domestic politics. Rather, the Kremlin sees that exacerbating the growing divisions in the American polity is a potent way of weakening America's role in leading and stabilizing the world order, an order that Russia would like to overturn.

Historically, the international order is forged by the most successful constitutional order existing at any one time. So it was with the Peace of Augsberg in 1555, the treaties at Westphalia in 1648, the Treaty of Utrecht in 1713, the Congress of Vienna in 1815, the Versailles and the San Francisco conferences, and the Charter of Paris in 1990.

That means the United States—the architect of the Charter of Paris that ended the Cold War—has a special responsibility to nurture the liberal tradition that has animated two kinds of constitutional orders envisioned for the nation, the liberal-imperial republic sought by Madison and Hamilton and the liberal-industrial democracy of Lincoln. The Declaration of Independence undergirds those orders, and I hope it will do so for any constitutional order in America's future. The most vulnerable link in the national strategy is America's confidence in its institutions, its heritage, and its goals. That is, a sense of purpose and the belief that the United States can and will do the right thing because—not in every case and every time—America has done so when it led in the past. Had the nation not lived—had the American state not developed as it has—the world would have been poorer, less free, and above all less hopeful. If America permits its current self-doubts to overwhelm its self-confidence, that fate may lie ahead.

Revitalizing the Freedom
of Religion

★ ★ ★

JONATHAN SACKS

Religious liberty was born in the seventeenth century during a turbulent era that resonates with our unsettled age. Then, as now, there had been a revolution in information technology: in our time, the Internet and instantaneous global communication; at that time, the proliferation of printing in Europe after the fifteenth-century breakthroughs by Johannes Gutenberg in Germany and William Caxton in England.

These technological revolutions set in motion vast changes, not just economic and political, but also cultural and intellectual.

Rabbi Lord Jonathan Sacks, recipient of the 2016 Templeton Prize, is the former chief rabbi of the United Hebrew Congregations of the Commonwealth. He is the author, most recently, of *Not in God's Name: Confronting Religious Violence*.

Then, as now, they provided the means of protest against the established powers, seen as corrupt, exploitative, and unjust. Then, as now, the protests sometimes took religious form: in the seventeenth century, with Martin Luther, John Calvin, and the Reformation; today, in the guise of al Qaeda, the Islamic State, or ISIS, and their allies, along with radicalized and politicized groups in other faiths, such as Hindu nationalists in India and Buddhist nationalists in Myanmar, in what political philosopher Michael Walzer has called a series of "religious counterrevolutions" in the Middle East and parts of Asia and Africa.

In both cases the new technology meant that movements that would otherwise have remained small and marginal were instead able to outflank existing power structures and shape the mood of a new age. The ideas expressed by Luther had been anticipated two centuries earlier by John Wycliffe in Oxford, but in the absence of printing, Wycliffe's influence was limited. By 1517, when Luther nailed his ninety-five theses to the door of All Saints' Church in Wittenberg, printing presses were able to flood Europe with his pamphlets by the hundreds of thousands. The sort of influence the Reformation achieved through the printed word, radical religious groups in our time are attempting to achieve by the Internet, social media, and other forms of electronic communication.

Luther's revolt touched off more than a century of instability and wars of religion, brought to an end only by the treaties of Westphalia in 1648. Today, in many parts of the world, wars of religion between faiths and sometimes within faiths are having the same effect. It was precisely in that earlier age, in 1651, that Thomas Hobbes described societal breakdown as "a war of every man against every man," in which there was "continual fear, and danger of violent death; and the life of man solitary, poor, nasty, brutish, and short." That is the situation in several failed or failing states today, and the ripples can be felt worldwide.

I have made this extended comparison not only because it is instructive in itself but also and especially because of that long-ago tumult's unexpected outcome. There were certainly those in the seventeenth century who feared that a new dark age was about to settle on the planet. But there were also those—most notably Hobbes, John Milton, John Locke, and Baruch Spinoza—who seized the moment and thought their way through to a new birth of freedom. Ideas were formulated regarding the social contract, the moral limits of power, the doctrine of toleration, and human rights. The era also envisioned the right to "liberty of conscience," or what today we call religious freedom.

More than a half century ago the Oxford philosopher John Plamenatz noted that, paradoxically, liberty of conscience as an idea came into being during one of the most intensely religious periods in European history. That age, he said, gave rise to fanaticism and persecution, but it was also the source of a new conception of freedom. "Liberty of conscience was born," he wrote in *Man and Society* in 1963, "not of indifference, not of skepticism, not of mere open-mindedness, but of faith." It came about through one simple move: from the idea that faith is supremely important, therefore everyone should have the one true faith, to the idea that faith is supremely important, therefore everyone should have the freedom to live in accord with the faith that he or she believes to be true.

That is how the concept of religious freedom arose in the aftermath of religiously inspired violence and war. It is how religious freedom could be reborn in our troubled time. No momentous change of heart by religious devotees is required, only historical circumstance and simple reflection.

Any period of prolonged religious conflict can be ended in one of three ways. The first is that the victorious party imposes its view on opponents, ruthlessly suppressing their rights if they persist in their views. That was the norm before the seventeenth century, and it remains true in totalitarian states today.

The second is to say, A plague on both your houses. Because religion is a source of conflict, let us ban it altogether, at least in public. If people must worship, let them do so in the privacy of their homes or places of worship but nowhere else. That was the view of Voltaire and the French revolutionaries: *ecrasez l'infame*, "crush the infamy." The first solution denies liberty to all but one religion, while the second denies it to all.

By contrast, the third view says, Today, our side holds power—we can impose our views on our opponents—but tomorrow they may hold power, and they may do to us what we did to them. Under those circumstances we would not be free to practice our religion, and that is an outcome we wish to avoid at all costs. Let us grant religious liberty to all who are willing to undertake to keep the civic peace. We will guarantee to our opponents the freedom to practice their faith, so long as they are loyal to the state and to the freedoms it secures.

"Liberty of conscience" secured the peace by guaranteeing religious freedom to all faiths regardless of who was in power. It emerged from prolonged, vivid, firsthand experience of religion's power to divide societies, to fuel violence, and to justify unspeakable brutality on the grounds that it was committed for the greater glory of God.

For many believers, religion is their most fundamental way of orienting themselves in the world. It forms their identity, their way of understanding their place in the universe, their mode of life, their memories and aspirations, their reference group and their loyalties. Hobbes predicated his version of the social contract on people's fear of death. The equation simply does not work for those of extreme faith who regard their religion as more important than life itself and who are willing to die as martyrs for the cause. That is why religion is so potent and why, throughout history, it has been exploited by rulers in pursuit of power.

We tend to forget this in societies that social psychologist Jonathan Haidt has described as WEIRD—Western, educated, industrialized, rich, and democratic. We inhabit a cultural environment shaped by four centuries of ever-deepening secularization. From the eighteenth century onward, "enlightened" observers have formulated a series of narratives about religion; each of them made sense for a while, but now all have lost plausibility.

One storyline said that religion in the West was dying—secularization was inevitable and irreversible.

Another: every society that sought to modernize would do so the Western way. Hence the secular-nationalist regimes that appeared, in the course of the twentieth century, in the Middle East, Africa, and Asia.

A third view: any religiosity that persisted in the modern world would do so in the post-Reformation way, as private creeds and voluntary associations.

Or this one: religions that wanted to survive would have to become accommodationist—that is, they would accept the prevailing secular consensus and adapt.

The shortest-lived narrative was the "end of history" thesis, that with the collapse of the Soviet Union and the end of the Cold War, market economics and liberal-democratic politics would slowly and peacefully conquer the world. People would be too engrossed in consumerism to fight for, let alone die for, any ideology, religious or secular.

Each of these narratives discounted religion as a significant factor in national or international politics. Yet shortly after the "end of history," Yugoslavia descended into ethnic wars involving groups that had coexisted for years, splitting apart essentially on religious lines, among Muslims, Catholics, and Orthodox Christians. In Iran in 1989 (the year the Berlin Wall fell), Ayatollah Khomeini delivered his fatwa against Salman Rushdie, declaring the novelist's *The Satanic Verses* blasphemous. Al Qaeda terrorists launched their first attack on the World Trade Center in New York City with a massive truck bomb in 1993.

The liberal-democratic West was blindsided. Religion could not be discounted after all. Today it is fair to say that not just religious freedom but freedom itself is at risk to a degree not seen since the 1930s. According to Freedom House's 2017 report, liberty as measured by key indexes suffered its eleventh consecutive annual decline, with the Middle East and Eurasia the worst offenders. Even in democratic nations, including the United States and in Europe, populism and nationalism—and the menace they pose to liberty—have risen to the highest levels in many decades.

Religious freedom, enshrined as Article 18 in the UN Universal Declaration of Human Rights, has suffered drastically. Since the rise of radical Islamist groups, Christians have been systematically persecuted throughout the Middle East and parts of Asia. During the Islamic State's two-year occupation of Mosul, Iraq's second-largest city, Christians were kidnapped, tortured, crucified, and beheaded. In northern Iraq, ISIS prosecuted genocidal attacks on the Yazidis, members of an ancient sectarian group. Egypt's Coptic Christian community has been subjected to regular terrorist attacks often targeting people at prayer.

In Nigeria in recent years, the Islamist terror group Boko Haram has captured Christian children and sold them as slaves. Christian men in the town of Madagali were beheaded, and Christian women forcibly converted to Islam and given to terrorists as "wives." Nor has Boko Haram limited itself to persecuting Christians. It has also targeted the Muslim establishment in Nigeria and is suspected of perpetrating the 2014 attack on the Grand Mosque in Kano, when suicide bombers and gunmen killed more than one hundred worshipers.

Sectarian religious violence in the Central African Republic destroyed nearly all the nation's more than four hundred mosques, according to a 2015 report to the United Nations. In Myanmar in 2017, hundreds of thousands of Rohingya Muslims and Kachin Christians were driven out of the predominantly Buddhist country by rampaging government forces. Some of the worst religion-fueled crimes against humanity have taken place in Syria, where 6.5 million people are internally displaced and 3.3 million have become refugees elsewhere.

"The state of affairs for international religious freedom is worsening in both the depth and breadth of violations," said the US Commission on International Religious Freedom in its 2017 annual report. "The blatant assaults have become so frightening—attempted genocide, the slaughter of innocents, and wholesale destruction of places of worship—that the less egregious abuses go unnoticed or at least unappreciated. Many observers have become numb to violations of the right to freedom of thought, conscience and religion."

Nor are these the only concerns. Even in the liberal-democratic West, persistent terrorist attacks have shown that, in a global age, conflict anywhere can lead to terror everywhere. And, in recent years, many Western nations have also witnessed a rise in homegrown anti-Semitism. Then there is a perceived threat of a different type: a highly aggressive secularism, combined with a hyper-individualized consumerist culture, is regarded by many religious believers, including Catholics, evangelical Christians, and Orthodox Jews, as endangering their own religious freedom and integrity.

These are, in short, troubled times. The West faces deep threats to freedom. Yet, as I have suggested, this should also be our deepest source of hope. For even amid the strife of the seventeenth century, in the midst of devastating, religiously motivated conflicts, great thinkers—some of them deeply if unconventionally religious—discovered that the path to liberty included religious freedom.

A technological revolution that had roiled Europe also provided the means for these thinkers to spread their message of hope and freedom. We need a similarly inspired technological adaptation today: just as religious freedom's enemies exploit the Internet and social media, so too should those who champion liberty tell the world untiringly about the blessings of religious freedom. When religion becomes political in the pursuit of power, it leads people to kill in the name of the God of life, to wage war in the name of the God of peace, to practice cruelty in the name of the God of compassion, and to hate in the name of the God of love. That is not faith but sacrilege. Faith lives in freedom, and freedom now needs its own defense of faith.

International Linchpins
of Stability

★ ★ ★

JOSÉ MARÍA AZNAR

On June 4, 1940, Winston Churchill delivered his "we shall fight them on the beaches" speech to the House of Commons. Even if invaded by Nazi Germany, the prime minister said, Britain would hold out until "the New World, with all its power and might, steps forth to the rescue and the liberation of the old."

The United States did step forth to save Europe. The liberation of the Old World was the result of a transatlantic alliance— cooperation between the United States and Europe that formed the heart of what became known as the West. Such cooperation also facilitated the rebuilding of war-ravaged Europe, created the multilateral infrastructure that nurtured unprecedented

José María Aznar is the former president of the Spanish government.

global prosperity, and established the military infrastructure, through the North Atlantic Treaty Organization, that deterred the Soviet Union.

This alliance of the United States and Europe spawned an entire network of global and regional institutions that were fundamental to peace and progress in the second half of the twentieth century. The institutions included the United Nations; the International Monetary Fund; the International Bank for Reconstruction and Development (now called the World Bank); the General Agreement on Tariffs and Trade, or GATT, which was expanded and institutionalized into the World Trade Organization in 1995; the Organization for European Economic Cooperation (a.k.a. the Marshall Plan); the Treaty on the Non-Proliferation of Nuclear Weapons; and the Partnership for Peace, which brought former members of the Communist Warsaw Pact into the Western fold.

These institutions were able to bring extraordinary blessings to hundreds of millions of people worldwide for two reasons. The first: like never before in history, the institutions encouraged globalized cooperation in matters that can overwhelm individual nations. The traditional tools of statecraft are often useless when a country faces challenges such as currency crashes, multinational trade disputes, international crime, weapons of mass destruction, natural disasters, terrorism, the threat of pandemics, or ethnic slaughter. The other reason why these global institutions created by the transatlantic alliance were so effective: they established a legal and legitimizing basis for the liberal world order.

The first half of the twentieth century was a disaster—two horrendous world wars bookending a global economic calamity. The second half was so much better almost exclusively because of the benefits that flowed from the establishment of an alliance between the democracies of North America and Europe. But, since the end of the Cold War, a central question has loomed: Can this alliance continue to exist in a strategically meaningful way? Anyone who recognizes how the world has gained from the alliance—the millions of people lifted from poverty, the lives saved, the dreams realized—should hope that the United States and Europe will remain compatible and capable of renewing this relationship, acting together to guide the geopolitics of the twenty-first century and to help steer the world from chaos.

Yet today this American-led Western order is under attack, from the outside and from the inside. The enemies of the liberal-democratic and transatlantic order can be broken down into three major categories:

- Illiberal forces that have been reinforced in recent years by fallout from the 2008 financial crisis. Populist voices have risen against our economic system, which is built upon free markets, limited state presence, individual innovation, and risk-taking. Under the guise of championing the downtrodden, populists inevitably pursue an agenda of higher state intervention, more public authority, and less individual freedom.
- National powers that think the distribution of power in the world does not favor them, which they regard as an insult to their status or as an impediment to their ambitions. These nations would like to be perceived as more important than they are today, and treated accordingly. They are working to achieve that goal by trying to impose themselves upon the world, picking fights over individual issues or undermining

the policies of those they consider rivals. I'm thinking primarily of Russia and China, but I won't exclude emerging nations like Brazil or Venezuela.

- Revolutionary forces, state or stateless, that would like to bring about a systemic change, a completely new international system. We can include here nations like Iran, with the ayatollah's nuclear ambitions, and the global jihad led or inspired by groups like the Islamic State and al Qaeda.

The good news is that these forces are different both in nature and in scope, and are unrelated in the majority of cases. The bad news is that their individual effects tend to be cumulative. This growing menace makes the transatlantic alliance more essential than ever, albeit in a new form. There is nothing, absolutely nothing, intrinsic to these threats that would lead me to believe that they cannot be overcome. On the contrary, I believe we have all the necessary tools at hand to defeat these enemies.

What is required? American leadership, a stronger Europe, and a common vision. Make no mistake, the world as we know it was largely shaped and sustained by liberal and democratic ideals. Essentially, these are American ideals. From the crucible of World War II, the United States emerged as the defining force in the international arena ideologically, economically, scientifically, strategically, and culturally. Unfortunately, we see nothing of the sort nowadays. What do we see instead? An internationally unpredictable American president, a Europe that is unable to overcome its many problems, and an eroding transatlantic link.

President Trump has promised a foreign policy that is nationalist and transactional, focused on securing narrow material gains for the United States. He has enunciated no broader vision of America's traditional role as defender of the free world.

The Continent's geopolitical order has been shaken both by Britain's decision to leave the European Union and by Donald Trump's election. These startling votes in two of the world's most open and market-oriented economies suggested dissatisfaction with globalization and economic integration. Both occurred in a period of high uncertainty and anxiety for European governments. The EU is at a crucial moment; it no longer suffers just a "crisis of growth" but a risk of destruction. Britain is leaving, and other EU countries, depending on the outcome of their own elections, threaten to follow—adding to the EU's burdens from terror attacks, the handling of the refugee crisis, and the American president's unpredictability.

It is true that Europe is a miracle of this evolution. Europeans went from killing each other by the tens of millions to rejecting the use of force under almost any circumstances. The ensuing decades of peace produced a culture of seemingly endless prosperity. With the creation of the European Union, many countries surrendered their currencies, believing in the euro. Unfortunately, Europe's material gains have not been matched by an increased sense of responsibility to manage the world. Under present circumstances, European nations are actually *less* likely to seek a major role in the international arena.

And that's why American leadership is as vitally important today as it was decades ago, when the post–World War II order was established.

If the United States were exhausted from fighting too long in too many places; if the United States were tired of fighting irregular wars or irregular enemies where victory is an elusive concept; if the United States were moving to an increasingly less engaged or less exposed posture in the world, rediscovering containment and strategic isolationism, then it would be understandable. But it would be a mistake.

Nobody is able to take America's place today, and probably nobody will for a long time. Those who defend the virtues of a multipolar world where the United States is just another regular country will soon find themselves in a nonpolar universe, spinning out of control. Besides, a more economically protectionist America will endanger any short-term recovery of the world economy—and give new impetus to the anti-capitalist axis connecting Beijing, Tehran, and Caracas.

We can limit some of the more dangerous risks, if not all of them. But we must have a clear vision of what is needed. I'll call it the Western World 2.0. The principal pillar of this Western World 2.0 would still have to be the transatlantic alliance.

The first step in that direction would be to reinvigorate the institutions that have been the cornerstone of the Atlantic world. Start with NATO. Some major changes must be introduced. Several years ago I proposed in a report called *NATO: An Alliance for Freedom* that the allies should develop a transatlantic homeland security component to fight jihadist terrorism. I also urged that NATO open its doors to those democratic countries, such as Japan and Israel, that were willing to contribute to the collective security. I still think measures like those—unlike President Trump's inconsistent remarks about the alliance—are the best way to ensure NATO's effectiveness in the twenty-first century.

Similarly, the transatlantic alliance must transform itself into something bigger. The Western world cannot be defined anymore as a geographical concept but must be reconceptualized as a community of shared values and joint actions. Strengthening ties with nations like India, Colombia, and Chile is paramount.

This community of shared values must also work hard to restore confidence in the economic system that has served liberal democracy so well. Without economic freedom, sustainable growth is impossible—and our societies depend on growth. I would like to renew the principles that have inspired our achievements of the past. And I would like to avoid repeating the mistakes of the past that unnecessarily prolonged previous crises. I do not believe that the best formula for solving a crisis of private indebtedness is raising the level of public indebtedness. Fighting economic turmoil with policies rooted in increased government spending, swelling deficits, and huge amounts of public debt is a serious mistake.

The twenty-first-century world does not need more socialism, nationalism, populism, or any other "-ism"; we had enough of them in the twentieth century, and we know how they turned out.

We in the transatlantic alliance should be proud of its achievements—and hold firm to a belief in its capacity to be a force for good in the world. The defense of the alliance's ideals cannot be a timid enterprise. People around this increasingly confusing world are waiting for answers. And the only valid answers are ours. From economics to education, from justice to culture, we hold the banner of progress, freedom, and security.

The transatlantic alliance is more than the sum of its parts, and it must remain so.

The University's Covenant
with Liberal Democracy

★ ★ ★

RONALD DANIELS

The strength and vibrancy of a country's democracy depend on the soundness of its institutions. Pride of place
and public attention are most often given to political and legal
institutions for advancing the competitive politics and rule of
law that are the signature of thriving democracy, and deservedly
so. But the university also plays a critical role, standing firmly
among the entities that are indispensable to securing the full
promise of liberal democracy and sharing in the responsibility—
and culpability—when liberal democracy itself is perceived to
be under siege.

Ronald Daniels is the president of Johns Hopkins University.

Few other social institutions rival the university in its capacity for independent truth seeking, knowledge creation, and the broad cultivation of an informed, engaged citizenry. If liberal democracy is the political manifestation of the Enlightenment's embrace of reason, fact, and truth as the basis for decision making, then the university is essential for holding those in power to account. Through its educative and research efforts, the university ensures not only that its students are prepared for citizenship but also that a nation's political and social structures operate on the basis of informed debate and reason, not passion and prejudice.

Higher education's link to liberal democracy draws support from empirical studies showing that democratic nations with higher levels of education historically are more likely to endure as democracies, and dictatorships with higher levels of education are more likely to transition to democracies, as Edward L. Glaeser, Giacomo A. M. Ponzetto, and Adrei Shleifer reported in "Why Does Democracy Need Education?" for the *Journal of Economic Growth* in 2007. But history is not destiny, and when liberal democracy is seen as vulnerable, as it is today, the university should expect scrutiny.

American universities have been subject to mounting criticism over the past decade, but the intensity of that criticism increased dramatically following the 2016 national election. Mark Lilla's lament (from the left) for the decline of the American university and its perceived submission to rampant identity politics is illustrative: "Relentless speech surveillance, the protection of virgin ears, the inflation of venial sins into mortal ones, the banning of preachers of unclean ideas—all these campus identity follies have their precedent in American revivalist religion," Lilla wrote in his 2017 book *The Once and Future Liberal*.

Andrew Sullivan (from the right) was similarly caustic in "We All Live on Campus Now" for *New York* magazine in February 2018: "When elite universities shift their entire worldview away from liberal education as we have long known it toward the imperatives of an identity-based 'social justice' movement, the broader culture is in danger of drifting away from liberal democracy as well." Sullivan added that "if you wonder why our discourse is now so freighted with fear, why so many choose silence as the path of least resistance, or why the core concepts of a liberal society—the individual's uniqueness, the primacy of reason, the protection of due process, an objective truth—are so besieged, this is one of the reasons."

The charge that the American university has been derelict in nourishing liberal democracy's promise is by no means novel. In the 1950s, the Red Scare placed higher education in the crosshairs, as a "National Council for American Education" pressed successfully for the purge of communists and socialists from the faculty ranks. The late 1960s and early 1970s saw education on many college campuses take a back seat to protest and violence. The 1980s and 1990s were marked by a critique of the academy from both ends of the spectrum, with the right focused on the perils of faculty and student radicalism, catalyzed by Allan Bloom's charge in *The Closing of the American Mind* (1987) that higher education has "failed democracy," and the left calling out the failure of the university to recruit traditionally underrepresented groups such as African Americans and Hispanics to student and faculty ranks. And the 2000s saw the emergence of sharp attacks on the expense, value, and pedagogy of higher education, with sharp cuts in public funding that are still being felt to this day.

With the benefit of hindsight, these admonitions that the university had lost its capacity to serve American democracy seem overwrought. But can we assume that the passage of time will restore perspective and confidence in institutions of higher education? Do universities even fully understand the reasons for the current backlash against them in the United States and elsewhere? Do the anxieties about higher education's role take on an added urgency amid worries about the health of liberal democracy itself?

At one level, of course, the broader currents of populism and suspicion of elites that are buffeting American society cannot help but reach the university; the rising polarization that now defines US politics is reflected in the public's view of higher education. A 2017 Pew Research Center survey revealed a yawning chasm between Democratic and Republican views about the role and contributions of American universities to the public good: 72 percent of Democrats versus 36 percent of Republicans believe that universities have a positive effect on the country. Even more striking is how rapidly Republican sentiment against universities shifted during the 2016 national election: as recently as September 2015, Pew reported, a majority of Republicans believed that universities have a positive effect. The velocity of this change says much about the capacity of political populism to stir the polity against civic institutions.

But attributing all the contemporary anxieties about the university's role in liberal democracy to a surge in populist sentiment is too easy, and it would absolve universities of responsibility to discharge the duties they uniquely carry.

One can trace no small part of the rising antipathy toward universities to the considerable media attention that has been focused on a cavalcade of free-speech incidents occurring on American campuses over the past several years. From the disinviting of commencement speakers to the suppressing of events featuring controversial speakers, these episodes stirred an intense public reaction. Some used them to decry the lack of political balance in the academy, but the more searing critique was aimed squarely at higher education's mission itself: If universities are dedicated to the creation of knowledge, the protection of truth, and the exploration of unpopular or renegade ideas, how could such censorious institutional actions be justified?

Despite equivocation by some universities, many have moved to reaffirm their commitment to free-speech ideals, shoring up their communities' understanding of why free speech matters, not least because it is essential to academic freedom and the broader role of the university in truth seeking. Yet there are many other dimensions to the discussion of speech in higher education—among them the ideological diversity of faculty (or lack thereof) and the decline of debates on campuses—that demand the same examination that the more conspicuous controversies involving speakers and protests have drawn. There will be challenges and even stumbles ahead, but universities are stronger for the recent scrutiny and criticism.

A separate but gnawing worry about higher education involves the reliability of science and research. Across several fields in recent years, scholars have been unable to replicate many foundational academic studies. After surveying 1,576 researchers online, *Nature* in May 2016 reported, "More than 70% of researchers have tried and failed to reproduce another scientist's experiments, and more than half have failed to reproduce their own experiments." A majority said there is a "significant crisis" of reproducibility. This is a problem for science, to be sure. But as these concerns spill into the public square, they also present a challenge for democratic ideals, contributing to an erosion of faith in facts and a growing mistrust of institutions and expertise on which democracy rests. Science by definition is, on some level, provisional and probabilistic—it assumes that new findings will refine and even displace our understanding of the world over time. But where objective fact is perceived as contestable, and fundamental science as discardable, people can far more easily retreat into misinformed opinion and disengage from shared discourse. Unless universities take seriously this concern, they risk losing their standing as bulwarks of science and reason.

Higher education's role as a liberal-democratic cornerstone is also endangered by the perception that the university is losing its power as a vehicle for economic and social mobility and for equality of opportunity. The university's capacity to enhance its students' income, socioeconomic mobility, health, and political participation—compared with those who do not earn a university degree—is significant and well established. To the extent that the university confers these benefits on the basis of talent, it honors and embodies the liberal ideal of equal opportunity, and, to the extent that the university indulges other bases of eligibility—such as wealth, privilege, or bias—it fails these same ideals. Economist Raj Chetty's recent work dramatically underscores the magnitude of universities' failure to dull the advantages of inherited privilege and wealth in determining access: elite universities, he found, have more students from the top 1 percent than the bottom 50 percent of the income distribution.

Over the past decade, universities have leaned into the work—both independently and collectively—of addressing the glaring disparities in socioeconomic participation that sap moral and political capital from their institutions. If universities intend to honor in words and in deed the ideal of equal opportunity for students of equal merit, they will need to take seriously the dramatic overrepresentation of students from high-income and legacy families. Of course, the frailties in liberal democracies' fidelity to these essential principles of equal opportunity extend beyond income and wealth to issues of race and gender and other underrepresented populations. It is certainly no accident that these issues have flared on our campuses at the same time as on the national stage; the critical task for universities is to work past many of the inflammatory debates and do the difficult work of building a pipeline of scholars and citizens that reflects the true diversity of the American intellectual experience.

Even as universities endeavor to make progress against these myriad challenges, there remains the largely unspoken need to connect the university's bedrock role in liberal democracy to its educative responsibilities. Amy Gutmann articulated this point in *Democratic Education* (1999): "Learning how to think carefully and critically about political problems, to articulate one's views and defend them before people with whom one disagrees is a form of moral education to which young adults are more receptive and for which universities are well suited." In the context of mounting disenchantment with the institutions of liberal democracy—particularly among young people who are expressing increased openness to authoritarian forms of government—is the university actively fostering students' understanding of and commitment to democracy's essential institutions? Does the university leave its students with an appreciation not only for the history of the American democratic model—the ideas that animated the founders and the complex institutions they devised—but also for the mechanics and pathways of contemporary civic engagement?

Few universities designate what constitutes an expanding core of critical knowledge, skills, and aptitudes that every student should possess to meet a democratic society's expectations of what it means to be an engaged and informed citizen. Even so, at other moments of stress for American democracy—in the nation's earliest days and in the aftermath of World War II—deliberate efforts were undertaken to establish a curriculum in defense of civic education and democratic engagement. The precariousness of the current political moment in the United States and abroad commands an urgent, unapologetic revival of previous efforts to equip students with a broad understanding of this experiment and the skills necessary to safeguard its success. Research into how universities can perform this role most effectively is also needed.

These are the fault lines now running through higher education's covenant with liberal democracy. If we in the university are to discharge faithfully our duties as an anchor of liberal democracy, we will need to reclaim our standing as an institution rich in dialogue and a diversity of ideas, reinforce our role as a stronghold for scientific reason and truth, make ourselves truly a place of equal opportunity rather than systemic advantage, and ensure we are doing all we can to foster our students' understanding of and commitment to institutions of democracy.

To address some of these concerns, the university will be able to draw on a literature and body of research that has formed over the years. Addressing others will require launching a conversation in earnest on our campuses about the precise nature of the problem and the optimal solutions. But the duty of the academy to democracy has never been more vital. To the extent that higher education has faltered in that duty in recent years, vigilance and dedication is needed—for the sake not only of the university but also for the liberal-democratic ideals it fosters.

Robust Speech, Robust Democracy

★ ★ ★

NANCY GERTNER

The First Amendment is at once an enormously powerful tool in promoting and sustaining liberal democracy, and at the same time a limited one. Its power has contributed to the robustness of American democracy for more than two centuries. Its limits are on display today in an unregulated social media controlled by private actors and when government officials, sidestepping First Amendment prohibitions, undermine speech indirectly. Still, without the First Amendment as a backstop America would be dramatically—*dramatically*—worse off, as seen in countries such as Hungary, Poland, and Turkey, where free speech is under attack and democracy is in retreat.

Nancy Gertner is a retired US district court judge and a senior lecturer in law at Harvard University.

The First Amendment's language is deceptively simple: "Congress shall make no law...abridging the freedom of speech, or of the press." Although the wording refers only to "Congress," the Supreme Court has made it clear that the First Amendment protects against incursions on speech from the government at all levels (federal, state, and local) and all branches (legislative, executive, and judicial). The amendment protects the nation as much from the tyrant, operating through the executive branch, as from democratic majorities, operating through legislatures. It keeps the government from being the arbiter of what the public should see or hear, precluding regulations that are based on content, whether the speech is criticizing an errant president, opposing abortion, or shouting ethnic slurs.

The amendment's role in promoting democracy could not be clearer. It is central to the principle of constitutional self-government. The tyrant doesn't have to consult anyone; under an authoritarian regime, the governed are expected to be passive. But self-government requires an active and engaged public, exposed to diverse ideas and information, so that citizens can participate in political decision making. The legal scholar Geoffrey R. Stone goes even further, suggesting that free speech is vital to promote the "character traits that are essential to a well-functioning democracy, including tolerance, skepticism, personal responsibility, curiosity, distrust of authority, and independence of mind." In 1963, legal theorist Thomas I. Emerson's *Toward a General Theory of the First Amendment* tied free speech to a democratic government's very legitimacy; when opposing views are suppressed, the cohesiveness of the society is undermined. Timothy Garton Ash, speaking in Hungary at

Central European University in 2017, underscored free speech's centrality in modern multicultural societies: "How can I know what it is like to be a Muslim, a Roma, a Kurd, a lesbian or a conservative Catholic, if we have not been able to explain it to each other?" The robustness of free speech may well be an important measure of the health and resilience of a liberal democracy.

But the First Amendment has its limits. As is typical of the Bill of Rights, its simple admonishments do not enforce themselves. They must be interpreted by an independent judiciary, often under extraordinary political pressures. Even in the United States, free-speech jurisprudence evolved across nearly 150 years. In 1789, for example, only seven years after the Bill of Rights became part of the Constitution, Congress passed the Alien and Sedition Act—laws that were never declared unconstitutional by the Supreme Court; they simply expired without renewal. The Alien Act gave the president the power to deport "all such aliens as he shall judge dangerous to the peace and safety of the United States." The Sedition Act provided for fines and imprisonment for "any person [who] shall write, print, utter or publish... any false scandalous and malicious writing or writings against the government of the United States or either house of the Congress of the U.S. or the President of the U.S. with intent to defame... or to bring either of them into contempt or disrepute."

During World War I, the Supreme Court held that speech condemning the military draft or praising anarchism could be punished; 2,000 people were imprisoned for their opposition to the war. It was not until the 1920s that the Supreme Court began to carve out meaningful First Amendment protections. In a concurring opinion that did not become the court's rationale until later cases, Justice Louis Brandeis wrote that the founders believed "that the greatest menace to freedom is an inert people; that public discussion is a political duty; and that this should be a fundamental principle of the American government."

Over the decades that followed, American courts gradually defined and strengthened speech rights. In 1931, for instance, the Supreme Court in *Near v. Minnesota* interpreted the First Amendment and Fourteenth Amendment to ban prior restraints on press publication, invalidating a Minnesota statute that permitted some officials or private citizens to sue to stop publication of a "malicious, scandalous and defamatory newspaper" unless the publisher proved that it was "published with good motives and for justifiable ends." During the 1960s, the Supreme Court made its commitment to speech even clearer, ruling that students wearing black armbands to protest the Vietnam War were protected by the First Amendment (*Tinker v. Des Moines*), as was speech advocating violence at a Ku Klux Klan rally, because the speech did not "incite to imminent lawless action" (*Brandenburg v. Ohio*).

That progress on speech rights now faces a significant challenge from President Trump, who risks undermining the First Amendment simply by undermining its judicial enforcers. He has threatened to replace federal judges with those whose ideology he supports, no matter how unqualified. He has attacked the credibility of federal judges—not just the decisions themselves but the decision makers. The Federalist Society, whose recommendations Trump has accepted for judicial nominations, has proposed a major expansion of the federal judiciary to afford him the opportunity of "undoing the judicial legacy of President Barack Obama." During the presidential campaign, Trump attacked Judge Gonzalo Curiel, suggesting that he was biased in a lawsuit against Trump University because of his "Mexican heritage." Judge Curiel was born in Indiana. After Washington district court judge James Robart temporarily blocked Trump's travel ban, the president called him a "so-called judge."

Under this kind of pressure, will even life-tenured judges stand and strictly enforce the First Amendment against government incursions? Or will they behave like the pre–Civil War Northern judges who were antislavery but nonetheless enforced the Fugitive Slave Act with a rigor that was not required by law?

The First Amendment is also limited precisely because it is a negative right. It only addresses what the government may not do to curtail speech. It may not jail, fine, or legislate against people or organizations based on their speech. It does not affirmatively oblige the government to maximize speech, to make certain that well-financed speech does not drown out poorly financed speech. Look no further than the case *Citizens United v. FEC* in 2012, when the Supreme Court eroded any meaningful regulation of campaign financing in an attempt to level the political playing field. The court held not only that the First Amendment applied to corporations donating money to political candidates but also that any such regulation had to be justified by a compelling state interest—a very, very high bar. With *Citizens United*, wealthy individuals, like President Trump, and corporations have unlimited access to the political process; their speech, in effect, is louder than anyone else's.

Perhaps most significant of all in this digital age, the First Amendment does not apply to private actors—private universities or companies, not even Facebook or Google, no matter what their power in the modern world. On the surface, social media democratizes free expression. But while everyone can post, or tweet, better-financed voices—friend or foe—are in the best position to manipulate the discussion with false and divisive information. The US indictment in early 2018 of thirteen Russian nationals shows how stolen identities, fake accounts, and compromised VPNs can flood the Internet with false information, masking their real source. Referring to sites like Facebook, Eugene Kaspersky, CEO of the Russian IT security company Kaspersky Lab, was prescient in 2012 when he told *Wired* magazine: "Freedom is good. But the bad guys—they can abuse this freedom to manipulate public opinion."

Although there are regulations governing television, radio, and print advertising, there continues to be little oversight of digital media, a remarkable omission given their extraordinary scope. The media-tracking Borrell Associates reported that in the 2016 presidential election more than $1.4 billion was spent on online advertising, a 789 percent increase over the 2012 election. Efforts to pass legislation requiring that companies at least be transparent about who purchased political ads and for how much have thus far proved unavailing. And suggestions—made by former Trump adviser Steve Bannon, among others—that Facebook and Google be regulated as would any public utility have not gained traction.

Nor does the First Amendment offer protection against all the ways that free speech is weakened not by direct prohibitions of this or that content but rather indirectly by limiting access to public information that can enhance the public debate: rules about how government information is classified, by whom, for how long; open-meeting laws; Freedom of Information Act policies; regulations governing who has access to public events; and so on. Months after Trump's inauguration, his administration announced that it would no longer disclose routine visitor logs maintained by the Secret Service, logs that had been published online by the Obama administration since 2009. (The Trump policy was since reversed in part through litigation.) Even travel bans—restricting who may or may not enter the country—can operate to reduce diverse voices and dissident opinions in the political discussion.

And obviously free speech can be chilled not just by what a leader does through formal executive orders and policies but by what he says or, more important, threatens. President Trump, using social media to bypass mainstream channels, flings words and phrases such as "treason," "un-American," and "enemies of the American people" in attacks on politicians of the opposing party or even dissident voices within his own party, and on news organizations themselves. Unhappy with coverage of him by the *Washington Post*, Trump has launched an unsubtle campaign against Amazon, whose founder and CEO, Jeff Bezos, owns the newspaper. In a typical tweet, Trump said in July 2017, "Is Fake News Washington Post being used as a lobbyist weapon against Congress to keep Politicians from looking into Amazon no-tax monopoly?" The company, Trump suggested elsewhere, "has a huge antitrust problem." A few months later, the president announced his opposition to AT&T's proposed acquisition of Time Warner, all the while criticizing Time Warner's property, CNN, which he calls "fake news." Whether related to Trump's comments or not, the Justice Department's intervention in November 2017 to block the AT&T–Time Warner merger showed that a president's threats can risk a real-world impact on speech. No matter how robust the First Amendment doctrine, or how ringing the Supreme Court's endorsement of free speech, such threats are difficult to contain.

With all this taking place in a country that has a strong First Amendment tradition, one does not have to go far to imagine what it is like in countries that do not. There we see laws directly limiting speech that could not pass muster here, and the apparatus of the state used to imprison citizens and journalists and to shut newspapers. Free speech is under duress in many places, but let's consider the examples of Hungary, Turkey, and Poland.

The penal code in Hungary prohibits incitement to hate, incitement to violence, incitement against a community, all so broadly defined that anyone might be liable to prosecution. It bars the denial of crimes "committed by national socialist or communist systems." And it makes defamation a criminal offense. Under a 2013 amendment to the penal code, anyone who knowingly creates or distributes false or defamatory video or audio recordings can face a prison sentence of one to three years. Under Recep Tayyip Erdogan's increasingly autocratic regime, Turkey has reportedly imprisoned journalists and prosecuted editors of national newspapers who face life sentences for working "against the state." Ordinary citizens have been arrested for

Facebook posts criticizing the government. In Poland, the election of a conservative government in 2015 has been followed by a gradual erosion of speech rights. Most notably, Poland in February 2018 declared it a criminal offense to refer to the historical fact that some Poles abetted Nazi Germany in perpetrating the Holocaust.

Beyond overt efforts to criminalize speech, these countries are also trying to commandeer the courts, no doubt in part so that further speech controls will be easier to impose. The governments in Hungary and Poland have sought to change the procedures for the nomination of judges so that the party in power can select judges without any support from the opposition party and to lower the retirement age to make space for its appointees. In Turkey, hundreds of judges and prosecutors were imprisoned after an attempted coup in 2016 as Erdogan rushed to consolidate his power. In March 2017, a Turkish court ordered the release on bail of a group of journalists who had been in pretrial detention for an extended period, but after criticism in pro-government media the decision was reversed and the judge involved was suspended from duty.

Traditionally, those around the world who found their freedom to speak limited, their news media under assault, would look to America and its First Amendment for inspiration. That may still be the case, and doubtless it will be again, but these days it is harder to imagine happening.

Alexis de Tocqueville noted two centuries ago that "Americans make up for their skepticism about government with their commitment to civic engagement." The First Amendment is a critical component of that civic engagement, even if beleaguered by a chief executive determined to undermine it. Defending constitutional speech rights is a basic duty of anyone—judges, legislators, citizens—who wishes to see the nation's liberal democracy flourish. In countries that lack a free-speech tradition and a robust civil society, those who might be tempted to doubt America's dedication to the First Amendment will be reassured that this essential liberal-democratic value is still cherished.

All the Difference in the World: The Qualities of Leadership

★ ★ ★

RICHARD NORTH PATTERSON

Like the distorted image in a funhouse mirror, the counter-example of Donald Trump compels us to consider the personal attributes of leadership essential to liberal democracy.

Far more than assertiveness or an instinct for the popular pulse, such leaders require specific qualities of mind, character, and spirit that enable them to advance and exemplify an ideal

Richard North Patterson is an author whose twenty-three books include the novels *Protect and Defend*, *Exile*, and *Fall from Grace*, and a nonfiction account of the 2016 presidential campaign, *Fever Swamp*. He is a columnist for the *Boston Globe* and *Huffington Post*, a member of the Council on Foreign Relations, and a former chairman of Common Cause.

that, however imperfectly, represents humankind's greatest potential and its highest aspirations.

A democratic leader must respect the institutions protecting that ethos, including the rule of law, an independent judiciary, a free press, and branches of government whose powers are circumscribed in the service of individual liberty. Such a leader must promote the values that are the sinews of civil society: tolerance, respect for difference in thought and belief, a regard for fact and reason, the desire to nurture the potential of all, the will to prevail against internal and external threats. Only when leaders and citizens share these attitudes can liberal democracy thrive.

Throughout history, often in extremity, Western leaders time and again have made manifest that democratic essence.

America started well. George Washington embodied the constitutional chief executive—fully empowered in that office yet respectful of Congress and its enumerated powers. As general and as president, he subordinated the military to civilian rule. He warned about placing party over country. By leaving the presidency after two terms, Washington established that the office should be greater than its occupant.

His imprint has informed presidential actions through American history. Harry Truman upheld civilian rule in 1951 when he relieved General Douglas MacArthur for statements that blatantly questioned administration policy in Korea. A decade later, Dwight Eisenhower, the illustrious former army general and ex-president, memorably warned that the "military-industrial complex" threatened the primacy of civilian rule. But Ike also knew that sometimes, in extraordinary circumstances, the military must become involved in domestic matters. Despite his reluctance to challenge Southern mores, Eisenhower in 1957 sent federal troops to Little Rock, where Arkansas was illegally blocking school desegregation. By enforcing the Supreme Court's ruling in *Brown v. Board of Education*, Eisenhower fulfilled his duty to respect American institutions and uphold the rule of law.

In acting without regard for how his order might play politically, Eisenhower exemplified another trait of individual character that typifies true leadership: the willingness to place the common good above personal or political advantage. In the 1960s, Lyndon Johnson honored this presidential tradition when he fought for civil rights legislation, even though doing so inflicted seemingly irreparable harm to his party's fortunes in the South.

George H. W. Bush's example is also instructive. Campaigning for the presidency in 1988, Bush pledged "no new taxes." He won the election, but by 1990 Bush realized that the swelling federal deficit could endanger the US economy and burden future generations with crushing debt. Surely aware that he was risking his political future, Bush reached a fiscally responsible budget deal with the Democratic majority in Congress. The deal of course included new taxes—and Republican conservatives were predictably infuriated. Right there, Bush might well have doomed his bid for reelection. But he helped pave the way for the prosperity Americans enjoyed under the man who defeated him, Bill Clinton.

So, too, did Al Gore put country above self. After a bitterly disputed 2000 election in which he won the popular vote, a dubious Supreme Court decision presented Gore with a fateful choice: honor the decision or continue to challenge the results.

Gore stood down, declining to exacerbate the rancor that could have delegitimized the presidency of George W. Bush.

The imperative of maintaining national unity fused with moral purpose was raised to the heroic by Abraham Lincoln. A lesser man might have crumbled under the Promethean weight of the Civil War's bitterness, bloodshed, and brutal military setbacks. Lincoln resisted pleas to make peace with the Confederacy and watched his personal popularity plummet. But he endured—emancipating the slaves, reuniting his country, and summoning the spirit of reconciliation embodied in his brief, indelible speech on the battlefield at Gettysburg.

America was fortunate to have a president who could surmount the trauma of the Civil War. The United States was blessed yet again when the Great Depression inflicted social wreckage so severe that it could have upended the entire economic system and liberal democracy itself—and Franklin Roosevelt met the challenge. After an inaugural address in 1933 that combined optimism and determination, FDR then launched "a presidential barrage of ideas and programs," historian Arthur Schlesinger Jr. once wrote, "unlike anything known to American history." This bold but pragmatic deployment of federal power buoyed Roosevelt's fellow citizens and quite possibly spared civil society irreversible damage fueled by mass hopelessness and demagoguery.

Like Lincoln, FDR fused the qualities of eloquence and decisiveness indispensable in a crisis. Equally important, both presidents had the capacity to perceive changing conditions, listen to advice, and adapt to the demands of the moment.

Sometimes the crisis is an external threat—and must be met with leadership committed to protecting democracy. The example of Winston Churchill's resolve during the dark early days of World War II requires no elaboration. But Churchill was buttressed by Franklin Roosevelt, who patiently surmounted American isolationism to enact the lend-lease program critical to Britain's survival against Hitler.

At the end of World War II, when America's notional Russian allies enslaved Eastern Europe, yet again Churchill gave voice to democratic resistance. Dismissed from office as Britain's prime minister, Churchill warned America in 1946 that an "Iron Curtain" had descended across Eastern Europe. Citing the failed appeasement of Hitler in the 1930s, he warned of the Soviets that there was "nothing which they admire so much as strength, and there is nothing for which they have less respect than for military weakness."

Churchill's clarity eased the way for Harry Truman the following year to assert American leadership in standing up to further Soviet aggression. "I believe we must assist free peoples to work out their destinies in their own way," Truman told a joint session of Congress, vowing to ameliorate the "misery and want" that breed totalitarian rule.

Hence America's massive economic assistance to postwar European countries. The purpose of what became the Marshall Plan, outlined by Secretary of State and retired army general George C. Marshall, was nothing less than to create the "political and social conditions in which free institutions can exist." America's investment in economic and political freedom underwrote a democratic Western Europe and the postwar liberal order that fostered human rights, stability, and peace while blocking Soviet expansionism.

Moral clarity and an unwavering commitment to democratic principles were displayed by European leaders who strengthened democracy's resurgence in two separate eras. West Germany's first post–World War II chancellor, Conrad Adenauer, helped construct a free economy while repudiating Prussian nationalism. Beginning in the late 1980s, Vaclav Havel helped Czechoslovakia to emerge from the thrall of Russia—first by leading a peaceful revolution, then by playing a pivotal role in dismantling the Warsaw Pact and expanding NATO eastward. Neither result was inevitable; visionary leaders enabled two wounded counties to transcend their bitter histories.

In turn, two American presidents facilitated the fall of Soviet totalitarianism. Echoing Churchill's moral rigor, Ronald Reagan in the early 1980s challenged the USSR to free the peoples of Eastern Europe. But, as the Iron Curtain began to crumble, it was Reagan's successor, George H. W. Bush, who demonstrated the homely but sturdy virtues of prudence, informed judgment, and quiet strength in exercising American influence.

By winning Mikhail Gorbachev's trust, George H. W. Bush negotiated the critical reduction of forces between NATO and the Soviet bloc. He underplayed America's reaction to Russia's slipping dominance, eschewing grandstanding in favor of easing the liberation of its satellites. After the Berlin Wall fell in 1989, he chose not to make a triumphant speech, wisely resolving, as he explained years later, not to "stick our fingers in Gorbachev's eye." Bush then persuaded France and Britain that putting aside atavistic suspicions and supporting the reunification of Germany was desirable because a unified Germany could become a Western democratic linchpin. His careful diplomacy with Gorbachev ensured that this metamorphosis would be possible. The many millions of Germans who moved from oppression to freedom benefited from George H. W. Bush's humility, wisdom, and foresight.

Empathy matters too. Jolted from passivity by the civil rights movement, John F. Kennedy in June 1963 issued a demand for racial justice that called on whites to imagine themselves as black. "If an American," he asked in a national television and radio address, "cannot enjoy the full and free life which all of us want, then who among us would be content to have the color of his skin changed and stand in his place?"

Another prerequisite of democratic leadership is the ability to inspire trust. As Eisenhower showed, this stems from a soundness of character—sincerity, candor, the resolve to keep promises and take responsibility, a palpable concern for the national welfare. Ike was seldom eloquent. But seldom did he give Americans reason to doubt his essential goodness.

Finally, a democratic leader must have the gifts to master unexpected peril. These include the ability to bolster public confidence, to seek out and understand advice from sometimes conflicting sources, to understand adversaries, to anticipate consequences. Underlying all this, such a leader needs to bring to bear on the emergency, no matter how dire, calm judgment and detachment from self.

President Kennedy displayed all these attributes during the Cuban Missile Crisis. His own missteps had helped bring about the crisis, but, during those thirteen days in October 1962, Kennedy's leadership came to the fore. He carefully sought advice, weighed the options, read his opposites in Moscow, and ultimately overruled a Pentagon plan that could have resulted in a catastrophic nuclear war. His decision to order a blockade and then negotiate a diplomatic solution required nerves of steel, but it succeeded in ousting Russian missiles from Cuba.

Any reckoning with the second Bush presidency means reckoning with Iraq. But George W. Bush made other defining presidential decisions worth recalling. In response to the 9/11 terror attacks, President Bush chose to embrace American Muslims—disdaining xenophobia and tamping down hysteria. When, in 2008, the economic meltdown threatened to collapse the global financial system, many argued that Bush's own policies were to blame. But he rose above partisanship and ideology to direct the massive federal intervention that helped prevent a global financial and political disaster.

Contrast these leadership qualities with those of President Trump. His chronic lying corrodes public trust. He shows little capacity for critical thinking. He regularly derides and humiliates those who occupy positions that should be filled by advisers whose counsel he seeks and respects. His actions are characterized by grandiosity, impulsiveness, entitlement, vindictiveness, grievance, a total lack of empathy, and an inability to interpret external reality.

This president's instincts are profoundly authoritarian. He attacks any institution that can hold him accountable—the media, the intelligence services, the Justice Department, the judiciary. He lashes out at critics or criticism, real or perceived; scorns advice that contravenes his instincts and desires; pits advisers against each other. His public statements are often untethered to fact or reason. He has no grasp of history, no patience for learning, no values that transcend his self-interest.

Trump's foreign policy mirrors this solipsism. He is bereft of strategy, unschooled in geopolitics, and seemingly oblivious to the complex aims of rival powers like China or Russia. He assaults the world with contradictory demands, transitory proposals, historical falsehoods, and juvenile bluster—alienating America's allies, emboldening its adversaries, inflaming regional tinder boxes, and degrading the coin of US leadership.

The sole consistent thread is his fondness for authoritarian and often murderous leaders. The most pernicious of these attachments is his bizarre affinity for America's odious antagonist, Vladimir Putin—particularly Trump's shocking dereliction and disloyalty in abetting Russia's continuing assault on American democracy.

In his scorn for democracy itself, Trump reimagines the post–World War II democratic order, through which the United States and its allies furthered global stability, free trade, and human rights, as a bad deal. The nation might have enjoyed unprecedented power and prosperity, but, in his mind, America was cheated. By replacing international cooperation with one-on-one bargaining for advantage, he has reduced the globe to the only model he can grasp: a Hobbesian landscape pitting one self-seeking adversary against the other. Meanwhile, the real world beyond his ken has grown ever more dangerous and dystopian.

The responsibility for changing this perilous state resides in the American people. An early protagonist of the democratic experiment, the Athenian statesman Pericles, warned, "Freedom is the sure possession of those alone who have the courage to defend it."

In the future, as in the past, America can—and must—do better. For the sake of the nation and for liberal democracy itself, American leadership makes all the difference in the world.

Interests Versus Values

★ ★ ★

BRET STEPHENS

To what extent should the conduct of American foreign policy be informed by the nation's moral and political values? It's an old question that was given new life in May 2017, when Rex Tillerson indicated where the president's priorities stood. "We really have to understand, in each country or each region of the world that we're dealing with, what are our national security interests, what are our economic prosperity interests," the then–secretary of state said in remarks to the diplomatic corps. "And then, as we can advocate and advance our values, we should."

Lest there be any doubt that Tillerson was speaking for the entire administration, H. R. McMaster and Gary Cohn penned

Bret Stephens, winner of the 2013 Pulitzer Prize for distinguished commentary, is an op-ed columnist for the *New York Times*.

an op-ed for the *Wall Street Journal* a few weeks later, fleshing out their vision of the president's concept of "America First." "The president embarked on his first foreign trip with a clear-eyed outlook that the world is not a 'global community' but an arena where nations, nongovernmental actors and businesses engage and compete for advantage," wrote the pair, who were then the national security adviser and the National Economic Council director. "We bring to this forum unmatched military, political, cultural and moral strength. Rather than deny this elemental nature of international affairs, we embrace it."

These and other expressions of the new administration's coldly unsentimental worldview raised eyebrows, both in the United States and abroad, as a radical departure from the more idealistic traditions of postwar American internationalism.

Yet, whatever else one might say about the new policy, it was hardly original. Its vision of the world is Hobbesian—international life as a perpetual and remorseless contest of strength. Its economic vision echoed the seventeenth-century mercantilism of Jean-Baptiste Colbert and others who thought the principal goal of economic policy was to accumulate wealth at the expense of other nations.

And its conception of how powerful countries should conduct themselves harks back to the argument made by the Athenian envoys to the besieged Melians in Thucydides's *History of the Peloponnesian War*: "Right, as the world goes, is only in question between equals in power, while the strong do what they can and the weak suffer what they must."

Such concepts of how the United States should conduct itself in the world are woven into its early history, from the Trail of Tears and the conquest of Mexico to the annexation of Hawaii, the Spanish-American War, and sundry intercessions in the developing world. Unsatisfied powers—longing for territory, resources, prestige, or the satisfaction of ethnic or historical claims—are adept at inventing self-serving principles to suit their material ambitions. Throughout the nineteenth century, America was an unsatisfied power.

Yet, for at least a century, the United States has been a satisfied power. Unlike China, the United States has no territorial or maritime ambitions. Unlike Russia, America does not seek to recapture an empire or to "redeem" ethnic cousins living in neighboring countries or to assert a "sphere of influence." Unlike Iran, the United States does not have sectarian regional ambitions or dreams of wiping other nations off the map.

America is often called an "empire," but that is wrong. Empires rule by force, not consent. What the United States has done is exercise a sort of global guardianship, generally through the consent of those guarded. It's true that the United States went into Iraq against the will of a brutal dictator. But the American troops left (and later returned) according to the will of Iraq's elected government. US troops remain in Afghanistan only because Afghans pleaded for them to stay. American military bases in Japan, South Korea, Germany, Italy, and elsewhere are there by the invitation of the host countries.

What, then, does it mean for the United States to "compete for advantage," as McMaster and Cohn put it, in the modern age? If America is not out for land or plunder, what does it want?

At the most fundamental level, the answer must be security, prosperity, and peace.

After World War I, American statesmen broadly took the view that a policy of relative isolation was essential for achieving all three. With some enlightened exceptions, such as the 1924 Dawes Plan to address the effects of the Treaty of Versailles, isolationism took the form of protective tariffs, neutrality acts, and rejection of international institutions. The result was a world adrift, then in crisis, and then at war. When Franklin Roosevelt asked Winston Churchill what World War II should be called, the prime minister answered, "the unnecessary war," because, as he explained, "never was a war more easy to stop than that which has just wrecked what was left of the world from the previous struggle."

The calamity of the war rendered three generations of American statesmen immune to the temptations of isolationism. Harry Truman, Arthur Vandenberg, George Marshall, Dean Acheson, and the other fathers of the postwar American order understood that the United States could not stay away from the world's agonies and expect to remain untouched by them. Engagement was essential. They knew, also, that such engagement would be feckless unless matched by American military and financial power. Declarations of good intent, such as the 1928 Kellogg-Briand Pact outlawing war, did nothing except create mirages of peace.

Finally, they understood that for the United States to exercise effective leadership, other countries would need a good reason to follow. Fear of the Soviet Union was one such reason, but not a sufficient one: in an age of ideological competition, millions of people in Western countries, and even more in the developing world, found more inspiration in communism than in capitalism.

That meant the United States would need to provide a compelling rationale for its leadership beyond fear of a common enemy. It could not close its markets while expecting others to open theirs. It could not use its preponderant military strengths to dominate the global commons solely to its advantage. It had to demonstrate a sense of responsibility over its possession of a nuclear arsenal intended for the defense both of itself and its allies. It had to at least participate in the work of international institutions, even if it found much to dislike, or disregard, about the outcome of that work. And America could not present itself as the great champion of free societies—including freedom of speech and civil liberties for all—unless it was seen as championing those freedoms at home.

Above all, the United States had to maintain fidelity to the creed of the American founding, which held that America wasn't simply a nation among others. It was, more importantly, an *idea* above others—of all men being born equal, with unalienable rights to freedom. It is what attracts immigrants to American shores and what inspires other nations to adopt the same idea as their own. It is America's power of *attraction*, sometimes called "soft power," that is as essential to its international leadership as is the "hard power" of military and financial wherewithal.

Critics of US foreign policy during the Cold War frequently point to its excesses, costs, crimes, and hypocrisies. Of these there are many, as men are not angels. Yet by comparison with the crimes of other great powers—the British massacre of Indians at Amristar in 1919 or the Soviet suppression of the Hungarian Revolution in 1956—the American record looks exceedingly good. Even if wars such as those in Vietnam or

Iraq were ultimately judged as follies, they were follies fought against tyrants.

Then, too, only the most acerbic or ideological critics would seriously oppose what the United States stood for, at least notionally, in the postwar era: free (or at least freer) government, civil liberties, market-based economies, the freedom of movement, the rights of religious and personal conscience. When the United States fell short, as it inevitably did, *it was falling short of its own ideals*. By contrast, when the Soviet Union or other dictatorships committed crimes, they were fulfilling their ideals.

What were the results of postwar American internationalism? The United States was able to maintain a global coalition of allies to defeat its most dangerous international rival without having to fight a third world war. Democracy and capitalism became, if not a global norm, at least an international aspiration. An ever-greater share of the world's population came to enjoy representative government and dramatic improvements in living standards. As the world grew richer and freer, the prospect of major-power conflicts of the kind that had typified human history for millennia diminished accordingly. Ever-smaller shares of national income were devoted to military spending.

A single example helps illustrate the point. Seventy years ago, in June 1948, President Truman chose to break the Soviet blockade of West Berlin through a logistically risky airlift, even as he knew that the United States was at a sharp military disadvantage and the Western exclave would be indefensible in a wider war. In breaking the blockade, Truman demonstrated a combination of firmness and benevolence that helped deter Soviet aggression, cement the NATO alliance, persuade Germans of American friendship, and support what would become a thriving advertisement for democracy and capitalism in the midst of the Communist world. Not surprisingly, it was in Berlin that the Iron Curtain collapsed forty-one years later without a shot being fired or a life being lost.

As for Americans, between 1945 and 2012, their average family income rose nearly threefold, in constant 2012 dollars, and average individual income more than doubled. An American businessman, traveling from, say, Tokyo to Dubai to Frankfurt, could feel reasonably sure that nearly everywhere he went English would be spoken in his meetings, his credit cards would be accepted, and his business would be sought after. The federal government continues to borrow trillions of dollars from abroad because foreign investors, public and private, see the United States as the safest destination for their capital. The American share of the global economy has remained remarkably stable since the rest of the world recovered from World War II, and the United States remains the global cultural trendsetter and technological innovator in nearly every facet of life. And America stands as an abiding pole of attraction to billions of people around the world who see it for what it is—in Lincoln's words, "the last best hope of earth."

All this came, and comes, with costs. As Donald Trump never tires of pointing out, the United States pays an outsize share of NATO's overall budget. International competition invariably creates losers along with the winners, which takes its toll on parts of American industry. US troops have fought and bled in distant wars for dubious allies. Not every immigrant to the United

States wants to pursue the American dream, and a handful of them actively seek to destroy it.

Still, all that pales next to what America achieved in the postwar period. It pales, too, next to any plausible alternative.

Would we rather live in a world in which another great power, such as China or Russia, exercises hegemonic power? Or in a new balance-of-power arrangement akin to the one that collapsed with such catastrophic consequences in Europe in 1914? Or one in which America got its way only through threat and coercion, instead of cooperation and persuasion? Even some of the most jaded enthusiasts for Trump's vision of America First cling, at some level, to the idea of America as a beacon of democratic values and rescuer of embattled nations. Could they sustain that belief in American moral superiority if US foreign policy were to be devoted exclusively to the advancement of selfish national ends at the expense of former allies?

In short, it turns out that the idealistic internationalism that defined the postwar US foreign policy consensus aligns most closely not just with America's democratic convictions and moral self-regard but with its core national interests as well. In raising a banner, and behaving in a manner that could turn former enemies into allies and friends, the United States found it easier to defeat its foes, broaden its appeal, sustain its morale, and shape the world as Americans wished it to be: freer, richer, and more peaceful.

Now all this is at risk. Under President Obama, the United States underwent an eight-year period of geopolitical retrenchment in the name of what was called "nation-building at home." Though his rhetoric was suffused with a high idealism and punctuated with moments of action, the net result of his presidency was to create a perception of American hesitancy and retreat that was quickly exploited by jihadist groups in the Middle East, by Vladimir Putin in Ukraine, and by China in the South China Sea.

Donald Trump has, if anything, been far more skeptical of America's global commitments than was his predecessor. Nearly his first act in office was to withdraw the United States from the Trans-Pacific Partnership, signaling an end to the era of American support for free (or freer) trade. Though he has not made good on his threats to withdraw the United States from NATO, he has created profound unease among the nation's oldest allies, from South Korea (which fears his intemperate bellicosity may trigger a war at its immediate expense) to Great Britain (whom he has repeatedly offended with gratuitous jabs at its anti-terror policies). His expressions of admiration for Putin may have raised political questions about potential collusion in the 2016 presidential election, but just as serious are the questions they raise about Trump's understanding of the dimensions of Moscow's revanchist designs and subversion of the liberal-democratic order.

The larger question is whether the "America First" slogan has a life beyond its current champions in the White House. Trump came to office on a wave of antipathy for a US foreign policy that was seen by much of the American public as weak, but so far he has merely substituted strategic retreat with moral retreat; substituted a belief that America was overextended militarily with one that the United States is overgenerous to its allies, who were freeloaders rather than partners. Neither view serves the long-term interests of American foreign policy.

It would be well if Americans once again understood the wisdom of the postwar consensus that matched American idealism to American power for the sake of maintaining a liberal world order in which we could thrive even as our partners did as well. That would require a combination of statesmanship and pedagogy that has been missing for several years.

"Whence then cometh wisdom?" Job asked. "And where is the place of understanding?" The answer lies in the nation's history—there for any current or future president to see if only he wishes to open his eyes.

Renew Democracy Manifesto

1. The modern world is at risk of losing its way. The liberal-democratic order is under attack from within and without. In response, a Committee has been formed to respond to the crisis. This document describes the crisis and outlines the responses necessary to meet it.

2. The historical arc toward greater global stability, freedom, and prosperity in large parts of the world is at risk of being bent back—toward political authoritarianism, economic stagnation, ideological extremism, and international disorder. The economic and political stability we have taken for granted for decades is eroding rapidly. The core principles of liberal democracy that once defined a centrist political majority across the free world are being pulled apart as once-fringe views from the left and right gain public acceptance.

3. Relentless partisanship has led major parties to abandon common cause, leading to the debilitation of vital civic institutions, including responsible news media and mainstream

political parties. Debates over immigration, education, health care, trade, national security, and taxes have been politicized to such extremes that the compromises needed to craft sound, sensible solutions are unlikely to be reached.

4. It is essential to defend and refine the values and institutions of liberal democracy before they are further crippled. These include: the integrity of democratic elections; freedom of the press, speech, conscience, religion, and assembly; equal justice under the law and the independence of the judiciary; the safety and security of individuals and nations; the ability to do business free of corruption or excessive government intervention; the right of every citizen to seek opportunity under the equal protection of the law; the free flow of goods, services, capital, and ideas across borders; a rational and humane immigration policy; a representative democracy that makes government accountable to its citizens; citizens who feel they are fairly treated and fully represented by their governments.

5. It is equally essential to defend liberal democracy against global adversaries—authoritarian regimes, terrorist groups, and the ideologies and theologies that underpin both. That requires a profound understanding of the nature of these threats and a willingness to confront them fearlessly, without jeopardizing bedrock rights of free peoples and the restraints of civilized governments.

6. The pillars of modernity are interlocking. Political stability and international security enable global trade and tremendous economic growth. A predictable and consensual rule of law creates the conditions in which entrepreneurs and

businesses flourish, fostering levels of affluence that in turn enhance the global appeal of liberal democracy. Responsible political and digital revolutions in previously closed or suppressed societies unlock the economic and intellectual potential of millions of people, making it more likely that similar revolutions will follow.

7. It is no coincidence that the twentieth century was the American century. Foundational principles of democracy, liberty, and human rights gained global sway thanks to the unrivaled growth of American prosperity and power. The United States promoted its values abroad in general with considerable success. Liberal democracy and properly functioning free-market economies became, if not a universal political norm, a widespread aspiration. The United States must continue to promote these values, and the institutions they sustain, at home and abroad.

8. In recent years these trends have slowed, stopped, or are in full retreat in parts of the world. Nationalists, neofascists, xenophobes, racists, and anti-Semites have received a surge of support. Neo-Marxism has found new champions in countries that owe their wealth to the opportunities provided by free-market capitalism. Protectionism is likewise gaining popularity in countries that have benefitted from free trade. Islamic extremism has gained sway through a combination of political appeal, social repression, and outright terror. Many champions of these movements have taken inspiration, or received political and financial support, from authoritarian regimes. Modern technology provides new weapons, new recruits, and new targets for the

forces of illiberalism, and they have moved far more quickly to exploit them than the free world has moved to defend itself. Conspiracy-mongers and fringe websites have spread "fake news" that supports their illiberal beliefs and that undermines faith in objective, commonly accepted truths.

9. There is little doubt that many of the problems being addressed by the advocates of illiberalism are real, including growing income inequality, economic dislocation, declining social mobility, high youth unemployment, a growing threat from terrorism, and social breakdowns that are the result of technological transformations and, in some cases, misguided government policies. But their proposed solutions range from the impracticable to the illusory to the immoral. Free societies cannot prosper by adopting the practices of closed societies. While extreme religious and nationalistic views play a central role in the rising tide of illiberalism, moderate religious and patriotic sentiment can be vital in counteracting social alienation and radicalism.

10. The extremists share a disdain for the globalism on which modern prosperity is based. Whether they are far left or far right, they believe in top-down solutions to problems that can best be resolved through greater freedom, competition, openness, and mobility. Both seek power without compromise or coalition and defer to the rule of law only when it strengthens their own position. These illiberal forces embrace divisive rhetoric that makes rational debate impossible. Indeed, they frequently reject established facts and scientific reasoning in favor of conspiracy theories and malicious myths. Liberal democracy must address the problems

of those disadvantaged by economic change with practical programs grounded in fact and reason.

11. The free world must rally in defense of free societies and their values and promote them where they are most urgently needed, and must reject intimidation or suppression of speech rooted in ideological rigidity or intolerance of political difference, as has occurred on college campuses and elsewhere. Western proponents of the liberal-democratic order must first promote these values at home and defend them abroad without paternalistically imposing them, or repeating past errors such as uncritical alliances with authoritarian regimes.

12. Political polarization has opened the door wide for active interference, even war, from outside powers. We must reject this dangerous path. We must not allow the political fringes to pull the center apart completely. To achieve this, there must be credible alternatives, real solutions, and an ongoing dialogue. We must rally to the values that unite us in order to preserve and optimize the institutions we depend on to navigate the issues that divide us. We must channel the surge of political engagement into forming a new and vital center, one that transcends party and policy.

13. There is still a center in Western politics, and it needs to be revitalized—intellectually, culturally, and politically. The center right and center left are still joined by a broad set of common values, including respect for free speech and dissent, a belief in the benefits of international trade and immigration, respect for law and procedural legitimacy, a suspicion of cults of personality, and an understanding that

free societies require protection from authoritarians promising easy fixes to complex problems.

14. The immediate need is to help restore political confidence and ideological balance to traditional center right and center left parties on both sides of the Atlantic. This does not require fundamentally "new" ideas. It requires fresh thinking about good ideas, a new way of arguing for sound principles of liberal democracy.

15. The aim of this Committee is to help generate this fresh thinking and to convene the best minds from different countries to come together for both broad and discrete projects in the service of liberty and democracy in the West and beyond.

PublicAffairs is a publishing house founded in 1997. It is a tribute to the standards, values, and flair of three persons who have served as mentors to countless reporters, writers, editors, and book people of all kinds, including me.

I. F. STONE, proprietor of *I. F. Stone's Weekly*, combined a commitment to the First Amendment with entrepreneurial zeal and reporting skill and became one of the great independent journalists in American history. At the age of eighty, Izzy published *The Trial of Socrates*, which was a national bestseller. He wrote the book after he taught himself ancient Greek.

BENJAMIN C. BRADLEE was for nearly thirty years the charismatic editorial leader of *The Washington Post*. It was Ben who gave the *Post* the range and courage to pursue such historic issues as Watergate. He supported his reporters with a tenacity that made them fearless and it is no accident that so many became authors of influential, best-selling books.

ROBERT L. BERNSTEIN, the chief executive of Random House for more than a quarter century, guided one of the nation's premier publishing houses. Bob was personally responsible for many books of political dissent and argument that challenged tyranny around the globe. He is also the founder and longtime chair of Human Rights Watch, one of the most respected human rights organizations in the world.

     ·   ·   ·

For fifty years, the banner of Public Affairs Press was carried by its owner Morris B. Schnapper, who published Gandhi, Nasser, Toynbee, Truman, and about 1,500 other authors. In 1983, Schnapper was described by *The Washington Post* as "a redoubtable gadfly." His legacy will endure in the books to come.

Peter Osnos, *Founder*